Seamless Neighbourhood

REDRAWING
The City of Israel

Motti Ruimy + Paul Kearns

A graphic slice of Tel Aviv – sea, sand, boardwalk,
Yarkon, boulevard and the White City of Tel Aviv

DEDICATED TO OUR DAUGHTER, ELLA

SEAMLESS NEIGHBOURHOOD – REDRAWING THE CITY OF ISRAEL
by Motti Ruimy + Paul Kearns

Published by Gandon Editions, the specialist producer and publisher of books on Irish art + architecture.

ISBN 978-1-910140-18-5

illustrations   all photography, graphics, maps and conceptual imagery are the
                 original artwork of Motti Ruimy and Paul Kearns
                 – base maps courtesy of Israeli Central Bureau of Statistics
                 – statistics courtesy of the Israeli and Palestinian Central Statistics Offices
production   designed and produced by John O'Regan and Nicola Dearey
                 (design © Gandon, 2018)
printing   Nicholson Bass, Belfast
distribution   distributed by Gandon and its overseas agents

GANDON EDITIONS, Oysterhaven, Kinsale, Co Cork
T +353 (0)21-4770830 / E gandon@eircom.net / W www.gandon-editions.com

This is the 398th book on art + architecture produced by Gandon Editions. Visit our website, or see our colour catalogue for information on 200+ titles in print.

other books by the same authors:

REDRAWING DUBLIN
by Paul Kearns + Motti Ruimy
a visual and statistical cornucopia that exposes the unconscious psyche of anti-urbanism that envelops city-making in Dublin
ISBN 978-0-948037-80-1 (Gandon Editions, 2010), 360 pages, 21.5x24.5cm, 400+ col illus, €33 hb

BEYOND PEBBLEDASH ... AND THE PUZZLE OF DUBLIN
by Paul Kearns + Motti Ruimy (with essay by Mick Wilson)
a pocket-sized compendium of ReDrawing Dublin, updated following the economic crash
ISBN 978-1-910140-03-1 (Gandon Editions, 2014), 224 pages, 170x110mm, 38 illus, €15 pb

see page 336 for more details

Sponsors

The authors and publisher gratefully acknowledge the support of the following institutions, companies and individuals towards the publication of this book:

WK NOLAN CONSULTANTS
ANON 1
ANON 2
DUBLIN CITY COUNCIL
CITY ARCHITECT'S DEPT, DUBLIN CITY COUNCIL
SCHOOL OF GEOGRAPHY, UNIVERSITY COLLEGE DUBLIN
LINDERS OF SMITHFIELD GROUP
REDDY ARCHITECTURE + URBANISM
McCULLOUGH MULVIN ARCHITECTS
KIERAN ROSE
Prof FRANCES RUANE

Acknowledgements

Zivit & David Aka and children
Maayan Amir
Marc Austan
Ido Bar-El
Meherata Baruch
Avinadav Begin
Amos Brandies
James Byrne
Eoin Collins
Ibrahim Daud
Nicola Dearey
Rachel Elan
Erez Ella
Embassy of Ireland, Tel Aviv
Yehuda Glick
Aliza Saidler Granot
Ali Grehan
Nili Renana Harag
Arin Kassen Hussain
Liat Izakov

Alison Kelly
Brendan Kenny
Nadav Lasser
Meital Lehavi
Gideon Levi
Merav Levi
Bruce Levin
Ester Levin
Rabbi Aharon Libovitch
Pat Linders
Shlomo Lotan
Liat Malka
Meir Margalit
Ahmed Mashrawi
Itay Mayer
Michal Meir
Alex Meitliss
Meital Michaely
Prof Gerald Mills
Daniel Mintz
Boaz Modai
Nurit Tinari Modai

Museum on the Seam, Jerusalem
Guy Nardi
Fahmi Nashashibi
Alon Bin Nun
Benny Nuriely
Paul O'Connell
Killian O'Higgins
John O'Regan
Annraí O'Toole
Adi Peket
Daniella Possek
Michal Shalev Reicher
Tim Reilly
Scott David Renwick
Ayala Ronel
Kieran Rose
Amit Rotbard
Sharon Rotbard
Eti Ruimy and children
Yehudit & Yaakov (Jacky) Ruimy

Tali & Lior Sagi and children
Eman Kasem Saliman
Matan Sapir
Ruti Sela
Carmit Shlomi
Iris Shoor
Stav Shaffir
Emily Silverman
Erez Tal
November Wanderin
Nathalie Weadick
Saado Zinab
Yahav Zohar
Ruth & Oren Zrihen and children
special thanks to Derek Stynes who wrote the maths of SELFIE

Seamless Neighbourhood

	Introduction	22
1	**Does Size Matter?**	**32**
1.1	Where is Tel Aviv?	33
1.2	The 'Lie' of the Land and the Lazy Eye of Geography	38
2	**Picture Tel Aviv**	**52**
2.1	The White City	53
2.2	Postcards from Tel Aviv	70
2.3	Mapping the 'missing' persons of 'Postcards from Tel Aviv'	80
2.4	508 Immutable Zonings	86
2.5	The Green City?	90
3	**Extensions**	**100**
3.1	Balcony Space	101
3.2	The soil of Israel and the rise of the Tel Avivian penthouse	110
3.3	Chasing space in the White City of Tel Aviv	116
3.4	Suicidal Geography	122
3.5	Taking Shelter Apart	126
3.6	Eleven and a half Rothschilds	138
3.7	Bnei Brak and the Architecture of Expansion	144
4	**Green Line Exurbia**	**154**
4.1	The Exurban Geography of Tel Aviv – Alfe Menashe	155
4.2	An Israeli City over the Green Line	168
4.3	Back Door to the Seamless Zone	176
4.4	Seamless Segregation and Greater Tel Aviv	180
4.5	The Tel Avivian Dead Sea Drive	186
4.6	Up the Road: the Semi-Detached City	192
4.7	Tram Space	202

Redrawing the City of Israel

5   Invisible Geographies   **210**

5.1   The Road to Ariel   211
5.2   The Shifting Ideology of a Simple Map   222
5.3   Mini Israel   228
5.4   Invisible Geography and the Census   232
5.5   Constituency Geography   238
5.6   Butterfly State   256
5.7   Settling for Less   264

6   The State of Tel Aviv   **276**

6.1   Bursting the Tel Aviv 'Bubble'   277
6.2   The world's first Jewish Global City?   282

7   Autonomy   **290**

7.1   The Looming Divorce:
       the 'State' of Tel Aviv and the 'State' of Jerusalem   291
7.2   The Geography of Regional Zionism   304

Conclusion   **316**

Appendix   **320**
The 120 single-seat member constituencies

References   **322**

Arriving into Ben Gurion Airport, Tel Aviv
The city centre of Netanya (25km north of Tel Aviv) is visible in the middle distance with the residential tower blocks of Ir Yamim in the lower foreground. Ben Gurion Airport is located 10km from the Mediterranean Sea and 10km from

The White (and not so white) City of Tel Aviv

The Carmel Market area of Tel Aviv, looking south-east, with the 34-storey Shalom Meir Tower (1965).

Driving south along Ayalon Highway Tel Aviv, with the 45-storey, pyramid-roofed Leonardo City Tower (2000), Israel's tallest hotel (157m) on the left

Carmel Market area of Tel Aviv

Arriving into Ben Gurion Airport

Introduction

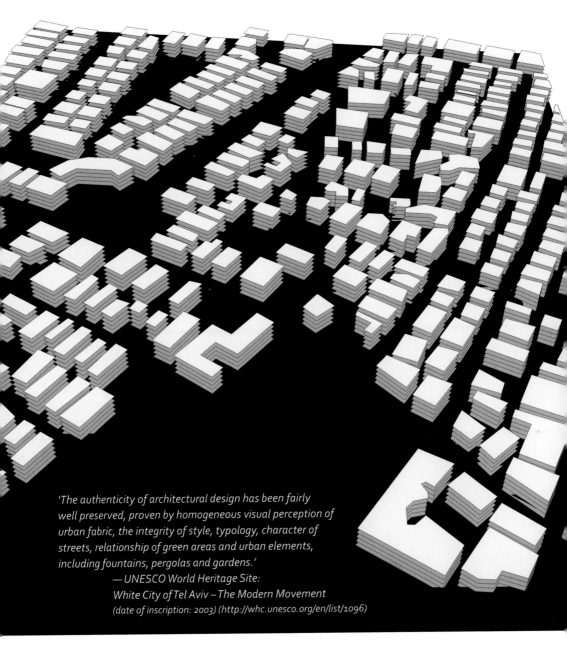

'The authenticity of architectural design has been fairly
well preserved, proven by homogeneous visual perception of
urban fabric, the integrity of style, typology, character of
streets, relationship of green areas and urban elements,
including fountains, pergolas and gardens.'
— UNESCO World Heritage Site:
White City of Tel Aviv – The Modern Movement
(date of inscription: 2003) (http://whc.unesco.org/en/list/1096)

Seamless Neighbourhood – Redrawing the City of Israel is a story of a city. That city is Tel Aviv. The story of any city, fact or fiction, is inescapably entwined with the author's own perspective. Every author's story necessarily reflects and encapsulates his or her particular interests, drafting and editing choices. It is illusory that an author can escape the path of subjectivity. What is not included in a particular story can often attract greater attention and generate a critique – a case of admission by omission.

The choice of subject for inclusion in this book reflects our academic background in geography, economics and fine art and our working knowledge as a practicing architect and urban planner. This is not to suggest to the reader that what follows is a deeply personal, revelatory journey, but as authors, the collection of observations that generate the story of this book is shaped by our personal experiences and is indivisible from our personal interests. We have endeavoured to creatively blend the diversity of this experience into an interdisciplinary framework of inquiry.

A frequent theme that unites the subject matter in this book is the desire to uncover stories of invisible landscapes, and to reveal the seamlessness of those inhabited geographies. Landscapes, and in particular man-made landscapes (where we build, what we build, where we ought or ought not to build, who lives where and why and how we travel) all form part of the basic building blocks of everyday inquiry for architects, planners and urban geographers. Landscapes are of course not just designed; they are primarily personally lived, experienced, consumed, tasted even. Their stories are particular and peculiar to each individual. We read our own everyday landscape according to a vast and complex ever-changing, bewildering array of often competing and often contradictory information. Much of it is personal to us. Much of it is informed or determined by our 'place' in society – what we do, where we live, who we know, our age, economic choices (or lack of them), ethnicity and legal status. While each of us generates our own mental map of space, the autonomy of our actions, our daily movement, can and often is unknowingly determined by others. Every day we make illusory choices from a supposed myriad range of personal options.

We simultaneously juggle different social roles and relationships – family, work, friends, neighbour, anonymous resident, citizen – and also navigate both literally and symbolically a hierarchy of different scales in our everyday lives. This includes everything from the immediacy of the walk to the local neighbourhood store, the sense of distance of travelling across the city, right through to the imagined geography of the nation state we live in. That awareness of diversity of scale and space includes an obvious sense of where we are physically, right now, at any one moment in time. It also includes how and when we visualise, imagine, even momentarily, where others are and what they may be doing. This constant back-and-forth flux, an ever-expanding and contracting imagined, real and negotiated space is how we all live, how we all operate consciously and subconsciously in our habitation of place.

Whilst there is nothing insightful or original about these observations, they provide a framework for how this book is structured. What we see and what we don't see, what we choose not to see or what is very consciously hidden from us, how we read, interpret or navigate our everyday landscape, real or imagined, is central to the unfolding journey of this book. In *Seamless Neighbourhood* we endeavour to reveal an obviously tiny slice or fraction of those landscapes. The structure of the book, in some ways, is an accordion-like experience of how we imagine and experience space – a constant back-and-forth journey, expansive then compressed, expansive again. Just as an architect in a design exercise may quickly go from the scale of an apartment layout – a kitchen, the location of a window to a particular view – to a neighbourhood scale of 500 housing units, every one of us lives and imagines, all of the time, differential scales of space, but in a less self-conscious or structured way. Our geography of scale, of space is utterly seamless. From deconstructing (or living) the sociability and functionality of a Tel Aviv balcony space to imagining (or driving through) the invisible whereabouts of a quasi-Palestinian autonomous state, our experience and imagination of scale is simultaneously always 1:1, and occasionally an unknowable, unfathomable or fantastical 1:1000 or 1:1,000,000 – one scale compartmentalised and enclosed, yet simultaneously overlapping with another that's a parallel bird's-eye view and Cinemascope in perspective.

An additional commonality of approach to the content of many chapters is an exploration of the seeming banality of data, particularly hidden or unimagined data. It's about making connections, decoding or quantifying landscapes. Imagining numerical space – whether it's calculating the totality of balcony space in Tel Aviv or measuring the distance of Rothschild Avenue to the West Bank, mapping the homes of Knesset members or drawing the 'invisible' ethno-gerrymandered constituencies of settler electoral geography – is part of the reality of the seamlessness of ordinary Tel Avivian city life in the midst of extraordinary Israeli political exurban geography. Imagining and quantifying hitherto unimagined space can create additional appetites or layers of enquiry, alternative ways of looking. It can open minds, provoke questioning.

Excavating the layers of a profoundly contested historical and geographical landscape to expose the myth-making of national narratives around everyday built environments is a common thread throughout the book. There are few books on Tel Aviv that substantially discuss the Israeli Occupation, and few books on the Occupation that meaningfully discuss Tel Aviv. This disguises the world Tel Avivians and other Israelis inhabit. A goal of *Seamless Neighbourhood* is to not simply blur the boundaries that separate these two domains, but to reveal the reality that they are not so self-contained. In this way the book can be viewed as a synthesis of a certain Tel Avivian narrative that emphasises what we call either 'The Historic Here' or 'The Contemporaneous There' spatial critique of the Israeli-Palestinian conflict with respect to the city of Tel Aviv. The narrative of 'The Historic Here' is a critique of the myth-making surrounding the origins of the White City of Tel Aviv, the myth that Tel Aviv emerged from the empty dunes or sand of the Mediterranean coast. The narrative of 'The Contemporaneous There' is a critical exploration of the settlement project and its architectural geography today, an architectural geography that is, however, largely viewed as separate, at a distance, over there, somewhat removed from the city of Tel Aviv. Whether 'over there' (15km to the 'Green Line' and beyond it) or 'back here' (100 years past), 'The Historic Here' and 'The Contemporaneous There' narratives are both inevitably distanced by either space or time. Political reflections, indeed moral responsibilities, are somewhat denuded or mitigated by the distance of history or geography. History and geography have partially, perhaps conveniently, absolved the city. Tel Aviv as a city has embraced a sense of self that is guilt-free. History and geography have colluded to generate a bubble of protection for self-identifying cosmopolitan Tel Avivians.

It's as if a Tel Avivian attachment, an affinity, a love even, of this liberal city somehow absolves. Politics is something else, it's elsewhere, it's over there. The reality of a seamless metropolitan urban Tel Aviv geography that includes settlements is largely viewed as apolitical.

Seamless Neighbourhood can be viewed as a partial synthesis of 'The Historic Here' and 'The Contemporaneous There' to frame the discussion around what we call 'The Contemporaneous Here'. This, in the context of Tel Aviv, is the reality of a city whose residents and commuters, shoppers or day-trippers, work and reside in an urban metropolis whose functional (geographic, social, economic) boundaries do not readily recognise the borders of the 1949 Armistice (Green) Line. In this way, 'Greater Tel Aviv' can be understood, for Jews at least, as a vast, albeit differentiated, but seamless neighbourhood. Greater Tel Aviv, with a population of 3.6 million people, is now home to more than 2 out every 5 Israelis.[1] This is a metropolitan conurbation that extends from Netanya in the coastal north to Ashdod in the coastal south. To the east, its metropolitan functional grip extends inland and uphill into the suburban commuter Israeli settlements of Alfe Menashe and Elkana across the Green Line. Some 20% of the residents of Ariel, an Israeli settlement which lies 17km inside the West Bank, commute to Greater Tel Aviv.[2] This seamless neighbourhood includes approximately 10% of all Israeli settlers, or Greater Tel Avivians, who reside in dormitory suburban settlements over the Green Line inside the West Bank.[3] Throughout the book we use the terms 'Greater Tel Aviv', 'the Seamless Neighbourhood', 'Contiguous Metropolitan' and 'the city of Israel' interchangeably.

So how big is Israel's largest city? How big and small can we make it? How elastic are its borders? In Chapter 1: *'Does Size Matter?*, we ask where does Tel Aviv really begin and end, and explore why the multiple answers to that question are so important to our understanding of the seamlessness of Israeli political space. 'Contiguous Tel Aviv' (page 46) maps out a contiguous belt of density, radiating out from the heart of downtown Tel Aviv (a minimum population of 200 people per km²), to reveal a metropolitan reach into the occupied West Bank. The capacity to try to look at a map, any map, differently and imagine the making of new geographies is an age-old cartographic game. In *'The "Lie" of the Land and the Lazy Eye of Geography'* we inverse, reverse, re-orientate and overlay various homemade Tel Avivian geographies to reveal their relative size to other global cities.

'Does Size Matter?' suggests that immigrants from the former Soviet Union (a country 10,000km wide) may in part be attracted to the politics of a 'Greater Israel' espoused by the Russian-dominated political party Yisrael Beiteinu after having absorbed the startling reality that their newly adopted home state is a mere 14km (9 miles) wide at its narrowest point. That narrowest point is just 5km north of the municipal border of Tel Aviv-Yafo.

In Chapter 2 we explore the DNA of the city by decoding land-use zoning and open-space hierarchies. We also map and photograph the multiple identities of the White City of Tel Aviv. *'508 Immutable Zonings'* reveals some of the 508 different zoning ordinances to be found in the Tel Aviv-Yafo municipal city plan, and asks who is empowered with the authority to alter, or invested with the skill to persuade those with the power to alter, these apparently immutable zonings. More importantly, who benefits from the opacity of this power of alteration?

Chapter 3 deconstructs and reconstructs various Tel Avivian built landscapes. In

'Balcony Space' we trace the evolution of the balcony in the social urban history of the city of Tel Aviv, exploring how the variation in taste of the Tel Avivian balcony has captured or reflected the contemporaneous zeitgeist of the Israeli state. *'Eleven and a half Rothschilds'* explores how Rothschild Boulevard occupies not only an important centrality of place in the geography of Tel Aviv, but also performs a meaningful hub for a very particular Tel Avivian mindset. In a celebratory challenge to that mindset, an imaginary Rothschild Boulevard is unfolded from the centre of Tel Aviv eastwards until it arrives at the 'front door' of the Green Line that separates Israel from the West Bank.

Chapter 4 explores the exurban geography of Greater Tel Aviv with respect to the occupied West Bank. *'The Exurban Geography of Tel Aviv – Alfe Menashe'* examines the multiple landscapes of the seamless suburban and exurban 'settlement' geographies on the fringes of Metropolitan Tel Aviv. The six ex-urban geographies – 'Green Line', 'Google', 'Identity', 'Picturesque', 'Windscreen' and 'Security' – each reveal their own stories; collectively they endeavour to present a picture of the multiple identities and the complexity of the seeming banality of the Israeli suburban dormitory landscape.

A seamless geography is a de facto uncertain geography, in the sense that Israelis are at times not quite sure of the geography of municipal or national borders, including the location of the Green Line. Few residents of any city notice when crossing municipal boundaries. Israelis are, however, often unclear as to where and when they cross the internationally recognised border between Israel proper and the West Bank. That uncertainty can fuse with a kind of equanimity and unknowingness when travelling across the open desert landscape of the West Bank. In *'The Tel Avivian Dead Sea Drive'* we take a Tel Avivian journey of day-trip geography. This is recreational travel into the occupied West Bank that is largely stripped of political meaning for its day-trippers. This is a day-trip geography that almost all Israelis have undertaken at some point in their lives. The Tel Avivian Dead Sea Drive is often very temporary; one's presence in the West Bank is almost fleeting – a few hours, a couple of days, perhaps just a few times over a number of years. Yet this apparently everyday recreational journey is woven into a more complex reality of the seamlessness of the Israeli Occupation. It is this ordinariness of the lived experience of the Occupation that we would argue psychologically anaesthetizes an Israeli (primarily Jewish) understanding of the Occupation itself. The municipal borders of Tel Aviv may be fixed, but the recreational boundaries of Tel Avivians are politically and conveniently blurred.

In *'Seamless Segregation and Greater Tel Aviv'*, we reveal that the 49 Jewish small villages or communities of Greater Tel Aviv inside Israel proper are, in fact, fractionally more homogeneous and segregated than Israeli 'Jewish only' settlement communities inside the occupied West Bank. This subliminally known patchwork pattern of 'Jewish only' or 'Palestinian only' villages and towns within Israel proper may partially inform the perception and thus possibly a residual passive acceptance of the continuation of the Occupation in the West Bank amongst Israeli Jews.

'An Israeli City over the Green Line' asks when is a 'settlement' not a 'settlement'? We explore how the fact that the majority of the 650,000 to 700,000 Israelis who live beyond the Green Line reside in neighbourhoods and suburbs of Jerusalem and Greater Tel Aviv serves not just to legitimise the Israeli settlement project, but more remarkably facilitates a linguistic political metamorphoses. This is a metamorphoses that allows a settlement to

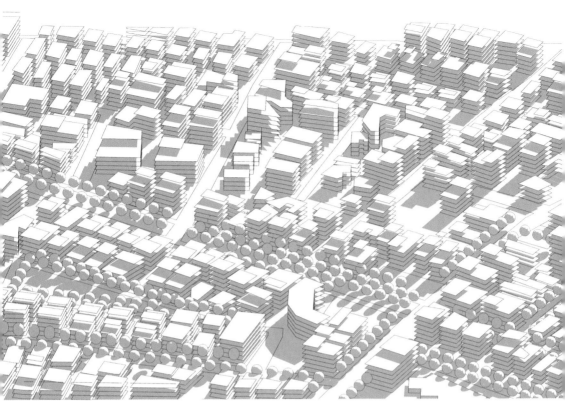

Decoding the layers of the White City of Tel Aviv

_____

evolve and mutate, to literally outgrow and somehow 'un-become' a settlement, and yet simultaneously remain geographically over the Green Line.

Chapter 5 makes visible Israeli invisible geographies. In *'The Road to Ariel'* we drive the seamless, uninterrupted journey along Route 5 motorway from the beachfront in Tel Aviv to the settlement city of Ariel. This is a journey that takes no more than 30 minutes. It is a journey of invisible geography, a high-speed, rarely congested, almost endlessly straight motorway connecting Israel proper with Ariel, almost halfway across the West Bank. This is a motorway with no signposts to tell you the names of local Palestinian towns and villages because there are no motorway exits to access them. They lie in forbidden territory. The motorway is designed not to connect to this invisible geography.

The invisibility of boundaries or absence of borders and constituencies masks the reality of other profound geographies. In *'Constituency Geography'*, 'What if the Knesset went local?' argues that the absence of a local area-based or territorial link to local elected councillors in Tel Aviv may not strike Tel Avivians as peculiar for the simple reason that in Israeli national elections the electorate votes in a single electoral constituency. This uniquely Israeli singular electoral geography has the effect of neutralising Palestinian political geography. The Palestinian voting bloc, indeed like all Israeli political groupings, are, whether by accident or design, literally 'geographically invisible' on election night.

In *'The Shifting Ideology of a Simple Map'* we contend that, in recent years, historical and self-conscious left-right cartographic map-making badges of identity have strangely started to mutate, reverse even. Where once to draw the contours of Israel as bounded by 1967 borders was perceived as an exercise in left-wing cartography, now it only serves to perpetuate the myth of two nations, Israel and Palestine, or, more perverse still, two Israels – the first, an imperfect but essentially democratic Israel that subscribes to western political norms and operates inside the Green Line, the second, an undemocratic Israel, a segregating and occupying military force that governs in the occupied territories. Irrespective of the application of two different legal jurisdictions (civilian and military), there is (and has been since 1967), of course, only one single de facto 'sovereign' state operating between the Jordan River and the Mediterranean Sea.

Every country perpetuates its own territorial myths through map-making; few perhaps are afforded the luxury or opportunity of designing myths on the scale of Mini Israel. Mini Israel was built at a scale of 1:125 to be precise, and extends over 35,000m², housing 350 large-scale models and buildings. In 'Mini Israel' we walk the miniaturized toy-like representation of the state of Israel where there are no borders, no settlements, no West Bank. The 'separation barrier' is conspicuous by its absence; there is no Green Line.

The increasing invisibility of the Green Line for many Israelis serves to erode or erase the geography of a future Palestinian state. In 'Butterfly State' we pin down six varieties of real and imagined butterflies to be found locally in Israel-Palestine. 'Butterfly State' seeks to create a visual appetite to look again, to look harder, to question one's assumptions, to open one's mind. Which butterfly states are real or imagined, natural or man-made? What can we see? What do we choose to see and not to see, and can invoking the temporal beauty of the butterfly reveal the tragedy of spatial stories and journeys we have chosen not to navigate? 'Butterfly State' is not simply a game of fantasy geography. The increasing invisibility of the Green Line in the life of most Israelis, and the increasing visibility of a separate proto-Palestinian state (a parliament in Ramallah, the trappings of government, a national separate vehicular licence-plate system) paradoxically serve to validate the existence of a quasi-Palestinian state and simultaneously consolidate the Occupation. This is a quasi-Palestinian state that is somewhere 'over there', not quite geographically discernible, but nevertheless a state that is almost politically tangible. It's this vague sense of 'somewhere-ness', we would argue, that assists in masking a comprehension of the reality of the contours of the geography of the Occupation. This is a Palestine that somehow manages to operate in a sort of schizophrenic duality. On the one hand, this is a Palestine that is hidden (behind walls and checkpoints); it exists but is not seen. This is a Palestine that Israelis are forbidden by law to visit (Area A under the Oslo Accords). On the other hand, the illusion of a Palestine state is promoted. It includes the superficial trappings of a state with a parliament in Ramallah. This Palestine is allowed to be seen but is not permitted to exist (as an independent state).

Equally invisible on the evening weather forecast are the Palestinian cities of the West Bank. Every major daily (Hebrew) national newspaper and all major national TV channels use a map of Israel in weather forecasts that is devoid of the Green Line. In Yedioth Ahronoth, Israel's largest selling daily newspaper, all major Palestinian population centres in the West Bank are omitted from the weather map. This omission, one could argue, is reasonable, as these Palestinian cities are 'technically' not inside Israel, nor have they been officially annexed by the Israeli state. The same, however, is true of the settlement city of Ariel.

The weather maps all include Ariel, which is a sixth the size of the adjoining next-door Palestinian city of Nablus. Nablus is invisible on the Israeli weather forecast.

This invisibility of Palestinian geography has a complex relationship with the consumption of the Israeli Occupation. There is a common and somewhat peculiar perspective amongst many on the Tel Avivian Israeli left that, in terms of the land, the majority of Israelis haven't really assimilated the settlements into their concept of Israel's territory in their everyday lives – that they, Israelis, don't go there; they have no wish to go there; 'there' becoming the almost unspeakable, unnamable 'territories'. This narrative presumably is intended to generate a sense of political comfort, detachment, a kind of hopeful or willful disengagement, an almost psychological resistance even. What this often can simply mean is 'people like me' or 'the people I know' choose not to go there. There is a risk that this left-wing Tel Avivian world view is erroneously extrapolated for the nation as a whole. Perhaps if a majority of Israelis don't go there – the settlements that is – it's simply because a majority have no reason to do so. They may have no family or work connections there. It may sound logically trite, but it is nevertheless true to say that, geographically and statistically speaking, the majority of people of any country do not actually go to vast swathes of many parts of the country they inhabit if they have no reason to go. The political detachment, distaste even, for the settlement project among wealthy north Tel Avivians is partly nurtured, we would argue, by the reality that few wealthy Tel Avivians are likely to have family or friends seeking cheaper, more affordable homes in those distant suburban settlements. Privilege and housing choice can accidently inform, perhaps conveniently reinforce, attitudes to geopolitical geography.

And where exactly is 'there'? The separation of the settlements themselves from the Occupation or control of wider open territory often betrays muddled thinking. One doesn't actually have to visit a settlement per se, pass its security gates, to consume the geography of the Occupation. The Tel Avivian day-trip drive to the Dead Sea is a visit through the Occupation itself. It is a day-trip geography consumed by many Tel Avivians leftists. And if most people do not travel to many parts of the occupied territories, maybe the reason is rather prosaic – they are forbidden or it's unsafe to do so, not because they are consciously acting out some form of personal political disengagement plan. Many Israelis living close to the Palestinian city of Qalqilya visited the city in the 1980s to shop, to go to the market. They do not go there now because the city is surrounded on three sides by an 8m-high wall. It's illegal to go there, and it is probably unwise to do so.

We would argue that Israelis do assimilate or consume the geography of the Occupation in their everyday lives. And they don't have to travel to a settlement to do so. The fact that every major newspaper and every TV channel presents a single Israeli geographic space, devoid of the Green Line and devoid of Palestinian cities, in their weather forecast maps is a not-so-subliminal and powerful message in normalising one continuous Israeli space. It is the very seamlessness of the Occupation that in part serves to sustain it. It psychologically anaesthetizes an Israeli (Jewish) understanding of the Occupation itself.

The Israeli occupation of the West Bank entered its 50th year in 2017. The political, economic, ethno-cultural and militaristic forces that weave together to sustain that occupation are undeniably complex. In *Seamless Neighbourhood* we identify two cartographic and apparently contradictory forces at work which paradoxically and simultaneously assist in sustaining that occupation. On the one hand there is the conscious wilful decoupling of Israel and the West Bank in mental mapping, and on the other an erosion or erasure of the Green Line on the ground and in map-making between Israel proper and the West Bank.

This is complex parallel and simultaneous process of psychological separation and physical integration. The imagined decoupling in map-making is fed by a leftist desire to separate, to disengage or withdraw from the West Bank. It perpetuates a myth of two Israeli states. This is an Israeli state west and east of the Green Line. The concept of an Israel proper and an occupied West Bank sustains a political illusion that there is 'a here' and 'a there'. This is the illusion perpetuated by many on the left of a democratic Israeli state west of the Green Line and an ethno-segregated occupied or undemocratic Israel state east of it. The constructed narrative of a 'democratic' motherland state and an 'undemocratic colonial' or client state may have some conceptual validity if they were separated by an ocean or continent. The seamless reality, however, of Israel and the occupied West Bank renders this constructed narrative somewhat senseless. This ongoing mirage of the decoupling of Israel proper from the West Bank is in part fed by the delusion of an occupation that is an interim or temporary arrangement. Fifty years of occupation in the life of a nation state just 70 years old is anything but temporary.

In Chapter 6, we reflect on the political state of the 'State of Tel Aviv' and the urban geography of the so-called Tel Avivian 'Bubble'. In 'The world's first Jewish Global City?' we chart the rise of Tel Aviv as a proto-global city, arguing that the ambition of Tel Aviv to gain a foothold on the ladder of international Global City status rankings cannot be divorced from its desire to escape the perceived constraints of both local Israeli and regional Middle Eastern political geography.

We conclude in Chapter 7 on the future challenges facing the city of Tel Aviv as it struggles to assert its identity in an Israel drifting politically rightward. In the 'The Geography of Regional Zionism' we map multiple imaginary Zionisms derived from the 2015 Knesset election to provide the territorial building blocks for a potential federal 11-state solution.

It is the present-day atomised, segregated and, yet, for many Tel Avivians, invisible and seamless built landscape that informs the outline of the possibilities of our decentralised autonomous federalism of the future.

The landscape narrative of many of the stories in Seamless Neighbourhood – 'The Road to Ariel', 'The Tel Avivian Dead Sea Drive', 'The Exurban Geography of Tel Aviv – Alfe Menashe', amongst others – could be viewed as analogous to the concept of 'negative space' in photography. They literally are the physical space that surround a more central subject to the story under observation. The subject in this case is the Israeli Occupation, including the physical landscape of walls, barriers, checkpoints, observation towers and road blocks that are experienced by Palestinians but mostly invisible to Israelis. Those Palestinian experiences are well documented by others elsewhere. Our interest in these so-called negative spaces is their possible role in consolidating and moulding the perceptions and attitudes of Israelis to both an apparent seamless geography of Israel and an invisible occupation of Palestine. In many ways Seamless Neighbourhood can be viewed as a geographer's and an architect's diary, both an imagined and real road trip of a city, an extended story of a greater and seamless Tel Aviv.

———

Ben Tsiyon Bouelvard, Tel Aviv

1 – Does Size Matter?

Winter on 'Jerusalem Beach', Tel Aviv-Yafo

1.1 – Where is Tel Aviv?

It is a superficially simple question, but a notoriously difficult and challenging one to answer for any city: Where does your city really begin and end? Where are its borders? How many people actually live there? So where exactly is Tel Aviv? And just how big is Israel's largest city?[1] Where does Tel Aviv begin and end? And why is it so important to our understanding of the seamlessness of Israeli political space? Ultimately Tel Aviv is as big or small as you want it to be. Tel Aviv is both a state of mind (the 'Bubble') that extends no more than a few square kilometres, and a vast, seamless neighbourhood extending beyond the width of Israel proper.[2]

A quick 'where exactly is Tel Aviv' Google search will instantly reveal the Wikitravel 'fact' that Tel Aviv is actually not Israel's largest city after all. Somewhat prosaically, Wikitravel states Tel Aviv is the second largest city in Israel. It is on the Mediterranean coast, about 60km north-west of Jerusalem and 100km south of Haifa.[3] Wikipedia tells us that the population of Tel Aviv is 432,892 (2015) and has an area of 52km² (20 square miles). This is the Tel Aviv of the municipality of Tel Aviv-Yafo. Its municipal borders, like most cities, are clearly and legally defined. They are, as in most cities, somewhat illegible on the ground. This is home to the city's tax-paying local residents and home to a very diverse and hetero-geneous population. This is the Tel Aviv of Mayor Ron Huldai, mayor of the city since 1998, who successfully sought re-election in 2013 for an additional five-year term.

For many Tel Avivians (indeed, many Israelis), 'Real Tel Aviv' is an altogether much smaller, socially cohesive and exclusive place. This is cliché Tel Aviv, a city happy to market itself as the Mediterranean fun-loving, laid back, hedonist Tel Aviv of the beach, leafy boule-vards, restaurants, coffee shops and nightclubs. 'Real Tel Aviv' is also sometimes colloquially referred to as the Tel Aviv 'Bubble' – a much-maligned, long-overused and sorely misun-derstood local moniker. The Bubble is an almost vapid two-decade-old (or more) pejorative to describe the supposed political detachment and self-delusion of Tel Aviv. The Bubble is for some a slur, for others a positive badge of civic or city local identity. For many it's simply a hackneyed phrase that has long outlived its original meaning.[4]

Both 'Real Tel Aviv' and the Tel Aviv 'Bubble' are a good geographical or territorial fit for another Tel Aviv, 'Bauhaus Tel Aviv'.[5] 'Bauhaus Tel Aviv' is also known as the White City of Tel Aviv on account its 2003 UNESCO world heritage status designation. The White City of Tel Aviv is home to the world's largest concentration of early International Style buildings.[6] Whatever you wish to call this few city blocks of the downtown central city area, this Tel Aviv is relatively wealthy and young, with half of the population aged between 20 and 34. This compares to just under a third for the city as a whole. Both 'Bauhaus Tel Aviv' and 'Real Tel Aviv' are also almost exclusively Jewish. They are also whiter, ethnically speaking, than

Tel Aviv as a whole.[7]

'Real Tel Aviv' extends perhaps as far north as Sderot Nordau; some locals may argue passionately that it extends no further than Arlozorov Street. It is bounded by Ibn Gabirol to the east and Rothschild Boulevard to the south, and is home to just 75,000 residents, approximately 20% of all Tel Avivians.[8] 'Real Tel Aviv' swings left at election time. This is Meretz territory, or 'Meretz Tel Aviv', the small party of the Israeli (largely Ashkenazi) liberal, progressive, secular left.[9] In the 2015 Knesset election, Meretz received just 3.9% of the vote nationwide. In the area centred around 'Real Tel Aviv' or 'Bauhaus Tel Aviv', Meretz received 25% of the vote in a contiguous small cluster of neighbourhoods, home to some 44,000 people, and its biggest concentration of the vote in the entire country.[10]

Tel Aviv, just like any city, is a city of contradictions and contrasts. Generally, a wealthier, 'whiter', more Jewish, 30- to 50-something, car-owning and relatively homogenous suburban north Tel Aviv gives way to a more complex, diverse Tel Aviv as one travels north to south. We have mapped out some of those in *Postcards from Tel Aviv* (Chapter 2.2). It could be argued that the northern suburbs are nothing more than a morphological inner extension of the suburban and wealthy city-suburbs of Ra'anana, Herzliya and Ramat HaSharon, while the largely poorer neighbourhoods of southern Tel Aviv have a lot more in common, both socio-economically and ethnically with the city of Bat Yam which borders Tel Aviv-Yafo further south.

Tel Aviv-Yafo, as the name suggests, is a fusion of two 'cities'. This a Palestinian and Jewish city. Palestinian Yafo, or Jaffa, has had more than 3,000 years of unbroken urban settlement. Its larger neighbour, Tel Aviv, is just 100 years old.[11] Culturally and historically, Tel Aviv-Yafo straddles many continents: 1 in 7 Jewish residents of the city trace their origins to Asia (including the Middle East), primarily Iran, Iraq and Yemen;[12] a further 10% claim first-generation North African heritage.[13]

From a European geographical co-ordinates perspective, Tel Aviv-Yafo is longitudinally west of Moscow and latitudinally north of the Canary Islands. From a Middle Eastern perspective, Tel Aviv-Yafo is south of Baghdad and east of Ankara. Geographically and culturally, Tel Aviv-Yafo is both a coastal Mediterranean city of 430,000 people and a vast Middle Eastern metropolis of 3.6 million people.[14] This is a Middle Eastern city where gay couples strolling hand in hand generally goes unremarked, and where both the practice and social acceptability of same-sex and shared parenting has almost become a badge of flag-waving cosmopolitan, local-neighbourhood identity.

This is also a Mediterranean city where the 20% minority Palestinian citizens of Israel can find it difficult to rent or buy property simply because they are Palestinian. Housing discrimination is both naked and indirect. Palestinian residents are ineligible for a first-time home-buyers' grant because they do not serve in the Israeli army – a not insignificant challenge in a city where local house prices have soared 152% from 2001 to 2016.[15]

This is a city many of whose residents are dismissive, indifferent and occasionally hostile to the rest of Israel, and in particular Jerusalem (the capital), a 40-minute bus ride up the road. A kind of fashionable elitist siege mentality permeates much of the wealthier parts of the city, a mentality that some would argue seeks to withdraw not from Palestinians in the West Bank, but disengagement from the rest of the Israeli masses living in peripheral suburbs and towns outside Tel Aviv. A significant proportion of these same Israeli masses actually live inside Tel Aviv – a 'Greater Tel Aviv'. This is a Greater Tel Aviv beloved of urban geographers and metropolitan municipal master-planners.

The Greater Tel Aviv area includes, but is not restricted to, the Tel Aviv District, the smallest and most densely populated of the six administrative districts of Israel. The Tel Aviv District has a population of some 1.3 million.[16] Neither the borders nor jurisdictional powers of the Tel Aviv District are likely to be of interest to too many people. Administrative districts are unsurprisingly unlikely to attract any sense of civic loyalty or recognition by the overwhelming majority of the residents who happen to live there. But where exactly is Greater Tel Aviv?

Metropolitan density provides a valuable prism with which to uncover where it actually begins and end. Tel Aviv-Yafo, perhaps somewhat unusually for the most central municipal authorities of a greater city region, does not fully encompass the densest part of Greater Tel Aviv. The densest part of Greater Tel Aviv stretches from Petah Tikva, a 'city suburb' 10km to the west of Tel Aviv-Yafo, into Bnei Brak, an adjoining western 'city suburb', before turning southwards to yet another 'city suburb', Bat Yam, 10km south of city-centre Tel Aviv. Geographically, a large swathe of Tel Aviv-Yafo does not form part of this high density arc. This high 'Density Tel Aviv' is home to some one million people.[17]

Greater Tel Aviv is, however, much bigger than either the bureaucratic Tel Aviv District or the 'Density Tel Aviv' of Petah Tikva-Bat Yam. Greater Tel Aviv is a vast, almost continuous, middle-density, polycentric conurbation with Municipal Tel Aviv-Yafo its undoubted core. This metropolitan Tel Aviv is home to some 20 autonomous municipal 'cities' or city suburbs that seem to blur and blend seamlessly into one another. Tens of thousands of residents of these municipal cities commute daily to Tel Aviv-Yafo to work.

Commuting is a useful analytical tool of the metropolitan reach of any conurbation. The proportion of workers of outlying suburban dormitory towns that commute daily to the downtown city (Tel Aviv) core is the most commonly used metric to delineate the territorial borders or edge of the Greater Tel Aviv area. The metropolitan reach of 'Commuting Tel Aviv' is now shown to extend southwards some 32km to the city of Ashdod, and northwards to the small town of Mikhmoret, 38km from the centre of Tel Aviv-Yafo.[18] This commuting metropolitan reach is revealed to extend eastward across the Green Line, deep inside the occupied West Bank. Some 20% of the residents of the settlements of Ariel, Elkana and Alfe Menashe commute to the Tel Aviv core. Ariel is located 17km from the Green Line and 38km from downtown Tel Aviv.[19]

The proportion of those in any exurban or suburban locality travelling to the core of any city masks a host of complex underlying sociological and economic commuting geographies, and Tel Aviv is no different. Like any city region, many are commuting considerable distances from towns and suburbs because spacious and attractive homes are unaffordable in the centre. Long-distance commuting is also a metric of employment accessibility. High-status, financially lucrative, creative or specialised employment is often only found at the centre of the most dynamic or largest city core in any conurbation. A commute to the centre of Tel Aviv from a distant wealthy suburb may simply reflect personal economic success and choice.

Greater Tel Aviv metropolitan-commuting number-crunching can, and very often does mask other local, particular, but very visible urban geographies. These are urban geographies of segregation, severance and enforced separation. An analysis of where Tel Aviv begins and ends cannot be divorced from the Israeli occupation of the West Bank. The fashionable academic language of 'fuzzy borders' and 'soft spaces' cannot be used to disguise the reality of impenetrable walls and hard-bounded places.[20]

The Palestinian city of Qalqilya is 20km north-east of Tel Aviv. Proportionally speaking, compared to nearby Kfar Saba in Israel proper, few residents of Qalqilya commute daily to work in Tel Aviv. Qalqilya is surrounded on three sides by an 8m-high concrete security wall (Israeli separation barrier). To enter or leave Qalqilya, a city of 40,000, its residents must queue for hours before funneling through the Eyal Israeli military checkpoint to the north of the city. Qalqilya is, in effect, severed from its natural commuting hinterland of Tel Aviv. An emphasis on commuting as a measure of Tel Aviv metropolitan reach assists in masking what we call 'severed urbanism', or 'truncated metropolitanism'. It normalises walls, barriers, checkpoints. Put simply, it normalises the Occupation.

Any commuting numeric used to define the boundary or cut-off point of metropolitan reach is necessarily arbitrary. Whether it's 10% who commute to the core, 20% or 40%, ultimately the number is subjective, no more than a mathematical prism of perspective. Density is no different in this regard. Both density and commuting as metrics have their limitations. A focus on commuting as a measure of metropolitan reach, even if unintentionally, risks making invisible the reality of a metropolitan occupation. It assists in erasing very real walls, barriers and military checkpoints. These walls, barriers and checkpoints currently corral tens of thousands of exurban residents, 'lost commuters', unable to commute easily because their freedom of movement is severely controlled.[21] It is estimated that 5% of the Qalqilya workforce work in Israel proper.

Density also risks masking the reality of severance and segregation. They mask functional relationships. Density maps do not reveal patterns of movement. Few Tel Avivians would consider Qalqilya to be part of greater Tel Aviv. The reason, however, is unlikely to be because of perceptions of geographical distance: the city is just a 20km or 20-minute drive away. This is a metropolitan Tel Avivian reach that is generally unimagined in part because it is dysfunctional – dysfunctional in the sense that it is artificially severed, cut off, blocked. In many ways this is an exurban geography that doesn't work, literally, but it is nevertheless a metropolitan geography that is more likely to provoke important questions on segregation, separation and the Occupation. Put another way, dysfunctional relationships are as valid a prism of analysis of metropolitan reach as are functional relationships, be they commuting, shopping or recreational day-tripping.

Metropolitan Tel Aviv is a largely seamless metropolitanism for Jews and severed urbanism for Palestinians living east of the Green Line. Israelis are generally not permitted to travel to Areas A and B (Oslo Accords) in the West Bank, and most probably have no desire to do so. Areas A and B make up 18% and 22% of the West Bank. Even including the Gaza Strip, Israelis are free to travel in 90% of historic Israel-Palestine.[22] In 'Contiguous Tel Aviv' (page 46) we have mapped out a polycentric metropolitan sprawl to generate a greater Tel Aviv region that has a minimum population of 200 people per square kilometre, whilst also forming a contiguous belt of density radiating out from the heart of downtown Tel Aviv. This greater contiguous Tel Aviv area we have termed 'METROTA' for Metropolitan Tel Aviv. Our METROTA extends seamlessly northwards along the Mediterranean coast to just beyond the northern suburban fringes of Netanya. The southern suburbs of the city of Ashdod, some 40km from the Dizengoff Centre in the heart of downtown Tel Aviv, forms the southern boundary of our METROTA. It extends eastward as far as the settlement of Ariel deep inside the West Bank. It's takes just 30 minutes to drive to Ariel from the centre of Tel Aviv. METROTA includes the West Bank Palestinian cities of Tulkarm and Qalqilya and the West Bank settlement towns of Alfe Menashe, Oranit and Elkana. It has an area slightly greater than the city of Los Angeles (1,469km² versus 1,290km²) but is home to one million fewer people (2.9 million versus 3.8 million). Greater Los Angeles has a population of 11.7 million compared to some 13 million for all of Israel-Palestine.[23]

Our last map of Tel Aviv is the 'Tel Aviv Strip'. The Tel Aviv Strip is located entirely west of the Green Line. The borders of this Tel Aviv to the east are the borders of the internationally recognised state of Israel. This Tel Aviv is often marketed as geopolitically vulnerable, wedged between the Mediterranean Sea and the predominantly Palestinian West Bank. This Tel Avivian metropolis is just 14km (9.3 miles) wide at its narrowest point. That narrowest point is just 5km north of the municipal border of Tel Aviv-Yafo. This is also the narrowest point of Israel proper. A distance of 14km wide is just half the average length of each of the 12 Moscow Metro lines;[24] the Sokolnicheskaya line (Line no. 1), which travels in a relatively straight line from north-east Moscow to south-west, is 32.5km long.

From the upper-floor balcony of homes in Petah Tikva, a city suburb in Greater Tel Aviv, just 6km from the Green Line, it is possible to simultaneously view to the west the skyscrapers on the Tel Aviv coast and to the east the homes of Palestinians in the West Bank. Some 40% of the Israeli population live in this small strip of coastal plain 60km long and, on average, 20km wide. This coastal strip is home to 3.6 million Israelis. They live on just 7% of the total land area of the Israeli state. This Tel Aviv Strip has a density of 2,300 people per square kilometre and is four times the size of the Gaza Strip. Gaza City is 71km south of Tel Aviv-Yafo. With close to half its population, the Gaza Strip has a density of population twice that of the Tel Aviv Strip at 4,900 people per square kilometre.[25]

There are of course, theoretically, an infinite number of Tel Avivs. Each can be constructed, designed or imagined according to a personal preference, logic, functionality or particular ideology. Whether Tel Aviv is delineated by a territorial border, expressed as a functional (or dysfunctional) relationship, or simply better revealed through comparative mapping, each equates to a different state of mind and place. Each is as elastic or illusory as the other. We have mapped and constructed just a few Tel Avivs. 'Tel Aviv-Yafo', 'Real Tel Aviv', 'Bauhaus Tel Aviv' or 'The White City of Tel Aviv', 'Meretz Tel Aviv', 'The Tel Aviv District', 'Density Tel Aviv', 'Contiguous Tel Aviv', 'Commuting Tel Aviv' and 'The Tel Aviv Strip' are all, irrespective of their scale, simply part of a bigger picture, a bigger story, literally a spatial hierarchy of Tel Aviv. All of them are constructed, all of them simultaneously artificial and yet real and inhabited. In many ways these different districts, commuting communities, neighbourhoods of a Greater Tel Aviv, can be best understood as a vast, differentiated, but seamless neighbourhood. It is this seamless neighbourhood we call 'The City of Israel', a city whose residents and commuters, shoppers or day-trippers work and reside in a metropolis whose functional (geographic, social, economic) boundaries, for Jews at least, do not readily recognise the Green Line.

––––––

Tel Aviv

Manhattan does Tel Aviv
Manhattan Island is 21.6km long; Israel is 15km wide at its narrowest point

1.2 – The 'Lie' of the Land and the Lazy Eye of Geography

The capacity to try to look at a map, any map, differently and see new geographies is an age-old cartographical game. Turning geography on its head, literally reversing the north-south axis, for instance (north-south is, in any event, an arbitrary exercise at a planetary scale) can at times provide a temporary, but refreshing dislocating sense of space, revealing unseen or new insights into scale, orientation and relative distances. Endeavouring to spatially see afresh what one perhaps has taken for granted is usually harmless, sometimes rewarding and occasionally quite revealing. Maps are also potentially powerful in constructing political arguments. In 'The "Lie" of the Land and the Lazy Eye of Geography', we inverse, reverse, reorient and overlay various homemade Tel Avivian geographies.

The DNA of geography is space and density. The reality of space, in particular the perceived lack of it, including the perceptions of the tyranny of proximity, is inextricably tied up with competing narratives of the Israeli-Palestinian conflict. Tel Aviv, technically Israel's second largest city but the nation's largest metropolis, offers a surprisingly often-overlooked urban spatial story in this laboratory of magnified national geography.

In a series of images (on page 42) we show the relative size of Municipal Tel Aviv-Yafo (52km^2), the Tel Aviv Strip, and various global metropolitan geographies. The Tel Aviv Strip is wedged between the northern portion of the occupied West Bank and the Mediterranean Sea. It is home to just over 3.3 million Israelis, or 40% of the population of Israel. The Tel Aviv Strip occupies just 6.8% of the land of Israel proper. It has a density of population of 2,300 people per square kilometre and is four times the size of the Gaza Strip. The Gaza Strip has a density of population of some 4,900 persons per square kilometre.

The state of Israel is a mere 15km (9.3 miles) wide at its narrowest point. That narrowest point is just 5km north of the municipal border of Tel Aviv-Yafo. A distance of 15km is half the average length of each of the 12 Moscow Metro lines. The Sokolnicheskaya line (Line no. 1) line which travels in a relatively straight line from north east to south west is 32.5km long.[1]

In 'London-Tel Aviv' and 'Dublin-Tel Aviv' we reveal, through comparative maps drawn to scale, the congested space of the contested geographies of the Middle East. A journey from Tel Aviv to Jerusalem, onwards to Amman (Jordan), then Damascus (Syria), Beirut (Lebanon), returning to Tel Aviv via the Israeli city of Haifa is some 598km. This perilous and impossible political journey around the Middle East is the equivalent in distance to a trip from the city of London to Cambridge, onwards to Birmingham, then Cardiff and Exeter, returning to London via Southampton. Similarly, this Middle East journey in the south-east of England it is the equivalent in distance to a trip from Dublin to Drogheda, onwards to Athlone, then Limerick and Cork city, returning to Dublin via Kilkenny.

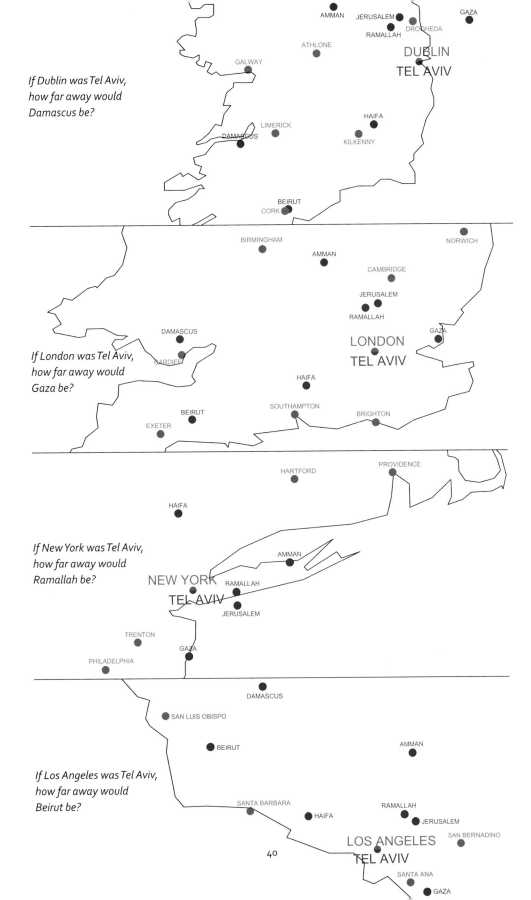

If Dublin was Tel Aviv, how far away would Damascus be?

If London was Tel Aviv, how far away would Gaza be?

If New York was Tel Aviv, how far away would Ramallah be?

If Los Angeles was Tel Aviv, how far away would Beirut be?

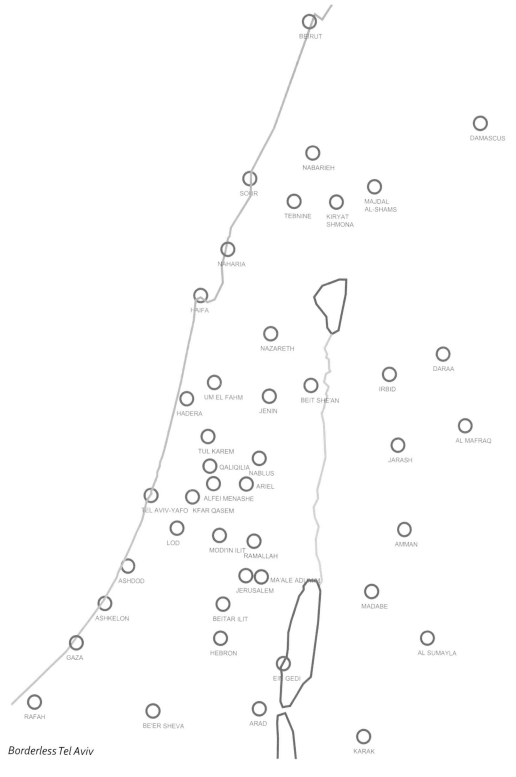

Borderless Tel Aviv

Mediterranean coast
Tel Aviv-Yafo Municipality
1949 Armistice (Green) Line
Jordan / West Bank border

The Tel Aviv Strip and the Moscow Underground / London / New York City (the five boroughs)

Manhattan (and Central Park) and Municipal Tel Aviv-Yafo (to scale) – Tel Aviv-Yafo (pop. 433,000) is 52km²; Manhattan (pop. 1.6m) is 59km²

Density

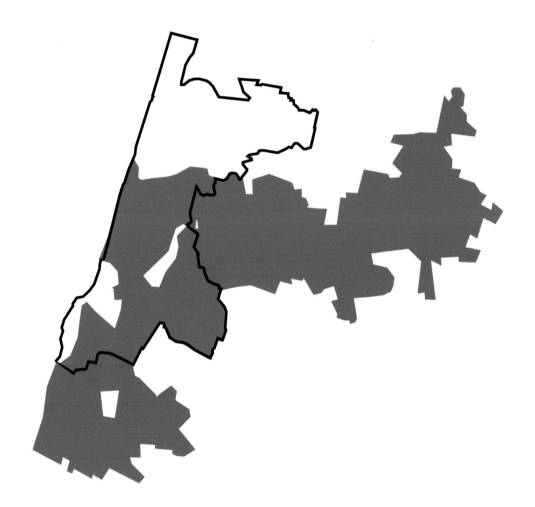

DENSITY TEL AVIV: 5,000 PERSONS PER KM²

Tel Aviv-Yafo, perhaps somewhat unusually for the most central or downtown municipal authority of a greater city region, does not encompass or monopolise fully the densest part of
Greater Tel Aviv. In 'Density Tel Aviv' we map a Tel Aviv with a minimum population of 5,000
people per square kilometre, forming a contiguous belt of density radiating out from the
heart of downtown Tel Aviv. That high-density population belt stretches from Petah Tikva,
a 'city suburb' 10km to the west, through to Bnei Brak, another 'city suburb', through part
of Tel Aviv-Yafo, before extending southwards to yet another 'city suburb', Bat Yam some
10km south.

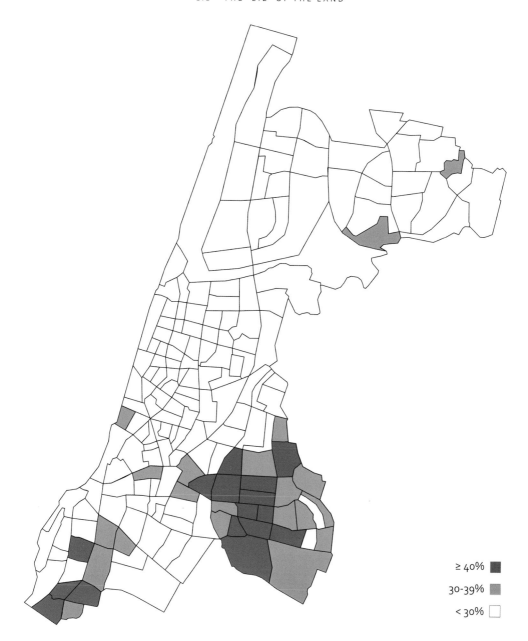

≥ 40%	⬛
30-39%	⬛
< 30%	⬜

MAPPING MIZRAHI

Just under 1 in 4 (24.1%) Tel Avivans are 'Mizrahi', or Jews of North African or Middle Eastern origin. Mizrahi Tel Avivans are to be found clustered in the relatively impoverished suburbs of Yad Eliyahu, Hatikva, Neve Tsahal and Yafo Dalet in the south and south-west of the city. With Tel Aviv property prices having risen 150% in the past 15 years, these areas are now being 'gentrified'.

Contiguous Tel Aviv

In 'Contiguous Tel Aviv' we map out a Tel Aviv with a minimum population of 200 people per square kilometre, forming a contiguous belt of density radiating out from the heart of downtown Tel Aviv. Contiguous Tel Aviv extends from Ashdod on the Mediterranean coast in the south-west to the 'severed' Palestinian city of Tulkarm in the north-east, with a contiguous finger of density extending east to Ariel, deep inside the West Bank. Contiguous Tel Aviv includes the Israeli-Palestinian cities of Kfar Kassem, Tira, Taibeh and Qalansawe, and the West Bank Palestinian city of Qalqilya. Our patchy contiguous or Metropolitan Tel Aviv (METROTA) has an area slightly greater than the city of Los Angeles (1,469km² versus 1,290km²), but is home to a million fewer people (2.9m versus 3.8m). Greater Los Angeles has a population of 11.7m compared to some 13m for all of Israel-Palestine.

persons per km²

≥ 30,000

20,-30,000

15,-20,000

10,-15,000

5,-10,000

2,5-5,000

1,250-2,500

400-1,250

200-400

no data

black-outlined area is Municipal Tel Aviv-Yafo

Roomy or Not?

In 'Roomy or Not?' we map out the percentage of homes with five rooms or more in the Greater Tel Aviv area (Contiguous Tel Aviv). Some of the largest homes are to be found in Alfe Menashe and Oranit – the largest of the two so-called quality-of-life settlements. Some 86% of homes in Alfe Menashe have five rooms or more. In Oranit it's 83.2%. Some 20% of Israeli homes have five rooms or more. In Hod HaSharon half of all homes have five rooms or more. There are few five-room homes to be found in central Tel Aviv or in the cities of Bat Yam (3%) or the Palestinian city of Qalansawe (3%). (Note: two rooms in Israel is usually a one-bedroom apartment with a separate kitchen.)

% of homes with
5 rooms or more

≥ 70%

40-69%

20-39%

10-19%

< 10%

no data

no data

Palestinian cities
in the West Bank

black-outlined area is Municipal Tel Aviv-Yafo

Ethno Tel Aviv

In 'Ethno Tel Aviv' we map out the proportion of local Jews and Muslims in our 'Contiguous Tel Aviv' or Greater Tel Aviv. Muslims form a majority in the west and north-west fringes of Greater Tel Aviv (Kfar Kassem, Qalansawe, Taibe, Tulkarm, Tira and Qalqilya) and in a number of small isolated clusters in the cities of Lod and Ramla, and Jaffa (Yafo) in Tel Aviv-Yafo. Qalqilya and Tulkarm are located east of the Green Line and the Israeli separation barrier.

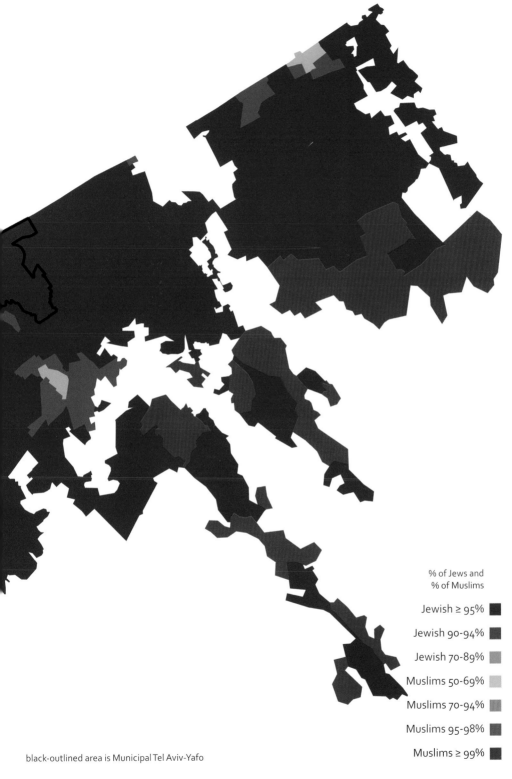

% of Jews and
% of Muslims

Jewish ≥ 95%

Jewish 90-94%

Jewish 70-89%

Muslims 50-69%

Muslims 70-94%

Muslims 95-98%

Muslims ≥ 99%

black-outlined area is Municipal Tel Aviv-Yafo

2 – Picture Tel Aviv

2.1 – The White City

The White City of Tel Aviv is famed for its Bauhaus or International Style architecture. In 2003, UNESCO declared large parts of the centre of Tel Aviv a World Heritage Site. The criteria and rationale for the UNESCO designation of 'The White City of Tel Aviv' primarily revolved around the simple fact that Tel Aviv possesses the 'the world's largest concentration of early International Style buildings'. In *'The White City'* we temporarily ignore the city's 'architecture' and instead provide a very brief glimpse or snapshot of the diversity of life inside the White City of Tel Aviv.

――――

Map of the White City of Tel Aviv (UNESCO)

opposite – Life in Tel Aviv

Chametz, the eight-day Passover ritual, is observed in almost all Tel Avivian supermarkets
Leaven food – any food that's made of grain and water that have been allowed to ferment and rise (bread, cereal, cake, biscuits, pizza, pasta, and beer) – is covered with plastic sheets and sales of them forbidden.

The legendary Palestinian Abouelafia 24-hour bakery at Yefet Street, Clock Tower Square, Jaffa
It has been operating since 1879, and is particularly busy during Passover when the sale of leaven goods is restricted elsewhere in the city.

Gay Pride, Tel Aviv
Gay Pride Tel Aviv 2017 attracted some 200,000 locals and overseas visitors to the streets of Tel Aviv. Heavily marketed by the city, it is regularly criticised (outside of Israel) as engaging in 'pinkwashing'.

Charles Glore Park fronting the beach, Tel Aviv

57

A Tel Aviv-Yafo resident is more likely to be over 75 years of age (7.8%) than aged 4 or under (7%). In Israel you are more than twice as likely to be 4 or under (10%) than over 75 (4.6%).

Some 14.2% of Tel Aviv residents are aged 65 and over (2008 census)
The city is steadily getting younger. In 1983 the proportion of over 65s peaked at 19.2% at a time when the city's
population had fallen to 325,000. The city's population today is 435,000.

Israeli Air Force cadets outside the HaKirya (headquarters of Israeli Defense Forces in Tel Aviv)

Inside a Route 6 shared taxi, Allenby Street, Tel Aviv. Some 31% of Tel Avivians are aged between 20 and 34, the figure for Israel as a whole is 23%.

61

Jaffa (Yafo) in south of the city
Some 93% of Tel Aviv-Yafo is Jewish. Jaffa has a small Muslim majority.

Outside the Central Bus Station in Neve Sha'anan, Tel Aviv
An estimated 40,000 'foreign workers' (documented, and undocumented) including asylum seekers, primarily from
Africa, live in Tel Aviv. They are not counted in the Israeli census.

Port of Tel Aviv. Just over 2 in 5 of all households in Tel Aviv are occupied by a single person. The figure for Israel as a whole is 21%.

Ben Gurion Boulevard, Tel Aviv

Frishman Beach, Tel Aviv

Rothschild Boulevard, Tel Aviv: elderly Israelis and their 'foreign workers' or full-time carers
1 in 25 Tel Avivians are aged 80 or over. It is estimated there are some 30,000 Filipinos working and living in Israel,
majority full-time care-workers mostly living in Israel's largest cities.

overleaf – Independence Day Celebrations, Rabin Square

Playing with the city of Tel-Aviv-Yafo

2.2 – Postcards from Tel Aviv

In 'Postcards from Tel Aviv' we paint a spatial picture of the lives of Tel Avivians, from 'Jewish Density' and '21st Century to Aliya' to 'Mapping Mizrahi' and 'Little Russia'.[1] In '21st Century to Aliya' we map where recent Jewish immigrants to Tel Aviv have chosen to live. It seems that newly arrived Jewish immigrants' urban choice is a coastal one. Some 7% of the Jewish population of Tel Aviv are 'recent' arrivals. This rises up to 20% near the city centre beaches of Gordon and Frishman. Wealthier suburban north Tel Aviv remains either unattractive or unaffordable, perhaps both, to newly arrived Jewish immigrants, with just 2% of north Tel Avivians made up of *olim* (new Jewish immigrant arrivals).[2]

Just under 1 in 4 (24.1%) Tel Avivans are 'Mizrahi' – Jews of North African or Middle Eastern origin. Mizrahi Tel Avivans are to be found clustered in the relatively impoverished south and south-west of the city.[3] Some 28% of all Tel Avivian Jews who were born abroad immigrated to Israel between the years 1990 and 2001. The overwhelming majority of these came from the ex-Soviet Union (USSR), mainly Russia and the Ukraine. There is a clear north-south Tel Aviv divide in where these immigrants settled.[4]

Just over 10 out of every 11 (91.7%) residents of Tel Aviv-Yafo identify (or are identified) as Jewish. Of the 168 separate statistical areas of the city, Jews are a majority in 161 of them (with Jews a plurality in one more). The Jewish proportion of the local population rises above 99% in 14 of these 161 Jewish majority areas. Only six of 168 statistical areas have a Muslim plurality (five of them with a slight Muslim majority). These are clustered around Jaffa and Adjami.[5]

Some 40% of all homes in Tel Aviv have just two habitable rooms. In 'Roomy or Not?' we map the density of small homes. In a few neighbourhoods, clustered around Florentine, 75% of all homes are two rooms or less.[6]

One in 8 Tel Avivians walk to work; not surprisingly 1 in 4 in the city centre walk to work.[7] Just 1 in 20 (5.1%) Tel Avivians are classed as 'unskilled workers'. They are spread pretty thinly across central and north Tel Aviv. A concentration is found in the neighbourhoods of Shapira and Neve Sha'anan where unskilled workers make up 1 in 3 of the adult population.[8]

Two in 5 (40.5%) households in Tel Aviv are single-occupancy households. Those who live alone are clustered in the south inner city (Florentine) and along the city-centre beach front.[9] For every 20 females in Tel Aviv there are 19 males. Men and boys, however, outnumber women and girls in 27 of the 168 small statistical areas of Tel Aviv. For the most part there is a distinctly north (female) / south (male) divide. Males are in a majority in an almost continuous geographic belt stretching from Jaffa to Florentine to the Old Central Bus Station area of Tel Aviv. Females outnumber males in the relatively wealthy north central neighbourhoods. These areas also closely correspond to those areas with the highest con-centration of elderly women.[10] One in 5 (19.3%) Tel Avivians are 17 years or younger. Children tend to be concentrated in either the suburban, wealthy and predominately Jewish north or the relatively impoverished and proportionally greater Muslim south. The central coastal strip of Tel Aviv is relatively childless: in many areas fewer than 1 in 20 locals are under 17 years of age.[11]

Just under half (44.8%) of all Tel Aviv households (in 2008 at least) are home-own-ing households. This rises above 75% in much of northern Tel Aviv. Home ownership is also high in 'poorer' south Tel Aviv, with the neighbourhood of Kfar Shalem having the highest home ownership of all, with 6 out of 7 (84.9%) households owning their home. The lowest home ownership is found in Florentine where less than 5% of households own their own homes.[12] Some 17%, or just under 1 in 6, Tel Aviv households have two cars or more. Perhaps not surprisingly this rises to above 1 in 2 households in wealthy suburban north Tel Aviv.[13]

Tel Aviv-Yafo could be described as a tale of five cities. In north Tel Aviv – 'whiter' Jewish families with children, living in owner-occupied larger homes, who drive to work. The city-centre beach front – recent immigrants, living alone, who walk to work. The south inner city – a disproportionate number of men and unskilled workers, living alone, in rented one-roomed homes. The south-west suburbs – a mix of Russian and Mizrahi families with children, who own their homes. Finally, Muslim or Palestinian families in Adjami and Jaffa.

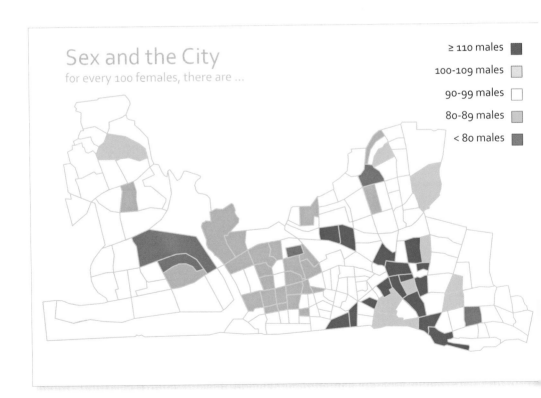

Little Russia percentage of Jewish population
immigrated 1990 -2001 (overwhelmingly ex-Soviet)

≥ 50%
40-49%
30-39%
15-29%
< 15%

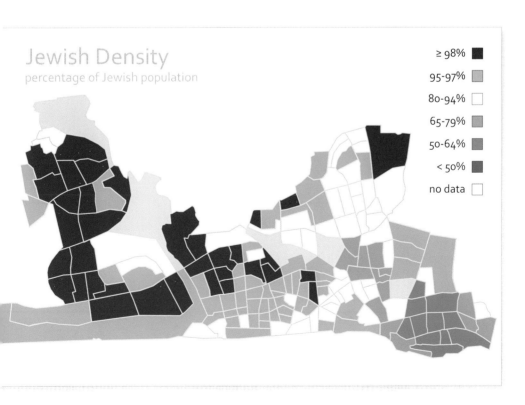

Jewish Density
percentage of Jewish population

≥ 98%
95-97%
80-94%
65-79%
50-64%
< 50%
no data

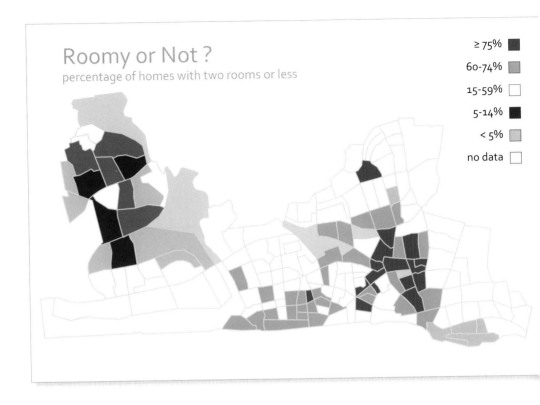

Roomy or Not ?
percentage of homes with two rooms or less

≥ 75%
60-74%
15-59%
5-14%
< 5%
no data

Walkers
percentage who walk to school or work

≥ 24%
20-23%
6-19%
4-5%
< 4%

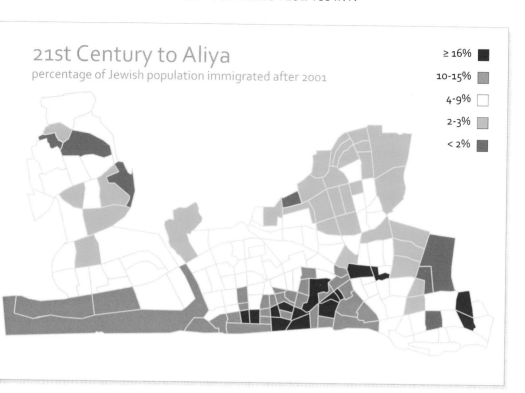

21st Century to Aliya
percentage of Jewish population immigrated after 2001

≥ 16%
10-15%
4-9%
2-3%
< 2%

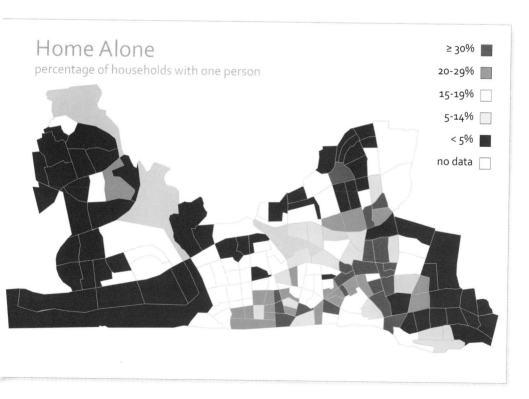

Home Alone
percentage of households with one person

≥ 30%
20-29%
15-19%
5-14%
< 5%
no data

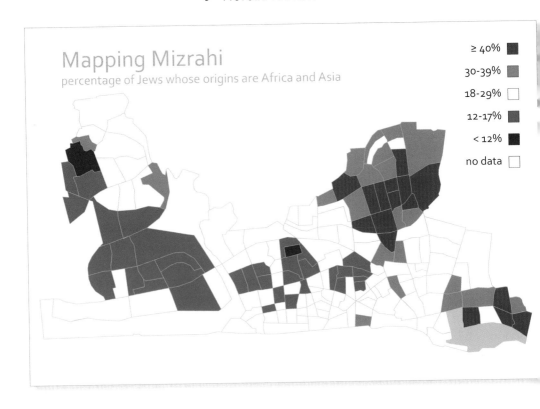

Mapping Mizrahi
percentage of Jews whose origins are Africa and Asia

≥ 40%
30-39%
18-29%
12-17%
< 12%
no data

Missing Children
percentage of households with children

≥ 30%
24-29%
12-23%
6-11%
< 6%

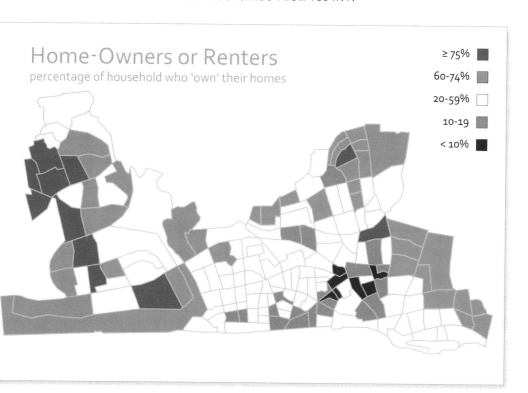

Home-Owners or Renters
percentage of household who 'own' their homes

≥ 75%
60-74%
20-59%
10-19
< 10%

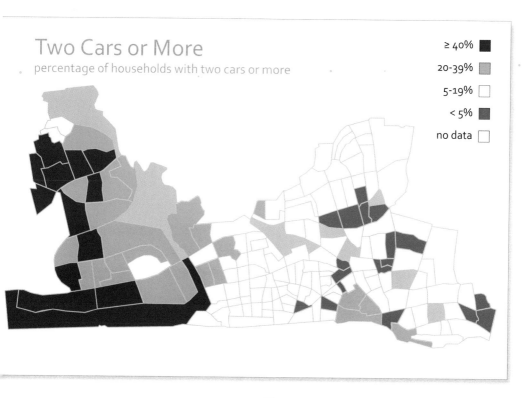

Two Cars or More
percentage of households with two cars or more

≥ 40%
20-39%
5-19%
< 5%
no data

Rooftop on Berdyczewski, Tel Aviv

previous page – Homes of Hatikva neighbourhood, south-east Tel Aviv

2.3 – Mapping the 'missing' persons of 'Postcards from Tel Aviv'

When is a long-term indigenous resident not a citizen, a recent new arrival not an immigrant, and an newly arrived immigrant an automatic citizen? What's the difference between a new arrival and a foreign worker, an illegal immigrant and an infiltrator? Just who gets counted by whom in officialdom in Israel, and who doesn't get counted at all? Put bluntly, who is made invisible by whom? All Jews living outside of Israel are entitled by virtue of being Jewish to emigrate to Israel and become Israeli citizens. Jewish immigrants to Israel are known as *olim* (the Hebrew word *olim* can be translated as 'going up'); the journey is known as 'making Aliyah'. Non-Jewish (documented) economic immigrants to Israel are primarily known as 'foreign workers'. The municipality of Tel Aviv-Yafo on its official website devotes its entire 'new residents' page to the *olim* only; 'foreign workers' are not mentioned.[1] It's not only the Tel Aviv municipality that appears to make 'foreign workers' invisible; the Israeli census doesn't count them at all. With the exception of the Palestinian municipal residents of annexed east Jerusalem, and the primarily Druze residents of occupied Golan Heights, the Israeli census does not count non-citizens of Israel in its once-in-a-decade headcount.[2]

Perhaps not surprisingly, the exact number of 'foreign workers' residing in Israel would appear to be unknown. Part of the uncertainty derives from the fact that a significant number of previously authorised workers have outstayed their work permits and remain in the country illegally, many of whom are assumed to be working without official permits. In addition, a significant number of people who entered the county legally on short tourist visas, but have outstayed those visas, are also assumed to be working without permits. These numbers do not include the tens of thousands of African residents who entered the country illegally, a significant proportion who now claim asylum-seeker status. Most of these immigrants came across the largely unprotected Sinai border. Undocumented African migrants who entered the country without a permit and who may be eligible for refugee status are often called 'infiltrators' in the mainstream Israeli press. To complicate matters, non-governmental organisations (NGOs) who work closely with both documented and undocumented immigrants often categorise or classify these various immigrant groups differently, with some grouping all foreign workers, documented and undocumented, together.

The Centre for Immigration and Migration Israel (CIMI) states there are 77,000 legal foreign workers, 16,000 illegal and a further 91,000 who have outstayed their tourist visas.[3] The African Refugee Development Center (ARDC) also says there are 77,000 foreign workers who have valid work permits. In addition, ARDC reports that there are 46,000 undocumented African immigrants who have entered the county illegally.[4] A 2013 report on the news website Ynet claims that there are 109,000 legal foreign workers and a further 93,000 who are undocumented.[5] The same Ynet report stated the number of undocumented

Neve Sha'anan neighbourhood, south Tel Aviv
Non-Israeli citizens, including 'foreign workers', both documented and undocumented, are not counted in the Israeli census of population.

African immigrants at 54,000. Other sources suggest up to 59,000, with an estimate of 17,000 living in south Tel Aviv.[6]

From this information we have generated a Tel Aviv map that includes both foreign workers (documented and undocumented) and those African immigrants who have entered the country without a permit many of whom seek asylum status. We estimate the total combined figure for these groups is 40,000. That's just under 10% of the total population of Tel Aviv. We call the map the 'Missing Persons of "Postcards from Tel Aviv"'. Our mapping series 'Postcards from Tel Aviv' (Chapter 2.2) takes it data from the Israeli Central Bureau of Statistics national Population Census of 2008 (the last full national census), a census that clearly does not count all the residents of the city. Those maps paint a distorted picture of Tel Aviv. As foreign workers, both documented and undocumented, are not counted in the census, they are also missing from all our maps. In mapping these 'missing' persons we correct that glaring omission of the visible lived urban reality in Tel Aviv.

Tel Aviv is a hugely diverse city, with immigrants, both Jewish and non-Jewish, coming from all parts of the world. In addition to the 10% who are not counted, most of whom were born outside of Israel, 27% of the Tel Avivian Jewish population were born abroad. This works out at around 33% foreign-born in Tel Aviv-Yafo.[7] The foreign-born population of New York City is 37%.[8] It is that diversity that contributes to the social and cultural dynamism of the city. 'Mapping the Missing Persons of "Postcards from Tel Aviv"' is a call to both the Israeli census and Tel Aviv municipality that all the residents of Tel Aviv, irrespective of their religion, origin, legal status or citizenship, should be counted.

Planning ahead for adequate social and housing provision in any city is a challenge. In a city where 10% of its residents are not even counted, it makes planning those services all the more difficult. But this is not simply about efficient planning. A decision not to count all residents – many of whom may have lived legally for years in the city – not only makes these residents invisible, it sends a clear 'official' message from the 'City' and 'State' on the values and importance of social integration.

In its 'Tel Aviv Global City – Work Process' manifesto,[9] the municipality of Tel Aviv-Yafo talks up its self-identifying 'values of pluralism and openness and never ending cultural vitality' (p.5), boasting of its 'pluralistic and unfettered atmosphere tolerance and informality' (p.23), and defines the Tel Avivian city character as a 'welcoming urban nature characterized by a rich mosaic of nations people and ethnic groups' (p.10). The 25-page document nevertheless shies away from once mentioning the words 'foreign worker', 'African' or 'immigration', let alone 'Palestinian', 'Muslim' or 'Arab'. Making visible invisible Tel Avivians remains a work in process indeed.

A NOTE ON OUR ASSUMPTIONS

We have necessarily had to make some bold assumptions in drawing upon all of the above sources of information. Averaging out different sources of data, we estimate that there are some 200,000 foreign workers living in Israel, and that some 12% of these live in Tel Aviv. This is a conservative estimate. Averaging out the varying sources of data on African migrants, we estimate there are some 53,000 living in Israel, with an estimated third of these living in Tel Aviv. This amounts to 18,300 residents. This closely correlates to the 17,000 estimate in Ynet news. Taken together, this community of non-citizens totals 42,300 residents or 10% of the population of Tel Aviv-Yafo. Those 42,000 missing Tel Avivians are not distributed evenly across the city. There is a known concentration of both foreign workers and undocumented Africans in south Tel Aviv. It is not unreasonable to assume a significant proportion are also likely to be living in neighbourhoods (southern and southeastern suburbs) in the city where rent is most affordable. In addition many care-givers reside in the home of their elderly 'patients/employers'. The areas of the city with the highest concentration of elderly living alone are centred on Kikar Hamedina in the 'old north'. Taking these factors into consideration and having regard to known counted local neighbourhood populations, we have mapped the 42,000 missing persons to produce a density map of missing Tel Avivians. In distributing our 42,000 accordingly, our density map generates concentrations of up to 35% missing Tel Avivians in Shapira and Neve Sha'anan. This 42,000 may well be as low as 30,000, but is likely to be much higher. If just 15% of foreign workers (both documented and undocumented) and 50% of African undocumented immigrants lived in Tel Aviv, the 'missing' persons numbers would rise to 56,000. Our 'Missing Persons' map does not include other temporary or long-term visitors such as tourists, overseas students, diplomats or non-Israeli spouses of Israeli citizens. The state of Israel in late 2017 and early 2018 was seeking to deport tens of thousands of undocumented Africans back to Africa, many to the state of Rwanda. The success or otherwise of this government policy, which at the time was proving to be highly controversial and meeting both significant political and logistical opposition locally, may inevitably affect the above assumptions on population concentrations.

_____

Mapping the 'missing' persons of Tel Aviv: making visible an invisible census

2.4 – 508 Immutable Zonings

In '*508 Immutable Zonings?*' we identify the 508 different zoning ordinances to be found in the Tel Aviv-Yafo Municipal City Plan. The entire city, block by block, building plot by building plot, is classified, colour-coded and sub-stratified until an almost unimaginable 508 different patterns of coloured boxes emerge to reveal the zoning ordinance for the city.[1] The 508 immutable zonings of Tel Aviv can be viewed as a divine 'blueprint' of immutable laws of spatial structure – a kind of planning DNA of the city. This is not simply a life map for the future, a plan, but the very genetic structure of the city itself.

In theory these 508 zoning ordinances – very subtle in their difference – provide for an extraordinarily specific prescriptive framework for future development. Each colour block is specific in its determination; each in effect describe a different type of use. Each of the 508 colour codes are then woven together to produce a vast matrix or jigsaw of building codes and guidance. Devising 508 different small colour patterns is in itself an exercise in creative imaginary design. Their specificity includes 64 different types of residential use.

Code 1211 is specific to 'Residential and Knowledge Industry' and is visually represented as thick pink and orange diagonal stripes. Code 1488 is specific to 'Residential, Employment and Docking' and is visually represented as thin turquoise, violet and orange diagonal stripes. Code 1494, 'Residential, Tourism and Transportation', thin red, pink and orange diagonal stripes; Code 1564, 'Trade and Rural Accommodation', very thick pink and grey diagonal stripes with thick green framed surrounding, and on it goes for 504 other uses.

Just as in the DNA of life, this complex interlinked system of coded blocks would appear to determine the spatial future or personality of the city. Much of this code is merely descriptive, telling us what is there already. It is for the most part spatial history revealed. It is designed, however, if not to predict, to determine the city's future.

The destiny of cities, of course, are never fixed. Opportunities can and often do arise. Tastes change. Demand and supply of almost everything can rise or fall daily, weekly, monthly. Change isn't always determinable or foreseeable. The very unexpected can happen. For good or ill, context and environment can make redundant or alter the best or worst of seemingly fixed, immutable planning destinies. This illusion of immutability is understood by the planners of Tel Aviv. Despite their painstaking efforts to interpret a vast, complex, colour-coded patchwork to determine the city's future, all is not as it appears to be. As in life, the city, its DNA hardwiring can mutate, alter, be altered. The mutations can eventually reveal themselves on the surface of the face of the city in the form of unexpected or unwanted extrusions or blocks of buildings, sometimes towers.

------

opposite – Just eight of the colour codes of the 508 Immutable Zonings

All 508 zonings – in theory immutable – are in fact, to some degree, utterly mutable. They can be changed, recoded, rezoned, rewritten. All plots of land in Israel are subject to national, district and municipal zoning plans commonly known by their Hebrew acronym TABA. In theory, the TABA determines how a property may be developed and what limitations or restrictions are applicable – its use, density, heights, etc.[2] In practice, the TABA is negotiable through discussion with the local municipality, colloquially known as the TABA change process (*halich shinnui TABA*). This potential to recode destiny is not unique to Tel Aviv (or Israeli cities for that matter). 'Rezoning', 'spot zoning', 'map amendments' – rewiring the DNA of a city has many names. This would appear to be inherently sensible as cities need to evolve. A patchwork of 508 different codes is, however, extraordinarily deterministic and arguably unworkable if a city, Tel Aviv city, is to unexpectedly evolve and change.

It does, however, beg the question why, if they can be radically altered through the (political) art of persuasion, do we have 508 zonings in the first place? Why be so fantastically specific and deterministic if that very determinism is so fluid? It is the very specificity that inherently makes the apparent fixed plan so unpredictable. Recoding to adapt is inevitable. And who then exactly is empowered with the authority to alter, or invested with the skill to persuade those with the power to alter these apparently immutable zonings?

The art or, indeed, power of persuasion to amend zoning requires considerable skill and expert knowledge. It is not unreasonable to assume that this expert knowledge demands considerable resources. Put simply, it may and often does cost a considerable amount of money. Understanding what is required to ensure a successful material alteration in the original TABA zoning can require the expertise of architects, planners, lawyers, engineers, indeed a potential whole range of professional and costly inputs. The greater the planning change, the greater the potential financial reward, the greater the incentive and logic to invest more time and money in persuading city officials to alter the plan. It is a system that is inherently designed, whether intended or not, to favour those who have access to the resources required to ensure a successful outcome.

This is a kind of city making by 'colour by numbers'. It has a superficial clarity and transparency. What could be more precise than 508 different potential land-use zonings or ordinances, except for the fact that those invested in painting the colours differently wield enormous power and influence, and do so in an opaque way. It muddies the democratic authorship of policy-making and the administrative execution of that policy. This is not simply a potential invitation for personal gain, favouritism or preferential treatment for developers or landowners, but also embeds the potential power of the ideology, personal preferences or peculiar policy whims or affectations of local planners or administrators. Ultimately this a recipe for an insider's charter. It makes sense to employ those consultants who are best capable of understanding the subtle interpretation of past TABA decision-making, including those with considerable insight into the nuances of how to persuade city planners and officials to approve the proposed changes. But who keeps tabs on the TABA changes?

———

Decoding the 508 Immutable Zonings
opposite – Berdichevsky Hotel, Berdyczewski Street, Tel Aviv

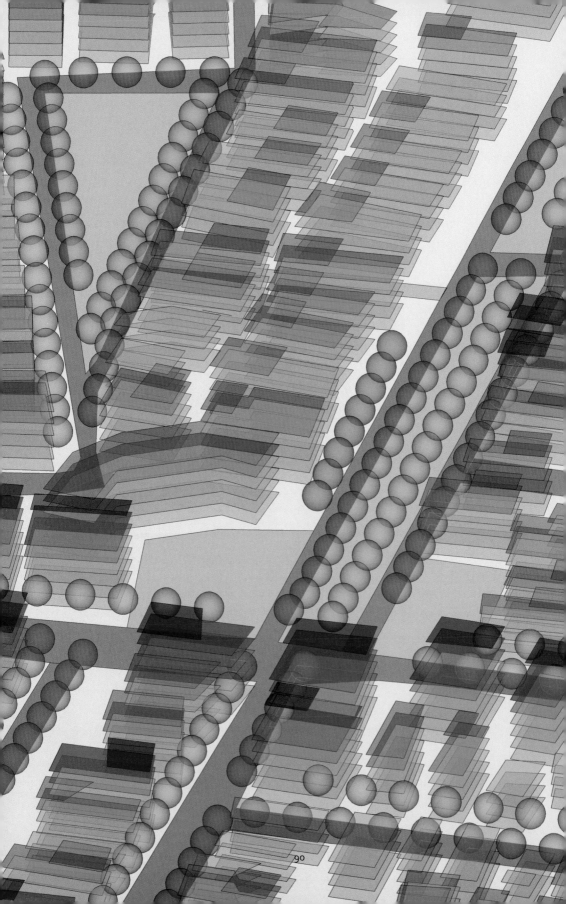

2.5 – The Green City?

So just how green is the White City of Tel Aviv ? When we say 'green' we don't mean some elastic terminology to guesstimate sustainability or ecological footprint, but the proportion of the city that is devoted to green open space. Tel Aviv-Yafo is a middle-ranking city relative to many European cities when it comes to the proportion of total municipal land area devoted to parks and public gardens. Some 18% of all land in the municipality is dedicated to green open space, a figure that includes the central green median strips on major roadways. This is a relatively low figure compared to the likes of Vienna (45%), Stockholm (40%), London (33%) and Dublin (25%), but compares favourably with Berlin (14%), Amsterdam (13%) and Paris (9.5%).[1] The municipality's own development plan sells itself somewhat short in quoting a figure of 13.9% because that figure excludes the vast majority of the Yarkon Park, a park that is classified as a 'Metropolitan Park' and therefore, peculiarly, is excluded from the green space calculation for Tel Aviv-Yafo.[2] Located closer to the northern suburbs of the city, the Yarkon Park at 350 hectares is by far the largest park in the municipality.

The distribution of green open space in Tel Aviv-Yafo, as in most cities, is geographically patchy. The southern neighbourhood of Florentine is particularly disadvantaged when it comes to green public open space. Florentine, historically a textile and small-scale manufacturing area south of the city centre, is perennially on the cusp of regeneration. Florentine is also home to a large student population. Just 1.2% of Florentine is devoted to green open space, the lowest percentage for any neighbourhood in the entire city. With a relatively high population density of 16,500 per km^2 (2.5 times the city's average) Florentine residents have just 0.7m^2 of green public space per person; that totals just 1.1 hectares.[3]

The relatively impoverished next-door neighbourhood of Shapira fares little better. According to the 2008 Israeli census, Shapira, home to 8,000 Tel Avivians, has just 2.4 hectares of public open space; that amounts to 2.6% of the total land area or just 3m^2 per resident. As the substantial local resident population of foreign workers and undocumented African immigrant population are not counted in the Israeli census (estimated to be a third of the local population), the per capita green open space is, in reality, substantially lower.[4]

This is not simply a story of social inequity. The relatively wealthy city centre or downtown area of Tel Aviv is also particularly devoid of green public open space. The largest green open space in the city centre, Gan Meir, is just three hectares in area: 47 Gan Meirs could fit into Hyde Park in London or 113 into Central Park in New York. New York and

opposite – Deconstructing 'green' open space in the White City: boulevards, balconies, pocket parks and communal gardens

overleaf – Rothschild Boulevard / Ben Tsiyon Boulevard / Sderot Hahaskala / Chen Boulevard

London of course operate on a different scale, but just 3.2% of the land of the city centre or central downtown area of Tel Aviv is devoted to green open space.[5]

A figure of 3.2% compares very unfavourably internationally. Almost a fifth (18%) of the most central part of London, an area of 16km^2 is green open space. This area includes Hyde Park, Regent's Park, St James's Park, Green Park and Battersea Park. Some 16% of central Manhattan from 34th Street to 116th Street in Harlem is taken up by Central Park. Even in central Berlin, in a 15km^2 area from Kreuzberg to Alexanderplatz to Kurfürstendamm, the Tiergarten (park) takes up 15% of the city centre.

In Tel Aviv, our park-less city centre we define as a 3.6km^2 area radiating out from Dizengoff Centre, extending to Arlozorov Street in the north to Derech Jaffa in the south, bounded by Allenby to the west and Sarona Market and Tel Aviv Museum to the east. This area approximates to about 7% of the total land area of the municipality and is home to 72,000 people (1 in 6 of the entire city's population). That works out at just 1.6m^2 of green public open space per city-centre resident. The city-centre area has a population density of 20,000 per km^2 – three times the city's average.[6]

Some of the most important public spaces in Tel Aviv – Habima Square or Rabin Square – aren't even 'green'; others, such as the infamous Kikar HaMedina (designed by Oscar Niemeyer), whilst green on Google Maps, is dusty scrub in reality, privately owned, with plans for residential towers. The municipality did open a great new city-centre park, Kiryat Sefer Park, in 2013; however, it would fit more than 40 times into the largest lake in Central Park (Jacqueline Kennedy Onassis Reservoir, 43 ha). Tel Aviv's beach isn't 'green', but is arguably the largest and most valuable public open space in the city. The municipality doesn't include the beach in its open-space calculations. The beach is also fairly accessible; we calculate some 175,000 residents (43%) are within a 15- to 20-minute walk of the beach.[7]

With an area of just 52km^2 Tel Aviv-Yafo isn't a particularly large city; it's a quarter the size of municipal Amsterdam (219km^2); half the size of municipal Dublin (115km^2); or less than two-thirds the size of municipal Copenhagen (86km^2). For a relatively small municipality, Tel Aviv-Yafo has 14km of sea frontage, most of it sandy beach. That compares very favourably to another beach city, Barcelona, which has a municipal area of 101km^2 and just 5km of sandy beach. As a relatively small city in terms of area, around a quarter of the city's population, 97,000 residents, are also within a 15- to 20-minute walk of the Yarkon Park, the city's largest and most attractive green open space, located at the relatively wealthy northern edge of the city.[8] Not surprisingly, some of the poorest neighbourhoods, in the south-west of the city – Hatikva, Yad Eliyahu and Kfar Shalem – whilst peppered with local green spaces, are the furthest away from the beach and the Yarkon Park.

Parks of course are just one part of the open-space infrastructure of any city. The humble balcony and space-efficient boulevard can play important roles. Boulevards and balconies are quintessentially Tel Avivian. In a city with few large-scale centrally located or downtown public parks, boulevards, balconies (along with roof terraces) and communally owned and communally accessed ground-floor gardens provide not just the open space infrastructure for Tel Avivians, they hugely shape social interaction in the city. Boulevards are arguably the great building blocks of the open-space infrastructure of Tel Aviv. In many ways, they define the public open-space character of the city.

Tel Aviv's leafy boulevards have a deceptive hold on the mental map of the city.

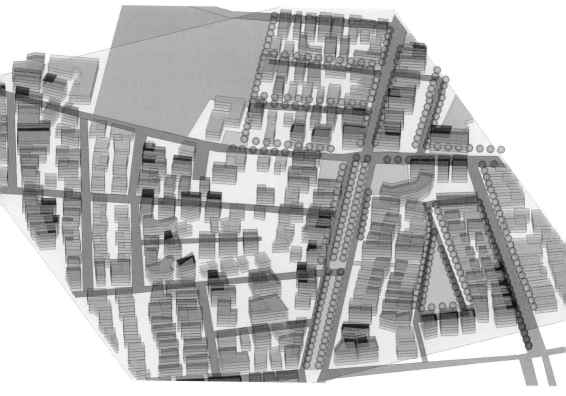

Three-dimensional open space

Calculating the city of balconies: 98,000 balconies is 49 hectares of balcony space, 16 times the size of Gan Meir Park (3 ha). Tel Aviv is also home to thousands of individual communal garden spaces which occupy most of the ground-floor plots of the ubiquitous 4/5-storey-over-pillar stand-alone apartment buildings, which, we estimate, add up to 375 ha of 'green' open space – 125 times the size of Gan Meir or 7.2% of the area of Tel Aviv-Yafo (52km²).[9]

There are five reasonably long and well-known boulevards in central Tel Aviv – Rothschild, Ben Gurion, Ben Tsiyon, Chen and Nordau – yet it feels as if there are many more. These five boulevards combined are just 4.8km in length, the same length as the 4.7km beach walk from the beaches north of Jaffa Port to the Metzitzim beach south of Tel Aviv Port. With an average width of just 20m, these 4.8km of boulevards have a total area of just 9.6 hectares.

Boulevards, unlike many parks, are not simply destinations, but pathways, urban journeys. Too many urban parks function as spatial cul-de-sacs. Successful boulevards, on the other hand, act like linear gravitational social magnets, drawing in activity, people, life from surrounding streets, and channelling them along on a constant travellator of human connection. The best boulevards provide children's play spaces, dedicated dog spaces, outdoor chess boards, cycle ways, coffee kiosks, benches, seats, trees, shade, grass, exercise equipment, mobile libraries and sun loungers. The main Tel Aviv boulevards provide all of these. In Tel Aviv they are the most pleasant way of getting from A to B.

Tel Aviv's boulevards are, for the most part, densely tree-lined. Tel Aviv, perhaps surprisingly to those not familiar with it, has relatively dense tree-canopy coverage – twice

that of Paris, and greater than leafy London.[10] The UNESCO-designated White City of Tel Aviv incorporates four of the great boulevards – Rothschild, Ben Gurion, Ben Tsiyon and Chen. The White City area also has one of the highest tree-canopy densities in the city.

Boulevards arguably occupy the highest rung in the hierarchy of the urban open space in Tel Aviv. They are publicly owned, publicly accessible and usable 24 hrs a day (unlike many parks). Their linear form provides for maximum viewing and visibility. They have an inherent efficiency of shape in terms of total space taken and relative to their accessibility or proximity to a large number of neighbourhoods. Boulevards punch above their territorial area in terms of positive urban impact. There is one Tel Avivian boulevard exception; ironically, its name is Jerusalem Boulevard. Jerusalem Boulevard has been long neglected. It is, in fact, something of a miserable walking experience, with few of the delights of Rothschild, Ben Gurion, Chen or Ben Tsiyon boulevards. Jerusalem Boulevard is somewhat forlorn and abandoned. Locals generally prefer to walk the side pavements of the busy street rather than the central median of the boulevard itself. Whist there are trees, the central median is largely cemented or paved in stone, in places blocked by ugly substations, parked cars and permanent municipal super-sized waste bins. Halfway along its route the boulevard curiously mutates: the walkable grey concrete (at the intersection with Nes Lagoyim Street) becomes a visually delightful green but unwalkable central median. Jerusalem Boulevard, potentially majestic given its natural and man-made geography, is located largely in Palestinian Jaffa (Yafo). Arguably, this is Tel Aviv's only 'Palestinian' boulevard.

There are municipal plans to run the Petah Tikva to Bat Yam light rail down through the middle of it, effectively obliterating the boulevard. The Tel Aviv light rail proposal (now under construction) is expected to open in 2021 (the Red Line runs through Jaffa). When completed, it will have taken 20 years from inception or serious planning to its first ticket ride. That is a very long time to have abandoned a neighbourhood boulevard, particularly when all the other boulevards in more central, wealthier, Jewish neighbourhoods have been the beneficiary of considerable welcome investment.

If the boulevard is undervalued because of its modest contribution to overall open-space area in the city, the domestic balcony is often completely overlooked. There are very few two-storey houses in Tel Aviv with a front and back garden. This is a city of apartments, and apartments tend not to have gardens. They do, however, have balconies. The humble private balcony space, whether partially enclosed, open, recessed, protruding, Bauhaus or not, plays an important role in the civilizing of residential city street life. Balcony spaces overlooking the street below plays an enormous if subliminal or often unacknowledged role in animating street life in Tel Aviv.

Few residents living in traditional suburban two-storey dwellings use their front garden space in the same way as the inhabitants of apartments with balconies. Suburban front gardens are often peculiarly forlorn and empty places; social activity is usually re-

_____

Jerusalem Boulevard curiously mutates from a joyless but walkable grey concrete boulevard path to a delightful but unwalkable green road median

opposite – Jerusalem Boulevard, Jaffa graffiti: "Here, it's not Rothschild"

stricted to the back or rear garden. Yet rear gardens of traditional two-storey houses are not just private in terms of access and ownership, but also very much hidden.

Urban balconies behave differently. Many Tel Aviv balconies directly overlook the street. The street below provides a constant stream of public theatre. There is, potentially at least, the possibility of two-way communication. If public open space can be understood as the so-called 'outdoor room' of the city, urban balconies are a uniquely transitional space between the private and public realm. The urban balcony is a place that invites the city inside the home, and a space that simultaneously opens the home outward to the city.

Planning and municipal open-space maps in most city-development plans tend to be flat and ignore the role of upper-roof terraces and balconies. Despite the fact that almost all municipalities have minimum standards for such communal or private open spaces, few ever collect or map the data when built. The Tel Aviv-Yafo municipality development plan interestingly has a maximum rather than a minimum floor-area requirement: no newly built balcony can be larger than 14m², and the total area of the balcony space in an apartment development cannot exceed 12m² per unit. Why?

With an apparent cap on balconies, how many balconies already exist in the city? With some 187,000 households (family units) in Tel Aviv and assuming a similar number of private residences (not always the same), the majority of which are in the form of varying typologies of apartment blocks, we estimate that there are 98,000 open balcony spaces in the city of Tel Aviv-Yafo.[11] In older blocks in the centre of the city, many balcony spaces have been enclosed and are thus temporarily lost. We estimate that there are a further 38,000 such 'lost' balcony spaces. Our calculations make assumptions on the number of balcony spaces according to size (number of rooms) of homes and the proportion of balconies likely to be enclosed according to their relative number in any one home and typology (age and location of blocks).[12] Assuming an average size of 5m², that amounts to 49 hectares of 'open' balcony space in Tel Aviv-Yafo. That's 16 times the size of Gan Meir (3 ha) or just over a third the size of Hyde Park, London (142 ha).

In our defined city centre of 3.6km², there are 44,000 households and 72,000 people.[13] In Tel Aviv as a whole, 40% of homes have just one or two rooms (excluding kitchen and bathroom), and just 25% have four rooms or more.[14] With an older typology of built fabric, and smaller homes, in our city centre, just 16.4% have four rooms or more and 62% two rooms or less. Given this typology and our assumptions, we calculate that there are some 11,000 open and 20,000 closed balconies. Assuming an average size of 3.5m² (slightly lower than city as whole), there are 38 hectares of balcony space in the city centre.[15]

It's worth restating that Gan Meir, the largest park in the city centre, is just three hectares, which means there is 13.5 times more balcony space than the largest green space in the city centre. But even if all of the green open space in the city centre is combined (11.6 ha), it amounts to just a third of the balcony space in the same area.

The White City of Tel Aviv may have a greater tree-canopy than many (non Tel Avivians) might assume, but in terms of open space it isn't particularly 'green'. So why does Tel Aviv put a cap on its balcony space? Perhaps that 'lost' 38,000m² of enclosed balcony space provides a clue. Enclosed or open, could the White City of Bauhaus architecture instead lay claim and celebrate another local moniker – that of the Balcony Capital of the world?

———

Port of Tel Aviv
Two in five Tel Avivians (175,000) are a 15- to 20-minute walk from the beach or coast

3 – Extensions

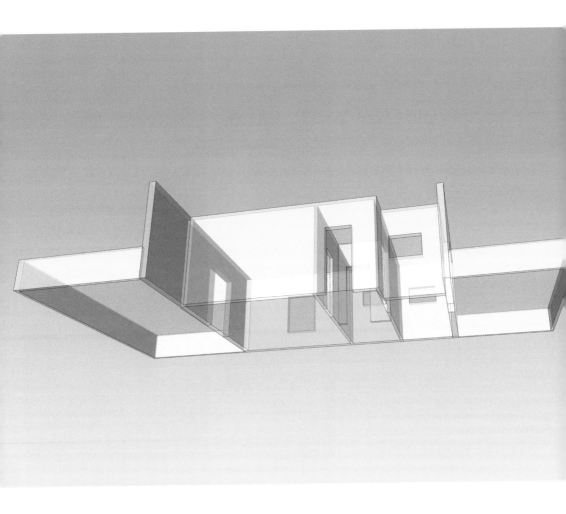

The rooftop apartment, 9 Berdyczewski Street, Tel Aviv

3.1 – Balcony Space

In *'Balcony Space'* we trace the evolution of the balcony in the social urban history of the city of Tel Aviv, exploring how the variation in taste of the Tel Avivian balcony has captured or reflected the contemporaneous zeitgeist of the Israeli state. From its humble origins as a decorative veranda, the status, scale and function of the Tel Aviv balcony space has evolved and mutated over the past 100 years. This has not been a linear evolution of increasing scale or complexity of space, but rather a chronological urban spatial story reflective of wider technological, architectural and socio-economic historic forces that have shaped this city over the past century. In *'Balcony Space'*, even a cursory observation and examination of the city's changing architectural balcony 'taste' reveals or mirrors critical moments in the social and political evolution of the Israeli state itself. So who or what were the critical social drivers or innovators in the evolution of the ubiquitous, but hugely diverse Tel Aviv balcony?

THE ORIENTAL WINDOW BOX (BALCONY)

Our starting point in the evolution of the Tel Aviv balcony story is the simple pocket veranda or window balcony box, less utilitarian and more architecturally decorative. The pocket veranda or window balcony box predates the modernist Tel Avivian era. Tel Aviv celebrated the centenary of its foundation in 2009. The oriental window box was colonial in architectural style – small, 'attached' and limited in its function. The visually decorative oriental window box provided limited utility to the buildings inhabitants. It was largely designed with the street viewer below in mind. *High point: 1900s – 1920s*

THE OPEN BAUHAUS BALCONY

The second evolutionary stage in balcony design is the arrival of Bauhaus architecture. The closure of the Bauhaus schools by the Nazis in the early 1930s resulted in an influx of architects to British Mandate Palestine to design and build what was to become, according to UNESCO, 'the greatest collection and concentration of International Style buildings to be found anywhere in the world'. Thus 1930s European political turmoil, an influx of Jewish immigration, International Modernism, Zionism, and the rather prosaic local practical need for a stripped-down construction technique, all combined to provide the context for this unique laboratory of simplicity and minimalism in design and construction materials. The result is Bauhaus or International Style Tel Aviv. The Tel Aviv Bauhaus balcony was born, architecturally integrated, light, open, airy, minimalist, curved, straight, projecting, internal, functional. *High Point: 1930s – 1940s*

THE SLIDING OPEN 'BALCONY'

Mass immigration to Israel in the early 1950s which saw the arrival of hundreds of thousands of Jewish immigrants from North Africa and the Middle East necessitated a new approach to housing design. Emergency housing needs pragmatic balcony solutions with minimal cost. The most pragmatic and minimalist solution of all was simply to omit them altogether. The open Bauhaus balcony was replaced with an extended ope in a breeze-block façade wall. A sliding window and rail system provided an opportunity for quick ventilation without losing valuable habitable living space. The sliding open balcony was utilitarian, democratic, and generally accessible to all. *High Point: 1950s – 1960s*

THE ENCLOSED BALCONY

The arrival of the air conditioner for the masses was the critical technological driver in the rise of the enclosed balcony. This was the era of 'negative' balcony space – the reversal of previous balcony incarnations. Balconies were in retreat. Stepping out onto the balcony for ventilation was substituted by the comforts of the internal air conditioner. Family and storage space was also at a premium and open balcony space was not a priority. Efficiency trumped leisure and pleasure; the domestic balcony was a luxury. *High Point: 1970s – 1980s*

THE COMMERCIAL BALCONY

Parallel to a decline of the domestic balcony, 1970s Tel Aviv saw the rise of the commercial balcony. The 1970s and '80s ushered in the era of mass-market tourist hotels. Balconies became fun (for holiday-makers at least). This was the era of the commercialisation of balcony

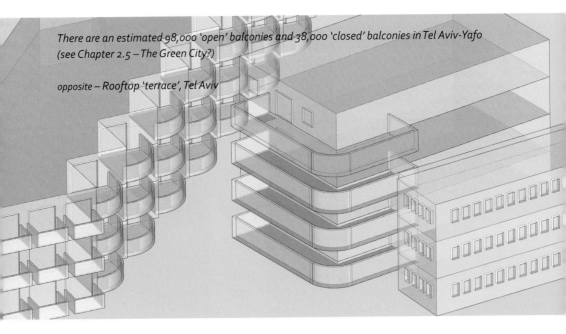

There are an estimated 98,000 'open' balconies and 38,000 'closed' balconies in Tel Aviv-Yafo (see Chapter 2.5 – The Green City?)

opposite – Rooftop 'terrace', Tel Aviv

space with the construction of thousands of small box balcony spaces for recreational use. Pocket balcony spaces determined entire architectural façades. The Renaissance (1975) and Sheraton (1977) hotels best exemplify this. *High Point: 1970s – 1980s*

THE SOCIAL BALCONY (TERRACE)

The burgeoning youth culture in the 1980s and 1990s, the so-called 'Shenkin era' of Tel Aviv, gave physical expression to new balcony phenomena – the temporary mass colonisation and occupation of entire roof terraces for fun. This was an era of accelerated youthful individualism and increased penetration of UK and US popular culture. Rooftop terraces had for the most part being used as places to dry the laundry and store the water tank. They now became home to cheap sofa dope-smoking parties. The socialisation, if social and collectivist in appearance, was resolutely individualistic. This was an era of improvised design. 'Architecture' was personalised and adaptive. Any decent roof space of a certain scale would suffice. *High Point: 1980s – 1990s*

THE STATUS BALCONY

The arrival of the status or high-consumer balcony coincided with the contemporary international rise of the global city. Downtown Tel Aviv, like many comparable (western) cities, has witnessed a new urban renaissance in the past 20 years. Living in the heart of the city is now convenient, desirable and increasingly fashionable and expensive. The status balcony is preferably large. Ideally, it's a vast wraparound space for dining, leisure and entertaining. It's conspicuous in its pleasure as it is an advertisement for the owner's taste and wealth. This is the Tel Aviv of wealth and personal comfort. *High Point: 2000s – today*

Bauhaus balcony, a little piece of 'reclaimed' White City of Tel Aviv

previous page – Balconies of Tel Aviv

Roof terrace on Marmorek Street, overlooking Habima Square, Tel Aviv

3.2 – The soil of Israel
and the rise of the Tel Avivian penthouse

The city of Tel Aviv was a low-rise city for the first 60 years or so after its 'official' founding in 1909. The first 'tall building' built was the 34-storey Shalom Meir Tower, completed in 1965. Things began to change significantly by the mid-1990s.[1] Despite its low-rise Bauhaus UNESCO World Heritage status designation in 2003, Tel Aviv is now a city on the up. Today the city has dozens of tall buildings, towers or skyscrapers above 100m.[2]

The city currently has 14 towers built or nearing completion above 150m, with at least a further six in advanced stages of proposal or approval, with many more under serious design consideration. The municipality approved the city's first 100-storey tower in early 2017.[3] The city has witnessed a transformation of its skyline in a relatively short time. Of those 14 existing or nearing completion above 150m, eight were erected during or after 2015. The Azrieli Sarona Tower, opened in 2017, stands at 238m or 53 storeys. The proposed Azrieli elliptical tower is 350m high or 80 storeys. Many of these towers are residential. Many are home to the very wealthy in Israeli society. Tel Aviv is not just witnessing a transformation of its skyline, but a revolution in the housing preference of its power brokers and political elites.

In 'The Soil of Israel and the Rise of the Tel Avivian Penthouse' we explore how the old Israeli left elite gave up the earth in search of the sky. This is the story of a move from the rural *kibbutzim* to an urban 'room with a view', but also the story of the parallel rise of a Neo-Zionist and messianic geography and its spatial implications for Israeli politics.

The evolution of property status in many western capitalist societies has steadily, over centuries, moved away from the horizontal accumulation of (primarily agricultural) land to the bricks and mortar of the detached mansion or estate house, and finally to the soaring status of the global city penthouse with towering urban views. This has accelerated in the past 20 years with the so-called 'rise of the city' A preference for terra firma has given way to a preference for *usque ad caelum* (reach for the sky). This happened in New York city as early as the mid-19th century, when local elites abandoned mansions in favour of spacious apartments overlooking Central Park. Property elites have been moving upwards in more ways than one ever since, and in so doing have generated or given way to new vertical geographies of status. Israel is no different. Its short 70-year history is a microcosm or condensed version of the historical move of the elites away from the land to the city townhouse and on upwards to the urban penthouse.

In Israel this vertical movement of a largely Labor Askenazi elite has manifested

---

Frug Street, Tel Aviv, with the 46-floor Frishman Tower behind, billed as the 'World's first Bauhaus Tower' (architects: Yossi Sivan and Rachel Feller, 2012)

itself in the slow but irreversible move away from the *kibbutzim* – and all its socio-emotional attachment to the soil and land – to the towering penthouse apartments of the Tel Aviv of the super rich. The last Labor Prime Minister to live a substantial period of his life on a *kibbutz* was David Ben-Gurion, the first Prime Minister of Israel. The last Labor leader to serve as Israeli Prime Minister, Ehud Barak, now lives in an upper-floor apartment in a residential skyscraper in the centre of Tel Aviv.[4] This isn't simply the changing preferences of a Labor elite, but a shifting electoral geography away from the *kibbutz* to the heart of the city. It's a general urbanisation and in particular a 'Tel Avivisation' of the Israeli left. It's a shift that has been taking place slowly for decades. Whilst the majority of voters in the *kibbutzim* remain loyal to the left, they make up a very small fraction of the total left vote today.

The electoral heart of the Labor party today is to be found in the new apartment blocks of north Tel Aviv. In these wealthy suburbs and in the adjoining wealthy municipality of Ramat HaSharon, the Labor Party (Zionist Union) in the 2015 Knesset election exceeded 45% of the vote.[5] The nationalist right-wing party of Prime Minister Benjamin Netanyahu, the Likud party, received just 18.2% of the vote in Tel Aviv compared to 23.4% nationwide. Labor received just 18.7% of the vote nationwide.

In many ways the old left has abandoned the land or soil of Israel in favour of the city. Domestic views of the Mediterranean Sea and the recreational sandy beach have replaced the sights of the working farm and the toiling soil of the *kibbutz*. The foundations of the Israeli Labor Party has, in effect, been uprooted and transplanted onto the 14th, 24th or 34th floor of the Tel Avivian apartment block, as far away from the dusty soil and agricultural toil as you can get.

If the old Labor Zionist left has abandoned an ideological attachment to the land, a messianic Neo-Zionist religious right has gladly taken up the baton. In a parallel political process, ironically facilitated, if not championed, by Labor itself, the rise of the settler messianic movement post-1967 in the occupied West Bank has reconnected (if it was ever lost) Zionism to the soil. The left has not just simply embraced a willingness to cede territory in favour of peace, it has, in the eyes of the messianic settler right, forfeited its attachment to and, thus, its moral right to politically abandon the land of Israel. For the 'left' today, land is simply territory, it's importance primarily informed by its real estate value and its geopolitical strategic depth. For the messianic right, the land, territory, is nothing short of biblical destiny. If the Israeli right's territorial mission is to now possess the land of Judea and Samaria (Jewish biblical West Bank), the Labor left is now reduced to seeking the purchase and inheriting the ownership of valuable real estate in north and central Tel Aviv.

The secular Ashkenazi elite, or establishment left, in Israel has had a historic political association with the land or soil, the most obvious being the self-applauding narrative of the pioneering social collectivism, Utopian story of the *kibbutz* movement. Today the *kibbutz* movement has been largely privatised, its children urbanised. From the appropriation of Palestinian land, followed by an appropriation of state development rights, the *kibbutzim* have worked the land of Israel for themselves for decades.

Somewhat perversely, in many ways the ideological heirs of the *kibbutzim* left are the messianic religious settler right. Both were, are, nominally collectivist in spirit, but

Gindi residential towers, off HaHashmonaim Street, Tel Aviv

relatively exclusive in their membership. Both were, are, Zionist pioneers, ideological, obsessed by the almost transformative power of the soil, and possessing an original unshakeable self-belief in Judaising the rural landscape. Both were, are, enormously successful in extracting considerable state resources for the exclusive benefits of its membership.

Both the settlers and the *kibbutzim* have acquired a scattered geography of subsidised housing, building tax-exemptions and quasi-do-as-you-please construction rights.[6] Regulatory 'national' land-use planning policy (whether in the pre-state Yishuv or in the occupied territories) has been usurped to favour members' collective economic or personal interest. Whether it's the erection of shopping malls on conveniently located *kibbutz* lands or the construction of settler housing on confiscated land, the Israeli state has colluded. In this allocation of state resources, the periphery, the largely Mizrahi and impoverished towns in Israel lost out.[7] They continue to lose out.

Perhaps most interestingly, both the *kibbutzim* and the settler project are dominated by Ashkenazi political parties or Ashkenazi elites. The settlement project was an Ashkenazi enterprise. The first settlements (1967 to 1977) were set up by Labor, a party founded and supported to this day primarily by Ashkenazi Jews – Jews who trace their origins to Europe. The settlement project was then sustained and significantly expanded by a Likud (Ashkenazi) elite. Today the settlements' primary electoral and strategic political champions in the Knesset, Habayit Hayehudi, is overwhelming dominated by religious Zionist of Ashkenazi extraction. The voters who are the greatest supporters of both settlement expansion and annexation are to be found in United Torah Judaism (UTJ), the political home, almost exclusively, of the Ashkenazi Haredi.[8] Finally, the residents of the most far-flung, ideological (non-Haredi) settlements are significantly disproportionally Ashkenazi. Israelis who can trace their origins to Africa and Asia (primarily Morocco, Tunisia, Libya, Iraq, Iran, Yemen) total 28.3% of the population. That figure drops to 24.2% for Tel Aviv. For the most ideological (non-Haredi), far-flung settlements (all located east of the Separation Barrier – Beit El, Ofra, Shilo, Eli, Talmon, Tekoa, Eli), the Mizrahi population ranges from 9.2% to just 15.3%.[9] The settlements are also home to a new wave of Ashkenazis, primarily North American Jews of European (Ashkenazi) descent. These North Americans make up just 4.4% of the Israeli Jewish population. In the seven settlements above, they number from 9% (Eli) to over 20% (Tekoa).[10]

Using any of these criteria, the settlement project is and remains an Ashkenazi political construct and electoral enterprise. This is a narrative that perhaps unsurprisingly tends to be overlooked or downplayed by today's leftist, predominately north Tel Avivian Ashkenazi Labor-voting middle class.

The 31-storey G Tel Aviv Tower (Gindi Tower), Ibn Gabirol Street
G Tower (architects: Gidi Bar Orian and Rani Zis) is home to Ehud Barak, the most recent Labor Prime Minister. Ehud Barak sold his previous home in the 31-storey Akirov Towers on Pinkas Street, Tel Aviv. Barak apparently bought five apartments in this 34-apartment scheme.

115

3.3 – Chasing space in the White City of Tel Aviv

Tel Aviv saw its largest-ever street protest in the city's history when, on the evening of Saturday 4th September 2011, 300,000 Israelis took to the streets in the so-called 'Social Protest Movement' (it's worth noting that Tel Aviv-Yafo's population at the time was just 415,000).[1] The demonstration was arguably the peak point in the Social Protest Movement that had started earlier that summer when a single tent was pitched on Rothschild Boulevard in central Tel Aviv in protest against rising rents and house prices. In the five years preceding the Social Protest Movement, house prices had risen 35% across Israel, with higher prices recorded in Tel Aviv.[2] In the five years following the Social Protest Movement, house prices in Israel have risen 35.5%.[3] House prices have risen 90% in Israel between 2007 and 2016.[4] It is difficult not to conclude that the Social Protest Movement had zero impact on Israeli house price inflation. It could even be argued that the explosive media attention in itself acted as a stimulus to increase prices even more – a self-fulfilling prophecy of further house-price increases driven by a combination of first-time-buyer panic buying and investor-driven speculation. It's impossible to really know.

Whatever the underlying cause or causes, at its most basic the surge in house prices is a case of too much money chasing too few homes. The year 2008 appears to be the 'lift off' date for the house-price surge. Property prices actually fell in Israel in the five years between 2003 and 2008 by 5%, then soared in the five years between 2008 and 2013 by a staggering 48%.[5] The list of usual suspects that drive up prices does not seem to explain the sudden house-price explosion. There was no surge in economic growth post-2008. The Israeli economy grew on average 4.5% in the five years 2003-2007 inclusive, but actually dipped slightly to 3.5% in the five years 2008-2012 inclusive.[6] There was no sudden spurt in immigration (Israel welcomed some 375,000 ex-Soviet immigrants in 1990 and 1991 alone – an almost 10% increase in the national population in just 12 months). Israel's population grew by 11.2% between 2003 and 2008 from 6.3 million to 7.4 million, and by a further 10.1% to 8.1 million between 2008 and 2013. There was no acute crisis of supply. Construction out-put didn't change dramatically either before, during or after 2008. In the five years 2003-2007, total housing construction averaged 32,262 per year. In 2008 alone it was 30,4558. In the five years 2009-2013 inclusive, total housing construction averaged 35,972 per year.[7]

Interest rates certainly have contributed. The Israeli Benchmark Interest Rate hovered between 4% and 6% between late 2003 and the middle of 2008. By the middle of 2009 the Israeli Benchmark Interest Rate had been slashed to below 1% and has rarely risen above 2% ever since.[8] Lower interest rates almost always help fuel a property surge as

---

The 35-storey Ron Arad building under construction, HaShalom Road, Tel Aviv

buyers and investors take advantage of cheap credit. These sharp interest-rate cuts were partly in response to a surging Israeli Shekel, which had increased by 20% against the dollar in less than three years (early 2009 to mid-2011).[9] The surging Shekel was primarily caused by a surge of capital inflows ($7 billion in the third quarter of 2013), borrowed at near zero interest rates in the USA and Europe and then ploughed into the local Israeli property market.[10] In addition to these surging 'legitimate' capital inflows, there is evidence of significant 'black' money flowing into the property market in Tel Aviv following legislative and banking changes in Israel and the USA following the 2008 global financial crash.[11]

Whilst there may be circumstantial evidence of a black housing market in the White City, and that massive capital inflows and low-interest rates have generated an equity bubble, an additional obvious and calculable probable cause of surging house prices is that the State was, and is, simply not building enough homes to meet demand, and that they are not building in the right locations. The average number of housing completions in the past three years (nationally) is 44,700.[12] According to the president of the Israeli Builders Association, with new household formations averaging 58,000 annually, the supply is insufficient.[13] Add in cumulative undersupply and the Builders Association says Israel needs to build 75,000 units a year.[14] For the Tel Aviv area the shortfall is even more acute.

Construction in the 'Tel Aviv District' has averaged 6,500 units per annum.[15] That equates to 14.7% of all State housing completions. But the Tel Aviv District is home to 16.2% of the population.[16] Tel Aviv is where people want (but cannot afford) to live, where employment and cultural opportunities are greatest, where housing demand is greatest; house prices jumping 150% since 2002 testify to that.[17] It is not unreasonable to argue that housing completions in Tel Aviv should be at least 10% greater than the current local population share, not 10% less. If the Tel Aviv District was to have this appropriate 17.8% share of house completions, it would need to be completing 8,000 new homes. Add in the unmet backlog spoken about by the Builders Association, and Tel Aviv should be constructing 13,4000 new homes annually instead of the current 6,500 annually – that's a full 100% more! The backlog in Tel Aviv District is even more acute, with average construction for the 10 years between 2001 and 2010 averaging just 3,900.[18]

So where is the State building? In 2000 and 2001 the population of the Tel District was 5.7 times greater than the Israeli or settler population of Judea and Samaria (West Bank excluding annexed east Jerusalem), but the State was actually building more homes in Judea Samaria than in the Tel Aviv District. By the mid-2000s the imbalance had been somewhat addressed. For the rest of the decade (2002-2010), twice as many new homes were constructed in the Tel Aviv District on average per year (4,236) than in Judea Samaria (1,929). But the Tel Aviv District, despite the rapidly growing population of the settlers, was still over four times greater than the Israeli (settler) population of the West Bank (excluding annexed east Jerusalem) by 2010.[19] Factor in the different family household sizes, and the anti-Tel Aviv housing construction bias is even more acute. A family of eight (two parents, six children), not untypical in Modi'in Ilit, the largest settlement in the West Bank, needs one home. Larger families don't equate to more homes; two couples, a couple with a child and an elderly person living alone – again eight people – need four homes.

In Tel Aviv-Yafo, 40.5% of all households have just one person living in them. In Modi'in Ilit (pop. 60,000) it's just 2%. In Beitar Illit, the second largest settlement, it's 2.2%.[20]

Beitar Illit and Modi'in Ilit are both Ultra-Orthodox Haredi settlements. In Tel Aviv-Yafo just 2% of all households have six or more people. In Beitar Illit 49.7% of households have six or more people. In Modi'in Ilit it's 46.9%.[21] Demand for housing in Israel, whether it's Tel Aviv or Modi'in Ilit, is unlikely to fall soon. Israel now has the highest fertility rate in the OECD at 3.1, higher than India at 2.4. The OECD average is just 1.7. Israel's fertility overtook South Africa in 1999, India in 2006, and Saudi Arabia in 2010.[22]

But where to build in Tel Aviv? With a population of 1.35 million, the Tel Aviv District is the most densely populated region in Israel (7,250 person per km²).[23] Israel is now one of the most densely populated countries in the world.[24] The answer, rather utilitarian, is to build towers where one can, and demolish, rebuild and densify almost everywhere else.[25] The city has even commissioned a study to explore plans to build (non- residential) space underground.[26] In 1986 there was just one building over 100m (Shalom Tower built in 1963). In 1996 there was a handful more. Today there are more than 70 towers over 100m. The city currently has 14 towers built or nearing completion above 150m, with at least a further six in advanced stages of proposal and/or approval, with many more under serious design consideration. The municipality in early 2017 approved the city's first 100-storey tower.[27]

The controversial TAMA 38 initiative dating from 2005 is a national plan facilitating the partial demolition and reinforcement of older residential blocks (built before 1980) susceptible to earthquakes. It originally permitted an additional floor (in places, two) of development over that which was reinforced/demolished.[28] Yet despite TAMA 38, the highrises and a decade of a skyline full of cranes, densities in Tel Aviv-Yafo as a city are not particularly high by international standards. At 8,300 residents per km² (pop. 433,000 and city area 52km²), Tel Aviv's density is higher than Greater London (5,600) and Berlin (4,100), but considerably below Paris (22,000) and Barcelona (16,000). Add in the fact that Tel Aviv is a middle-ranking city in terms of green public open space (18% of municipal land area), with very little green open space in the city centre where densities are usually higher, and the overall density of 8,300 is even less 'impressive'.[29] Paris admittedly has little green open space – just 9% of its municipal land area. New York (five boroughs), however, has a density of 11,000 people per km² and 27% green open space. Paris and Barcelona are cities with substantial neighbourhoods of six to eight stories. Tel Aviv is essentially, notwithstanding the construction of over 70 towers over 100m in the past two decades, a city of four-storey apartment blocks.

With substantially less green space than London (33%), Vienna (45%) and Stockholm (40%), and lower on average residential-building block heights than Berlin, Paris and Barcelona, Tel Aviv arguably has a middling density of population.[30] A revised TAMA 38 dating from 2016 facilitates multiple-floor additions, seven or eight floors to replace an existing typical four-storey block. Each additional floor, if implemented across just 20% of all blocks in Tel Aviv, would generate 9,350 extra homes.[31] That's almost 1.5 times the annual amount of homes built in the entire Tel Aviv District on average per year from 2014 to 2016.[32]

There is, however, something else going on. It is an open secret that Tel Aviv homes, particularly those in the centre of the city, are small. In Israel 18.3% of all dwellings have just two rooms or less (generally neither a small separate kitchen nor a bathroom is considered a room in Israel). In Tel Aviv, however, that figure is as high as two homes in five (40.4%).[33] In the centre of Tel Aviv, from the beach to Ibin Gabirol Street, and from the Yarkon

Park to just north of Florentine, covering some 61,000 households with a population of 98,000 people, a total of 59% of all homes have two room or less.[34] Very small homes actually tend to reduce and not increase the overall density of population in a city. Building tiny homes to try to densify the population, leads to the law of diminishing returns, from a municipal policy perspective. A simple example: take a small apartment of 40m², just about tolerable for an individual. Two such apartments is a density of one person per 40m². However, a 70m² home for a family of four generates a density of one person per 17m² – fewer homes, but over three times the density. Add in additional services (corridors, lifts, etc) required to serve smaller units, and the density differential becomes even greater.

So which comes first in Tel Aviv, the 40.5% who are living in single-person households or the 40.4% of homes that are two rooms or less?[35] Housing policy on size of homes doesn't (generally) determine household formation. Tel Aviv needs to build more homes. We argue that to increase densities and reduce house prices, Tel Aviv needs to build not just more homes, but, perhaps counterintuitively for some, more family-sized homes in the city centre. Whether there is a bubble in the Bauhaus City and whether or not that bubble was driven by international capital flows in the 'black economy' Tel Aviv in 2017 had a higher property-to-income ratio at 19 than New York (10.3), Paris (16.5) or Tokyo (17.5).[36]

The locally famous MY BABY store is 20,000m² of retail and amusement space for children in the Druze village of Yarka in northern Israel. Israel has the highest fertility rate in the OECD at 3.1, higher than India at 2.4. The OECD average is 1.7. Israel's fertility overtook South Africa in 1999, India in 2006 and Saudi Arabia in 2010.

The Dolphinarium, Tel Aviv beachfront
This is the site of the Dolphinarium discotheque massacre on 1 June 2001 in which a Hamas-affiliated suicide bomber
blew himself up outside a nightclub killing 21 Israelis, 16 of them teenagers.

3.4 – Suicidal Geography

The city of Jerusalem, perhaps for reasons of convenience (proximity to the West Bank) has had a greater number of suicide bombings than Tel Aviv. Tel Aviv, nevertheless, suffered 16 separate terror attacks, the vast majority suicide bombings, between 1994 and 2006. That's approximately one every eight months over the 12-year period. Ten of these attacks occurred during a two-year period between June 2001 and April 2003. Excluding the suicide bombers themselves, 117 people were killed in the wave of bombings.[1] Are there any particular spatial patterns to discern? Which Tel Avivian neighbourhoods experienced the most attacks? Did the pattern change over time? And does the geographical distribution give us potential clues into the urban mind-set of the bombers?

Early suicide terror attacks tended to be scattered geographically, with a significant number striking at the very heart of the commercial centre of the city. The first three attacks in the 1990s all occurred just a few hundred metres from each other, close to or on Dizengoff Street, in the very heart of the city centre. Over time, however, 'suicidal geography' tended to gravitate southwards to the more socially disadvantaged neighbourhoods of the city. A spatial clustering is evident in and around the old Central Bus Station. This area is also home to many Israeli 'foreign workers', including undocumented immigrants, many of whom were fatal victims in the attacks. The reason for this gravitation southwards to the bus station is difficult to establish, for the very prosaic reason that the suicide bombers are dead and they didn't leave clues in any suicide notes as to the factors that may have informed their preference in geography of their suicide attacks in the city.

The area in and around the city's main bus station has the attraction, from the bombers' perspective, of maximum deadly impact. Like bus stations the world over, it is generally very busy with a high density of pedestrian movement on the streets outside. It is also not unreasonable to surmise that many Palestinian suicide bombers may have themselves arrived by bus from the West Bank, terminating at the old Central Bus Station. In addition, the areas in and around bus stations tend to be more familiar to new arrivals or recent past new arrivals in any city. It is a local geography that is generally better known by visitors and immigrants than by the long-established residential population.

The geographic movement southward is also likely to have been informed by the 'success' of past suicide attacks. Following the first wave of suicide attacks, there was an inevitable increase in security and a general heightened sense of terror awareness across the city. A young Palestinian with a back pack or suspicious package or padding is likely to have, eventually, attracted the attention of anxious residents or vigilant security staff. The suicide bomber may have simply chosen to minimise the risk of a failed mission by choosing not to walk or catch a taxi to the heart of the city centre.

Unlike the larger department stores and more upscale restaurants in the city centre, the shawarma and falafel kiosks and cheap cafés clustered around the bus station were less likely to be in a position to employ full-time security personnel at their entrance. During this period, many of these upscale restaurants and larger retail stores in the commercial heart of the city employed security staff at the entrances. Detonating the suicide bomb at the point of arrival close to the bus station in this busy pedestrian area was simply a logical choice for the suicide bomber. The geographic concentration of attack in this area is indeed stark. Five of the last eight suicide bomb attacks were carried out in and around the old Central Bus Station. Interestingly, few however occurred on the buses themselves.

If Jerusalem suicide bombers tended to explode themselves and others on buses, the Tel Avivian suicide bombers instead favoured places of eating and drinking: 12 of the 16 terror attacks took place just outside or in restaurants, food markets, cafés, bars or clubs. It would appear that eating at a cheap falafel café in the poorer neighbourhoods in the southern side of the city was in late 2005 the riskiest place to encounter a suicide terror attack. Indeed, one such café, Rosh Ha'ir, had the bizarre misfortune of being struck twice in the space of two months. The first terror attack in January 2006 destroyed the café and injured 31, the second in April, once again destroyed the rebuilt café, this time killing 11 and injuring 68 people .

In the intervening 10-year period, 2007 to 2016 inclusive, there have been 'just' five suicide bomb attacks and four deaths arising from those suicide attacks across Israel. None took place in Tel Aviv. Between the year 2000 and 2006 inclusive, 624 people were killed in 148 separate suicide bombers attacks in Israel.[2] Since the Second Intifada, which began on 28 September 2000, and the end of 2016, some 9,449 Palestinians and 1,206 Israelis have been killed in political related violence and terror.[3]

———

The geography and sequencing of Tel Aviv suicide bombings 1995 to 2006 (transparent: earliest, to opaque: latest)
The first, Dizengoff Centre, in 1996; the most recent, two separate bombings in Rosh Ha'ir restaurant in 2006, near the Central Bus Station. (Tel Aviv's main boulevards shown in green.)

opposite – Rosh Ha'ir restaurant in south Tel Aviv, site of two 'shawarma suicide bombings'
The first bombing on 19 January 2006 injured 31, killing only the suicide bomber; the second on 17 April killed 11 and injured 68.

3.5 – Taking Shelter Apart

In Hebrew, *machaseh* is the most common word for 'shelter', and specifically refers to a place someone flees to for protection. The Hebrew word *miklat* is also commonly used for 'shelter', but is more loosely understood as referring to a physical structure. Most dictionary definitions of the word 'shelter' are likely to include references to something that provides cover or protection, a refuge or haven, perhaps even an establishment or structure that provides temporary housing for homeless people. In *'Taking Shelter Apart'* we explore, deconstruct and reproduce the architecture of shelter in the Greater Tel Aviv urban landscape. We both isolate and contextualise everyday, ordinary, but occasionally politically charged simple shelter-like structures in the Israeli landscape. What do we see? What do we not see? When do we stop looking?

'Shelter'
a. Something that provides cover or protection, as from the weather.
c. An establishment that provides temporary housing for homeless people.
2. The state of being covered or protected.
b. A refuge; a haven.

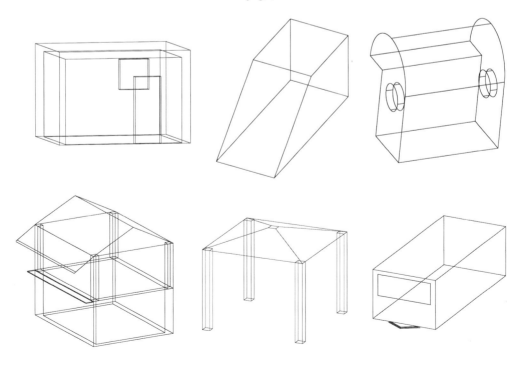

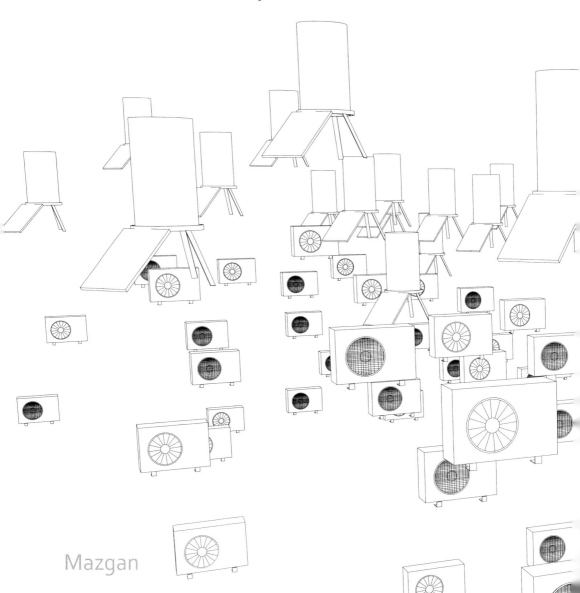

Mazgan

In 'Mazgan' we strip away the Tel Avivian urban rooftop landscape leaving only the air conditioner (mazgan) and the water barrel. 'Mazgan' reveals the visual density of everyday objects, reflecting the spatial pattern of the density of lives lived below the rooftops. It temporarily allows us to look beyond, to peel back a layer, and strip away. What do we see in the everyday city landscape? What's hidden? What's imaginable? Dismantling the everyday landscape by imagining its varying components in isolation can, almost counter intuitively, allow us to decode unexpected connections, the building block, including the hidden glue of city-making. Perhaps nothing provides more 'shelter' from the searing Middle East heat than the humble mazgan or air-conditioner cooling box. The mazgan is not unique to Tel Aviv, but its ubiquity does give a certain character to Tel Aviv city streets. Like many objects in the Israeli landscape, this is an architectural ubiquity hidden in plain sight.

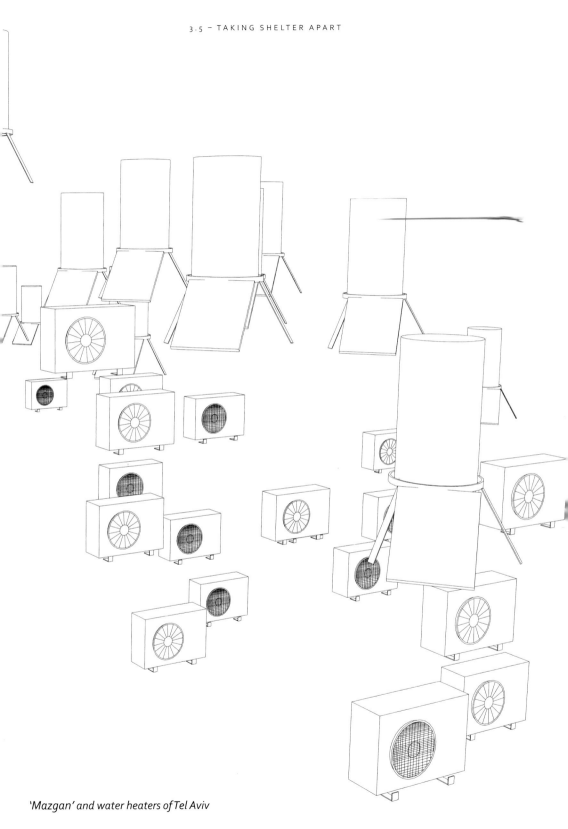

'Mazgan' and water heaters of Tel Aviv

'Mazgan' roofscape, central Tel Aviv

Caravan

The modest caravan is generally universally recognisable. It possesses ordinariness and simplicity. A caravan is a holiday home, a temporary refuge; for some, it is long-term residential accommodation. The caravan is sometimes mobile, sometimes fixed, compact and versatile. The caravan, or *caravanim* in Hebrew, is also an Israeli term referring to a portable building. The unassuming caravan or caravanim assumes a profoundly different meaning when parked or perched on a settler outpost in the West Bank. The erection of *caravanim*, in many cases on disputed land, is often the first step towards the establishment of a fully fledged, state-recognised Israeli settlement. Caravans in Israel are imbued with a sense of frontier and occupying geography. They are literally staging posts in settlement expansion. Dotted on hilltops in the occupied West Bank, these modest box homes are the architectural flag-waving equivalent of medieval colonial watchtowers.

——————

Caravan settler outpost of Migron, 14km north of Jerusalem, West Bank
(peak population 300, evacuated in 2012)

opposite – Bus stop, Dead Sea, West Bank: "Live high in the lowest place"

132

Bus Shelter

The Israeli bus shelter is a small object of functionality that performs an outsized and out-sourced role in the landscape, perhaps unwittingly. This humble structural cover (there are a few interesting different typologies) is familiar. A bus shelter is comforting. It is the famil-iarity, the Hebrew signage, the banality of the bus timetable information that gives it a pow-erful role in anchoring how space is literally read. On the streets of Tel Aviv, the bus shelter is simply a bus shelter – a place of shade and cover when waiting on a bus. In the sparse rocky hills of Samaria or in the searing heat of the desert of Judea, the humble bus shelter communicates something more. It communicates the ordinariness of Israeli presence. It's comforting (for Israeli Jews). It isn't a barrier, a road block, a security tower, and for that rea-son it is a powerful signifier. A non-threatening, familiar bus shelter in the otherwise occu-pied West Bank strips the landscape momentarily of visible military occupation.

The red-tiled roofs of an Israeli hilltop settlement are for many politically charged. They are, however, secure behind security gates. The Israeli bus shelter, on the other hand, is vulnerable, isolated, often empty, and apparently neutral in its banality. Its very simplicity and innocuousness communicates the implicit ordinariness of an 'Israeli' landscape. The rugged and rocky West Bank is a beautiful natural landscape, a landscape that can in parts be devoid of any visible human inhabitation. That very beauty and the banality of an isolated bus shelter can combine to desensitize the viewer to the political reality of occupation.

133

Israeli bus stop, Route 1, 10km east of Jerusalem, West Bank

Bomb Shelter

The Israeli bomb shelter is to be found all over Israel. They are, for obvious reasons to Israelis, ubiquitous in the southern city of Sderot. Sderot is located a kilometre or so from Gaza, and has been subject to more rock attacks than any other Israeli city. Perhaps to the untrained eye they are invisible. To those more familiar with the Israeli built landscape, these shelters intentionally or otherwise, they tell their own stories. They serve to remind Israelis of a Zionist narrative of the constant threat, the need for constant vigilance, the enemy beyond. They are adaptable and multifunctional, doubling up as synagogues, community centres and art galleries.

———

Tel Aviv lifeguard hut

opposite – A public shelter in Tel Aviv

Safe Room

The Israeli domestic 'safe room' (*mamad*) is a close architectural relative of the Israeli bomb shelter. The literal translation of *mamad* is 'protected space'. Found in most homes, and certainly in all new residential construction, the safe room is usually a single, centrally located room of reinforced concrete with blast-proof windows, designed to withstand rockets and unconventional weapons attacks. In times of emergency, the safe room is stocked up with dried and tinned foods and government-provided gas masks. For the rest of the time it is simply another room in the home – a child's bedroom, a study, a spare room.

Other ubiquitous 'shelters' in the Israeli landscape include the beach and lifeguards huts, boulevard kiosks and the short-lived homemade *sukot*. 'Taking Shelter Apart' is a simple story of the apparent ordinariness of objects in the built landscape and the sometimes extraordinary stories they can reveal about how Israelis perceive those everyday lived landscapes.

———

3.6 – Eleven and a half Rothschilds

In *'Eleven and a half Rothschilds'* we unfold an imaginary Rothschild Boulevard from the centre of Tel Aviv eastwards until it arrives at the 'front door' of the Green Line that separates Israel proper from the West Bank. The densely tree-lined boulevard, dotted with kiosk cafés and children's place spaces, gently unwinds in a 1.7km slow-moving arc from the commercial grittiness of Herzl Street before terminating at the grandness of the Israeli National Theatre and Concert Hall in the recently refurbished Habima Square.

Little over two decades ago, Rothschild Boulevard seemed somewhat lost or peripheral to the city centre, a city centre whose gravitational pull remained firmly anchored further north along Dizengoff Street. Today it occupies not only an important centrality of place in the geography of Tel Aviv, but also performs a meaningful role for a very particular Tel Avivian mindset. Rothschild is both a municipal urban spine fringed by gleaming new 40-storey 'starchitect' towers and trendy restaurants, and a civic stage set where liberal or progressive Tel Aviv finds expression. It was the site of the first tent encampment in the anti-government social justice protests in the summer of 2011.

It's not surprising then to discover that the progressive left-wing Meretz party of Israel, a party that receives just 4% of the vote nationwide (20th Knesset elections in 2015), and one that is perceived, pejoratively by many Israelis, as a very 'Tel Avivian' party, should receive its highest vote share in the immediate streets and neighbourhoods of Rothschild. In the 2015 elections to the Knesset, the party received in excess of 25% of the vote in a contiguous small cluster of adjoining neighbourhoods (home to 44,000 people) and its biggest concentration of the vote in the entire country.[1]

Strolling the length of the boulevard is one of the quintessential Tel Avivian urban experiences. In many ways this is the confident and very public face of progressive, socially liberal and economically secure Tel Aviv. The Occupation seems both far away but simultaneously niggling, not least in the minds of many of its local self-conscious and self-identifying leftist residents. But just how far is this comfortable liberal place of refuge, this strolling or perambulating boulevard, from the Occupation in the West Bank, and how many imaginary Rothschild Boulevards would it take to actually get there? In our *'Eleven and a half Rothschilds'* we build a kind of fantasy or fantastical urbanism by unfurling a magical city boulevard carpet to reveal memorable, perhaps unimagined distances.

It is not uncommon in the Israeli-Palestinian conflict to invoke distance (or indeed the lack of it) as an apparent weapon of geographic fear or threat. Greater proximity is often implicitly meant to communicate greater danger. Sometimes geographies remain hidden,

Habima Square, Tel Aviv

A kiosk café on Rothschild Boulevard
If laid end-to-end, how many Rothschild Boulevards would it take to reach the West Bank?

Unwalkable: "Sorry we could not calculate walking directions from Habima Square to Dayr Balut"
(Google Maps)

_____

their realities only revealed through imagination. Our *'Eleven and a half Rothschilds'* is a metaphorical extension of urbanity, a wilful collapse of traditional geography, a city portal invitation or extension eastwards.

The West Bank is 20km directly west of Habima Square. There are thus just 11½ imaginary Rothschilds between Habima Square and the West Bank. Walking at a leisurely pace it takes 22 minutes to stroll the entire length of Rothschild Boulevard. By our calculation it would take four hours to walk 11½ Rothschilds from Habima Square to the occupied West Bank. This is marginally shorter than the length of Manhattan (21.5km). Our 11½ Rothschilds, if extended directly westwards, arrives at the Green Line 1km west of the Palestinian village of Dayr Balut (pop. 3,000). The Israel separation barrier surrounds the village on three sides, so logistically it isn't possible to walk freely from Habima to the centre of Dayr Balut. Google says our 11½ Rothschilds from Habima Square to Dayr Balut is literally unwalkable. Yet Google also says the next-door settlement of Pedu'el is a walkable (albeit an eight-hour) circuitous stroll from Habima. It would appear Google can't find its way around the Israeli separation barrier. Dayr Balut doesn't have a 1.7km tree-lined boulevard dotted with kiosks. It does have three fruit and vegetable stores, two bakeries and, with a third of its residents under 15 years of age, four schools and a kindergarten.[2]

_____

top — Under construction, 11½ Rothschild's to the Green Line. What if?

bottom — Habima Square, Tel Aviv

A bakery in the city of Bnei Brak, 3km east of Tel Aviv
The largely Haredi city of Bnei Brak is the densest city in Israel. Over half the city's area has a density of 35,000
people per square kilometre, higher than that of Kowloon, Hong Kong.

3.7 – Bnei Brak and the Architecture of Expansion

Bnei Brak is both a suburb of greater Tel Aviv and a municipality in its own right, directly abutting the municipality of Tel Aviv-Yafo, its centre just 6km from the heart of the Bauhaus city. Bnei Brak is just one of the dozen self-administering cities or local councils in the Tel Aviv District.

Bnei Brak is different. This is, uniquely in the regional context of greater Tel Aviv, an enclave city of Haredi or Ultra-Orthodox Judaism. This is no ordinary enclave. This is no small religious community, but a relatively homogenous city of 180,000 people. Bnei Brak is the third largest city within the hierarchy of the regional and local government in the greater Tel Aviv area.[1] Its religious and cultural demography is reflected in its electoral politics. In the 2015 Knesset election, whilst a plurality of Tel Aviv-Yafo and the adjoining city of Ramat Gan voted Labor (Zionist Union), some 83% of Bnei Brak voted for Religious Orthodox parties (59% for the Ultra-Orthodox party United Torah Judaism, and 24% voted for Shas, Religious Orthodox party of the Mizrahi). Just 1% of Bnei Brak voted for the centre-left Labor or leftist Meretz party. Some 47% of Tel Aviv voted for Labor and Meretz; conversely just 5% of Tel Aviv voted for UTJ and Shas.[2]

What makes Bnei Brak particularly special is not that this is a city of Harridim (Religious Orthodox Jews), although it is by far Israel's largest (there are many such Haredi population concentrations across Israel and the West Bank), it is the city's density of population and its inhabitants' creative architectural responses to the inevitable pressures of overcrowding. Bnei Brak is the densest city in Israel; it has been ranked the sixth densest city in the world.[3] With an area of some 7km², and a population of 180,000, Bnei Brak has a density of population of 24,000 persons per square kilometre. This is comparable to Kolkata and Mumbai in India.[4] The municipality of Tel Aviv-Yafo, with a population of 433,000 and an area of 52km², has a density of 8,300 people per square kilometre. Greater Tel Aviv has a population density of 5,000 people per square kilometre.[5]

The northern residential neighbourhoods of Bnei Brak are relatively mixed, both religious and secular. In the densest and more religious areas of Bnei Brak, an area that makes up 60% of its municipal territory and 80% of its population, the density of population rises to 35,000 people per square kilometre.[6] This is a comparable density to that of Kowloon in Hong Kong.[7]

It is not unusual for Haredi families in Israel today to have 10 or 12 children. The proportion of households with four of more children in Tel Aviv is 4.4%. In Bnei Brak the proportion of household with four of more children is 41.5%.[8] Some 21.2% of the residents of Tel Aviv-Yafo are under the age of 19 years old; in Bnei Brak just over half (50.8%) of the entire city is under 19 years of age.[9] All of these children must sleep somewhere. Space is at a premium in Bnei Brak. Unlike Kowloon in Hong Kong, there are few tall buildings in Bnei Brak. This is a city of three- to four-storey buildings. Overcrowding is not uncommon. Some 2.4% of Israelis reside in households with a housing density of two persons or more per room. In Bnei Brak this rises to 18.8%.[10]

Bnei Brak is also one of Israel's poorest cites. The Israeli Central Bureau of Statistics gives the city a 'socio-economic' ranking of just 2 (out of a possible 10). This is Israel's largest poor city and it is getting poorer. (It had a socio-economic ranking of 3 in 2008). It is by far the poorest city in Israel with a population over 100,000.[11] It is also a Haredi city, somewhat uniquely located in the greater Tel Aviv area where property prices are highest and rising fast. House prices rose 150% in Gush Dan (Greater Tel Aviv area) between 2001 and 2016.[12] Bnei Brak also has some of the smallest homes in Israel with just 12.7% having five rooms or more.[13] For the relatively impoverished households and families of Bnei Brak, a solution to the overcrowding lies partly in the creative extension of existing homes to generate a whole new architecture of extensions. Most of these extensions are modest, they are ultimately all unique to the particular extension opportunities afforded to them. Many are built without planning permission. They make their own spaces, but they can be loosely grouped into a number of clear typologies. In *Bnei Brak and the architecture of extensions* we grouped those extensions into three simple typologies: the roof bungalow, the box extension and the room on stilts.

———

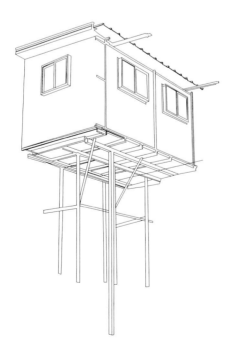

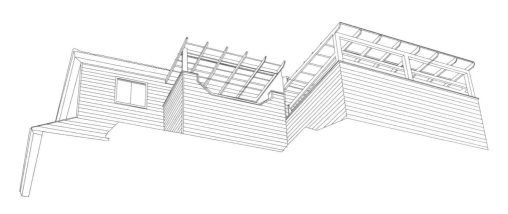

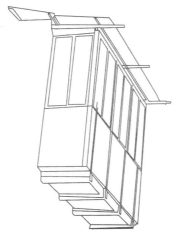

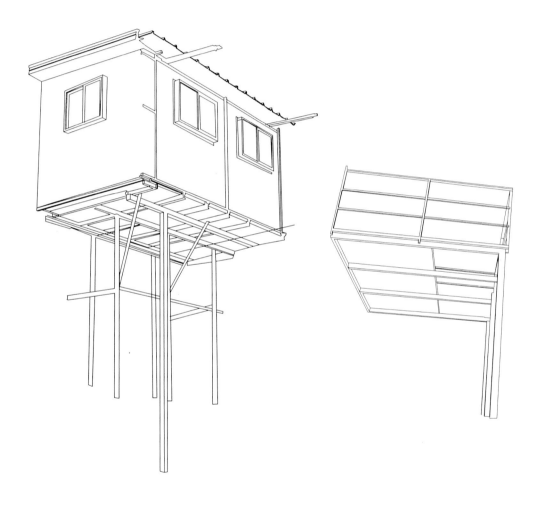

Domestic extensions in Bnei Brak

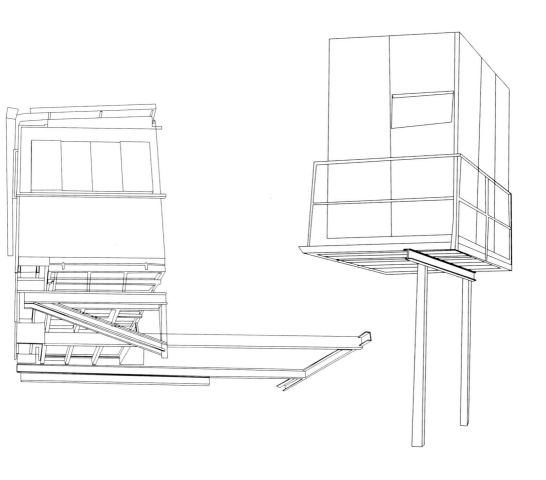

4 – Green Line Exurbia

'Hidden' security outside the settlement of Alfe Menashe, West Bank
Israelis drive by, perhaps oblivious to a small decorative wall that protects them and disguises a subterranean tunnel linking the Palestinian town of Hable (pop. 4,000) and the Palestinian city of Qalqilya (pop. 40,000) 1km further north. Both Palestinian communities are surrounded by the 8m-high Israeli separation barrier. The 'Palestinian only' tunnel provides the only link below a predominately settler-used road above.

4.1 – The Exuburban Geography of Tel Aviv – Alfe Menashe

Alfe Menashe is an Israeli 'settlement' with a population of around 8,000 people, located 3km over the Green Line inside the West Bank. It is a 15- to 20-minute driving commute from downtown Tel Aviv; many of its inhabitants work in the Greater Tel Aviv metropolis. With its neat rows of detached and semi-detached houses and manicured green lawns, this is the quintessential dormitory or suburban Israeli settlement. Alfe Menashe has been characterised as a 'quality-of-life' settlement by Peace Now.[1]

These so-called quality-of-life settlements are those settlements where, it is argued, the chief motivation for choosing to live there are quality-of-life issues, primarily the relatively cheap but highly desirable spacious housing. All the quality-of-life settlements are located just a few kilometres or less over the Green Line. Most are within a 15-minute drive of downtown Tel Aviv. Other quality-of-life settlements in the exurban fringes of Tel Aviv include Oranit, Beit Aryeh, Nili, Na'ale and Sal'it. Alfe Menashe and Oranit, the largest of the two quality-of-life settlements in exurban Tel Aviv, also have the largest homes in Israel. Some 86% of homes in Alfe Menashe have five rooms or more. In Oranit it's 83.2%.[2]

Depending on how one defines their social and territorial geography, quality-of-life settlements comprise between 15% to 35% of all settlements.[3] The voting pattern in a significant number of these settlements closely reflects the overall national voting pattern, with centrist and centre-left parties receiving a substantial portion or plurality of the vote. Perhaps proximity to the Green Line, a secular outlook, and 'rejection' of the avowedly ideological settler party, Habayit Hayehudi, are necessary quality-of-life thresholds.

If these are the criteria, Alfe Menashe is typical in this regard. In the 2015 Knesset election, this settlement closely mirrored Israel as a whole. Some 42% of Alfe Menashe voters plumped for the right-wing Likud and Habayit Hayehudi (the latter receiving just 10% of the vote), 29% for the centrist Kulanu and Yesh Atid parties, and 23% for the centre-left Zionist Union and progressive leftist Meretz party. This is not too dissimilar to how Israel overall voted – 35% for Likud and Habayit Hayehudi, 16% for Kulanu and Yesh Atid, and 23% for Zionist Union and Meretz.[4]

Our six chosen exurban Alfe Menashe landscapes reveal multiple stories of the seamless suburban and exurban geographies on the fringes of metropolitan Tel Aviv. These six landscapes, 'Green Line', 'Google', 'Identity', 'Picturesque', 'Windscreen' and 'Security', are variously traced, reproduced, constructed, presented, painted and revealed. Each one tells its own story; collectively they present a picture of the multiple identities and complexities of the banality of the Israeli suburban dormitory landscape adjacent to the Green Line.

The exurban landscape of Alfe Menashe is clearly a landscape of seamless segregation that is simultaneously visible, invisible and hidden in plain sight. This is a built land-

Alfe Menashe (pop. 8,000), 3km east of the Green Line, was founded in 1983.

The so-called 'quality-of-life' settlement of Alfe Menashe has the third highest proportion of large homes in all of Israel with 86.4% of all homes having five rooms or more. Only Tel Mond (87.8%) and the small community of Kfar HaOranim (87.8%, pop. 2,100) ranks higher. In Tel Aviv-Yafo just 8.4% of all homes having five rooms or more.

scape of intentional, accidental and incremental layers that fuse together to partially mute and muddy the political picture of the reality of the Occupation. A unifying theme in these six landscapes is the role played by motorway signage in guiding, informing, literally leading the exurban Tel Avivian through the daily grind of the commuting landscape. This is a seemingly ordinary and banal road signage that scrambles urban hierarchies and makes invisible Palestinian geographies.

The 'quality-of-life' settlement of Alfe Menashe, 3km east of the Green Line, with the Palestinian village of Hable in the distance
Alfe Menashe is the second wealthiest community 'in Israel', where a plurality of voters voted for the Likud Party in the 2015 Knesset election. The wealthiest Likud-voting community is Oranit, another 'quality-of-life' settlement, just 5km to the south.

Green Line Exurban Geography

'Green Line Exurban Geography' is both an imaginary boundary and a very real border circumscribing the everyday movement of Palestinians who reside east of the Green Line. The 1949 Green Line or armistice border is both an invisible and visible, and at times a deliberately obscured border. Alfe Menashe lies just 3km east of the Green Line. For the Israeli citizen and almost exclusively Jewish residents of Alfe Menashe, travelling east from Israel to Alfe Menashe, the Green Line effectively does not exist on the ground. It cannot be seen when crossing it.

Driving east along Route 55 from Israel proper to Alfe Menashe in the West Bank, it is possible to catch a glimpse, through dense shrubbery, of the Israeli separation barrier in the distance. The separation at this location is an 8m concrete wall separating the Palestinian city of Qalqilya from Israel. It is built for the most part along the Green Line, directly parallel to the Israeli motorway (Route 6). Pinpointing the exact location of the Green Line where it hypothetically severs Route 55, is impossible without employing GPS geography. Its invisibility, however, is both traceable and mappable. We photographed its exact but imaginary ghost-like invisible location just beside a bus stop, some 400m east of the intersection of the Route 55 flyover crossing Route 6.

———

Crossing the Green Line, outside Alfe Menashe

Google Exurban Geography

Google Geography, as read and consumed on a daily basis by Israelis, reveals a remarkable geographic difference between Palestinian and Israeli towns. The settlement suburb of Alfe Menashe, home to 8,000 people (2015), has more than 60 individual streets names identified by Google Geography. The Palestinian city of Qalqilya, home to 45,000 people , the largest West Bank Palestinian or Israeli city within a 10km radius of Alfe Menashe, would appear to be a rather placeless or nameless city. There are no street addresses in Google Qalqilya at the same scale of map that shows 60 individual street names in Alfe Menashe. Qalqilya's streets appear as a massive network of blank white roadways devoid of place names, with the single exception of a 'main street' (in English).[5]

The streets of the nearby Palestinian town of Hable are equally nameless. In fact, all Palestinian cities in the West Bank in the immediate vicinity of Alfe Menashe are mysteriously stripped of their street identities. Perhaps nameless West Bank Palestinian city geography has no particular meaning or significance for Israelis. Israeli citizens are, after all, legally forbidden to visit or access Palestinian cities (Areas A, Oslo Accords). 'No Name' territory is a simple natural extension of 'No Go' territory. The forbidden becomes invisible, the invisible simply forbidden. This is subliminal faceless geography. Places with no names become non-places. By extension, forbidden non-places have nameless nobodies living in them. Invisible and nameless, they become a dehumanising geography.

Identity Exurban Geography

The ethnic or religious homogeneity of towns and cities both east and west of the Green Line is striking, if not surprising. Ironically, when mapped, it serves to make the Israeli and West Bank landscape appear rather seamless. This is one extensive and extended indivisible patchwork of Jewish and Palestinian segregation, with a similar pattern existing either side of the Green Line.

Alfe Menashe was established as a settlement in 1983. Alfe Menashe is over-whelmingly Jewish (98.1% to be exact). The 'settlements' of Oranit (pop. 5,700) and Elkana (pop. 3,400) just south of Alfe Menashe are 99.2% and 99.6% Jewish respectively. Across the Green Line in Israel proper, however, the 'religious-ethnic' homogeneity of towns, villages and neighbourhoods is remarkably similar to that of the West Bank.[6]

The 'city' of Kfar Saba, with a population of 83,000, lies just 6km west of Alfe Menashe and is 96.2% Jewish. Israeli (Jewish) suburban settlements, in the broadest sense of that word, look remarkably similar. The Israeli town of Rosh HaAyin, with its rows of red-tiled suburban houses, is a housing typology common to the settlement suburbs of Alfe

---

The seamlessness of segregation either side of the Green Line, where the vast majority of residential communities are either Jewish (blue) or Palestinian (green)

opposite – The invisible streets of Google Qalqilya

Menashe or Oranit, just 2km away. Rosh HaAyin is 98.8% Jewish.[7]

The Israeli-Arab or Israeli-Palestinian town of Jaljulia (pop. 8,400) located just 2km south-east of Kfar Saba and 5km south-west of Alfe Menashe, is 99.6% Muslim. Kfar Kassem is commonly identified as the largest 'Israeli-Arab' or Palestinian town or city closest to Tel Aviv. Kfar Kassem has a population of just over 18,000, and is 99.9% Muslim.[8]

The scale of a settlement in the broadest meaning of that term, or its 'typology' or 'ideological' affinity, would appear to matter little. Four small *moshavim* (Neve Yamin, Tsofit, Elishama and Hagor) all located inside Israel proper and scattered between the larger towns above, each with a population of around 1,000 residents, are 97%, 98.4%, 98.8%and 99.1% Jewish respectively.[9]

This Jewish and Palestinian geography is a 'known' patchwork of segregation and separation. It is a known segregation that blurs the separation between Israel proper and the West Bank. There are few truly 'mixed' Jewish-Arab towns or cities in Israel-Palestine. There are none in the exurban geography of Greater Alfe Menashe.

———

Looking west to the skyline of Tel Aviv (20km away in the distance) from the settlement of Alfe Menashe, 3km east of the Green Line
The Palestinian town of Hable in the middle foreground (surrounded on three sides by the Israeli separation barrier) provides an almost serene pastoral scene. When the Occupation began in 1967 there was just one building in Tel Aviv higher than 100m. Today there are 70 buildings over 100m (Tel Aviv, Ramat Gan, Giv'atayim).

Picturesque Exurban Geography

In '*Picturesque Exurban Geography*' we present a framed picturesque almost pastoral land-scape of layered horizons, distance and foreground, a seemingly seamless exurban land-scape reminiscent of metropolitan Los Angeles. A hazy, decidedly urban downtown skyline of Tel Aviv, its skyscrapers can be seen in the distance. In the middle distance is a low rise and vast suburban sprawl, and the immediate foreground is dotted with farming and exur-ban villas scattered in the surrounding foothills. What's not visible in this seemingly ordinary or urban-suburban-exurban metropolitan landscape is the unseen borders and barriers, walls and fences that demarcate political space and curtail personal movement.

This is a landscape geography that looks west. For many exurban, so-called 'qual-ity-of-life settlers', the distant glimpse of the silhouetted skyscrapers of downtown Tel Aviv provides an anchoring, normalising comfort. It's a panorama that orientates the viewer. Many settlers residing in these hills commute to Tel Aviv on a daily basis. The city in the dis-tance and the imagined suburban sprawl that separates the foothills of the West Bank is punctured somewhat by the visual inconvenience of Palestinian villages and a separation barrier that can be occasionally glimpsed. But even the Palestinian village in the foreground, with its water tower and farm buildings, an imagined rural idyll, provides a kind of anodyne pastoral, almost subservient or supportive landscape role. This is picturesque exurban ge-ography stripped of the inconvenience of territorial politics.

Driving east along the exurban motorway of Tel Aviv where political geography, the Green Line and the Occupation become inevitably blurred.

Rosh HaAyin and Petah Tikva are in Israel proper. Ariel is an Israeli settlement located 17km inside the West Bank.

Windscreen Exurban Geography

'*Windscreen Exurban Geography*' is a snapshot of the daily experience of travelling through the landscape of Alfe Menashe. This is geography on the move, typical exurban geography visually consumed and navigated on a daily basis through the car windscreen. It is a kind of stop-go traffic-light geography, a drive-thru landscape where momentary glimpses of signage through the rear- or side-view mirror dominates the visual consumption of space.

Driving around the western fringes of exurban Tel Aviv, inside Israel proper, one eventually becomes enmeshed in the political messaging of motorway signage. The rules governing motorway (freeway) or dual-carriageway (highway) signage are universally standard – blue for motorways, green for highways. An urban hierarchy of place names appears and disappears. Very large, but distant cities appear regularly. Signage for smaller towns appear less frequently, but rapidly increase in frequency the closer the approach to town. An 'exit' sign for any location, no matter how small, appears in rapid succession, and so on.

But the ordinary 'rules' governing the hierarchy of place-naming on motorways are perverted in exurban Tel Aviv. In the 'Windscreen Exurban Geography' of Alfe Menashe, Palestinian towns, no matter what their size, appear less frequently than they should. Local Jewish cities that are actually smaller than local Palestinian cities appear more frequently on the motorway information highway. In addition, the motorway sign in the exurban geography of Alfe Menashe blends and blurs Israeli and occupied West Bank settlement geography. The internationalisation and standardisation of motorway signage inevitably assists in eroding (arguably, is actually designed to erode) international barriers or borders. This banality, familiarity and standardisation is co-opted, perhaps accidently, in flattening or obscuring political geography. It blurs the Green Line and the Occupation. The settlement city of Ariel becomes just another destination written in standardised white on a blue background. The sign for Ariel sits alongside Rosh HaAyin. Rosh HaAyin is an Israeli city located 15km west of downtown Tel Aviv. The city of Ariel, however, is an Israeli settlement located east of the Green Line, 17km inside the West Bank. Their differing political geography is erased by the rules to ensure a common motorway signage.

There is, of course, no time available to read annotated motorway political footnotes when whizzing by at 80 or 100km an hour. Motorway signage is perfunctory. There is no opportunity to inform the driver that Ariel is actually a city inside the occupied West Bank. The motorway signage doesn't distinguish between those local towns and cities in Israel proper, Tel Aviv, Rosh HaAyin, Kfar Saba, and those over the Green Line, Ariel, Elkana, Alfe Menashe. The necessary clarity in the internationalisation and standardisation of motorway signage perversely blurs the geography of Greater Tel Aviv's relationship to the Occupation. This is a metropolitan motorway network that doesn't, cannot, distinguish between contested narratives of political geographies. This is not to suggest that the Israeli state has somehow consciously co-opted international rules governing the motorway network in exurban Tel Aviv to mask the legibility of the Occupation. Motorway geography performs that task effortlessly.

Invisible security: hidden underground tunnels link the Palestinian city of Qalqilya and village of Hable

Security Exurban Geography

'Security Exurban Geography' is a landscape of multiple Israel built security layers, much of it unseen by exurban Israelis. This is a landscape of looping walls as the Israeli separation barrier snakes, twists and turns across a hilly typology, carefully weaving its segregated pattern. The separation barrier is clearly visible from the air but often disguised at eye level. The wall of course – particularly in this location – is rarely seen by Israelis. It is instead consumed, peripherally at times, by fractional glimpses, sometimes at a distance, whilst travelling at high speed along Route 6. The Israeli separation barrier abutting and surrounding the Palestinian city of Qalqilya is masked as a green landscaped motorway sound barrier when viewed by Israelis driving along Route 6. When viewed from Qalqilya, the same barrier is an 8m continuous wall of concrete running some 2km along the same (of course, inaccessible) motorway. Qalqilya, once easily and freely accessible to Tel Avivians, is now cut off from the rest of Israel. This city of 45,000 people, just 20km from the centre of Tel Aviv, is within the natural orbit of metropolitan Tel Aviv but has little economic or social connection to Israel's largest metropolis. Qalqilya has had to adapt as a city to Israeli-imposed severed urbanism. It has effectively been politically amputated from its natural economic and social hinterland.

     Security geography also includes the gated-community barriers to all Israeli settlements. Some security geography is particularly adept at hiding itself: it is virtually im-

possible to tell, when driving across it, that there is an underground passageway linking two Palestinian urban centres. This passageway, a small tunnel under Route 55, provides a direct link between the town Habla and the city of Qalqilya, allowing for the 'free movement' of Palestinians below ground. It also facilitates the free movement of settler traffic driving above. Security risks are, at a stroke, significantly reduced. Palestinians and Jews are segregated by underground and overground exurban geography.

The permanently manned Israeli security checkpoint separating the West Bank and Israel proper is located 3.5km inside the West Bank on Route 55. This checkpoint is therefore 'invisible' to the residents of Alfe Menashe who have themselves a seamless drive from Tel Aviv to the front gate of their own settlement. Drones, camera towers, listening devices and satellite systems all provide an additional blanket of 'invisible' security. It is the Israeli settlements themselves, however, perched for the most part on hills with their red-tiled roofs, sprinkler lawns and suburban malls that provide the ultimate 'eye on the street'. Perhaps this is the most invisible of all – an entire town of watchful eyes, ever vigilant, hidden in full view.

———

The 8m-high Israeli separation barrier surrounding the Palestinian city of Qalqilya made invisible (along Route 6 in Israel proper) by motorway planting (just outside Alfe Menashe)

opposite – The 8m-high Israeli separation barrier miniaturised and flattened but made visible for artistic visual consumption in the Tel Aviv Museum (2017)

The balcony of an apartment in the Haredi settlement of Beitar Illit
Some 63% of all residents in Beitar Illit are under 17 years of age, with 79.1% of all females over the age of 15 married. For the state of Israel as a whole, the comparable figures are 31.4% and 54.2%.

overleaf – Pisgat Ze'ev Mall in Pisgat Ze'ev, the largest settlement suburb of annexed east Jerusalem, 6km north of west Jerusalem city centre (pop. 50,000)
Some 40% (254,000) of all settlers live in suburban annexed east Jerusalem. A further 19% (121,000) live in additional suburban settlements surrounding Jerusalem. 6% (38,000) of settlers live in settlement suburbs of exurban Greater Tel Aviv (see Chapter 5.7 – Settling for Less).

4.2 – An Israeli City over the Green Line

When is a 'settlement' not a 'settlement'? The answer to this question would appear, super-ficially at least, to be a rather simple and reasonably clear one. A 'settlement' in the context of the Israeli-Palestinian conflict is a catch-all euphemism for all, irrespective of size, Israeli-built, almost exclusively Jewish residential developments constructed in the occupied ter-ritories of the West Bank or the Gaza Strip. Those who reside in these settlements are often simply referred to as 'settlers'.

In Israel it would appear, at times and in certain places, however, that a 'settle-ment' is not quite a 'settlement' thus a 'settler' not quite a 'settler'. The Hebrew word for 'settlement' is *htnachlut*. For many Israelis, including many of those who actually live in 'set-tlements' in the West Bank, a settlement or *htnachlut* would appear to have an altogether more fluid meaning. The scale, location, ideological affinity and built typology would all ap-pear to infuse the word with different significance and identity.

For the international observer, the scale of a settlement, its sheer size, its location, including its distance from the Green Line, its ideological or political outlook (secular, Haredi or religious Zionist) are all critical and diverse factors in classifying or understanding the ge-ography, history and typology of a settlement. Whilst the origin and diversity of Israeli set-tlements is complex, what is not in doubt is the fact that their very existence over the Green Line automatically qualifies them as a settlement. Put simply, all Israeli-built, almost exclu-sively Jewish residential developments built across the 1949 Armistice (Green) Line are de facto settlements.

A long-established, large, secular settlement built close to the Green Line is self-evidently visibly different from a recently constructed outpost of caravans and water towers erected on some hill deep inside the West Bank. They both however remain 'settlements'. Settlement 'outposts' are clearly understood as smaller, 'proto' or 'embryonic' settlements, the latter usually built by those with a self-professed messianic or ideological motivation. A settlement 'outpost' in Hebrew, *ma'ahaz* translates as 'a handhold'.

There is, however, a subtle, but fundamentally different understanding of the term 'settlement' or *htnachlut* that permeates everyday Israeli consciousness. This differ-ence of understanding goes beyond a mere differentiation of scale or geography. For many in Israel a settlement would appear to have a remarkable inbuilt capacity to evolve and mu-tate, to literally outgrow its own *sui generis*, to somehow un-become a settlement yet re-main geographically over the Green Line. This post-settlement metamorphosis doesn't occur through some political sleight of hand or pen by either redrawing the border or uni-laterally declaring Israeli 'annexation'. This is something much more fantastical, almost darkly magical. This (potentially) occurs when the settlement physically expands to support

a significant number of homes and residents with all the attendant social infrastructure of a typical 'normal' Israeli neighbourhood, small town or suburb. By 'normal' we mean an Israeli town inside Israel proper, inside the Green Line. The construction of a high school or two, a supermarket, a shopping centre, perhaps a medical centre of a certain size or a third level college or university, collectively and cumulatively assist in the transformation.

A settlement of a certain scale, no matter what its origin or how it acquired its land for construction, has the inherent inbuilt capacity to evolve and outgrow its inherent or literal – and for many Israelis – implied pejorative meaning. There would appear to be a critical point when a settlement emerges, butterfly-like, from its *htnachlut* pupa into what is commonly referred to as 'an Israeli city over the Green Line'. It is as if by increasing in scale and morphological and social complexity, the very legal status of the *htnachlut*, its political origins, its historic DNA itself changes. If it begins to look and feel normal, it somehow normalises, legitimises or absolves itself from any past indiscretions, perceived or otherwise. Looking and feeling normal, as in exhibiting the common characteristics of a typical Israeli town or suburb, is critical to this morphological semantic transformation.

The secular, dormitory settlement suburbs of Oranit, Alfe Menashe and Ma'ale Adumim all qualify as 'Israeli cities over the Green Line'. The Harridim or Religious Orthodox settlement of Beitar Illit, despite its proximity to the Green Line – and thus near guaranteed inclusion into Israel proper in any future redrawing of the border – perhaps unfairly doesn't qualify. The settlement 'city' of Ariel, with a population of 18,000, despite being 17km inside the West Bank, complete with its own university, is an 'Israeli city over the Green Line'.

For many, the larger the settlement grows the quicker the likelihood the settlement is simultaneously and mysteriously stripped of its ideological origins. The foundation of a new settlement is commonly viewed as a profoundly ideological act. The enlargement, however, of an existing settlement (particularly one close to the Green Line) is usually dressed up in the language or needs of banal dormitory suburban expansion. The irony is that the larger the settlement grows, the greater the likely negative impact on adjoining Palestinian communities. This invariably happens through Palestinian community severance or through the confiscation of Palestinian land, or both.

The transition from *htnachlut* to 'Israeli city over the Green Line' has no corresponding official equivalent. This isn't an officially documented or recorded process. The state does not confer additional legal status on any 'Israeli city over the Green Line', rather an almost seamless psychological change occurs, a kind of transitional 'adoptive suburbanisation'. Unofficial adoptive suburbanisation replaces the need for official territorial annexation. The settlement of Pisgat Ze'ev was annexed by Israel (it forms part of Municipal Jerusalem). The settlement of Alfe Menashe has not been annexed. Both, however, are generally perceived as 'Israeli towns or cities over the Green Line'. Both Alfe Menashe and Pisgat Ze'ev are viewed by many Israelis as non-ideological settlements.

There are many different terminologies employed to distinguish the real and vaguely pejorative *htnachlut* or settlement, and the implied non-threatening, benign, anodyne 'Israeli city over the Green Line'. The latter is often imbued with a dry, matter-of-factness. They include 'existing major Israeli population centres' or 'large settlement blocs'. They are embraced as somehow familiar, suburban, almost welcoming.

There are, perhaps, few words in the lexicon of contested settlement construction terminology that sound as non-threatening, normalising, and safe sounding than the word 'suburb'. Suburbs are familiar, comfortable, comforting, boring even. It is therefore not surprising that the Israeli Prime Minister, Benjamin 'Bibi' Netanyahu, in his speech to the US Congress in 2011 chose to invoke the 'suburbs' in his defence of the Israeli settlement project. 'The vast majority of the 650,000 Israelis who live beyond the 1967 lines reside in neighbourhoods and suburbs of Jerusalem and Greater Tel Aviv.'[1] Netanyahu's statement, whatever the political motivation, was in many ways a mere statement of fact. Cleverly employing the local comparative suburban geography of greater Washington, Netanyahu went on to say, 'Israel is one of the smallest countries in the world. Mr. Vice President, I'll grant you this. It's bigger than Delaware. It's even bigger than Rhode Island. But that's about it. Israel on the 1967 lines would be half the width of the Washington Beltway. But Israel on the 1967 lines would be only nine miles wide. So much for strategic depth.'[2]

The suburbanisation of the Israeli settlement project neatly serves as a kind of closed looped logic. Suburbanisation is both a rationale for settlement construction and a defence for their existence once built. Land is first cleared to prepare for the construction of much-needed Israeli family homes; these homes, once occupied, become de facto suburbs of nearby Israeli cities. The legitimate need for and the act of building suburban homes is intended to politically legitimise and sustain the expansion of settlement suburbs.

Territorial appropriation becomes infrastructural occupation before mutating into a kind of 'banal', suburban, invisible, borderless conurbation. Further normalisation is facilitated by an ongoing socialising and suburbanisation of the 'settlement'. A settlement even-

Ma'ale Adumim, a settlement 7km east of Jerusalem, is a classic example of an 'Israeli city over the Green Line'

The banality of suburbia: housing construction in the settlement city of Ma'ale Adumim in 2017 (7km east of Jerusalem; pop.38,000 and rising)

tually becomes an 'Israeli city over the Green Line' through the banality of everyday daily life. The simple daily drudgery of the commute to work, the weekly shopping trips to the nearest large shopping centre, family visits across the invisible Green Line all combine to blur and blend settler life with normal Israeli life. The Green Line for many Israelis, particularly for those living in Greater Jerusalem or in the suburban fringes of Tel Aviv, is virtually invisible. Unless you are a stateless Palestinian living under Israeli occupation, and therefore need Israeli permission to cross it, the Green Line plays a largely meaningless role in the lives of those who live near it. The Green Line is invisible to many settlers who live east of it.

It is this very invisibility of the Green Line that further facilitates the political normalisation of large settlement blocs. Morphological continuity generates a seeping socialisation that has blurred the suburban geography of the fringes of greater or metropolitan Tel Aviv. Where Tel Aviv really begins and ends has itself become inseparable from how and where Israel itself circumscribes its own borders. This blended metropolitan suburban settlement expansion has a profound impact on how many Israelis perceive the reality of the Occupation and thus the wider Israeli-Palestinian conflict.

Distance is not the critical issue here. Ariel, with its recently accredited State University, is the quintessential 'Israeli city over the Green Line'. The drive from Tel Aviv to Ariel along Route 5 is a quick and seamless 30 minutes. This is not so much a 'civilian occupation' but rather a 'seamless occupation'.[3] It is that perceived seamless of the Occupation, a seamless landscape, that we believe anaesthetizes and sustains an indifferent tolerance of the reality of the Occupation for the Palestinians living inside the West Bank.

HOW MANY SETTLERS ARE TEL AVIVIAN OR JERUSALEM SUBURBANITES?

We estimate there are approximately 38,000 settlers living in suburban-exurban or Greater Tel Aviv (25km radius), including Alfe Menashe, Oranit, Elkana and Sha'are Tikva. This amounts to 6% of all settlers. Another 38,000 live just 10km further east. They include, amongst others, Ariel (18,000) and Karne Shomron (7,000). Most of these settlements function as dormitory suburbs; 4 out of every 5 workers in the settlement suburbs of Greater Tel Aviv commute outside their settlement to work – Ariel 78%, Alfe Menashe 78.7% and Oranit 83.4%. Half (52%) of all Israelis work outside their municipal locality. In Tel Aviv-Yafo, the heart of the largest metropolitan region in Israel, 34.2% of the workforce works outside the municipality. Tel Aviv-Yafo is surrounded by multiple municipalities of varied size and complexity. Some 250,000 settlers live within annexed Jerusalem (40% of all settlers). A further 121,000 settlers live within a 12km radius of downtown Jerusalem, but are located outside the city's municipal boundaries (19% of all settlers). These include Ma'ale Adumim, Beitar Illit, Har Adar. Depending on geographical definitions and commuting thresholds, it could be argued that 65% or 413,000 of all settlers live in suburban commuting distances of either Greater Tel Aviv or Jerusalem. Jerusalem, technically Israel's largest city (its largest municipality), is surrounded on three sides by the West Bank; just 10.7% of Jerusalemites work outside the city.[4]

The 'imaginary' borders of the Green Line and the hard walls of the Israeli separation barrier: welcome to the Seamless Zone (a few hundred metres from the Green Line in the northern West Bank).

opposite – The Seamless Zone may be seamless for vehicles, but apparently not for mechanics (Israeli warning outside the town of Barta'a).

4.3 – Back Door to the Seamless Zone

Crossing the Green Line between Israel and the West Bank can be rather straightforward for Israeli citizens. For most Israelis travelling eastward by car – from Israel proper into the West Bank – the journey tends to be seamless along one or other continuous Israeli-built motorways. There are numerous 'seamless' motorway routes that effortlessly connect – without disruption or acknowledgment of any border crossing – Israel and the West Bank. These include, amongst others, Route 5 from Tel Aviv to Ariel, Route 443 from the outskirts of Tel Aviv to Jerusalem, and Route 55 from Kfar Saba to Alfe Menashe and Karnei Shomron.

The Green Line on the ground is, for the most part, invisible, imaginary even. Travelling by car, one isn't even aware when crossing over or passing through it. Only by employing the car's GPS system can one be reasonably clear when and where the Green Line actually 'exists'; otherwise it appears to have evaporated leaving nothing more than a trace of an illusory, abandoned ghost border.

The Green Line does however assert itself, for security reasons, in certain locations when travelling westward from the West Bank into Israel proper. For most Israelis the experience of passing through these border controls feels little different to navigating a (non-paying) motorway toll barrier. Most of the Green Line border controls are, in fact, not located on the Green Line itself, but hundreds of metres, sometimes a few kilometres inside it. Whilst most Israelis cross or pass through the Green Line along national motorway or

highway routes, there is a second altogether more discrete and oddly ephemeral Green Line transfer route or passage. This is a twilight borderless area, an almost surreal portal that allows – relatively unchecked – the free movement of people between the backdoor of Israeli-Palestinian towns inside the state of Israel into the open territory of the Israeli-occupied Palestinian West Bank.

In 'Back Door to the Seamless Zone?' we trace the peculiarly invisible and seamless border that 'separates' Israeli-Palestinian towns from Israeli-occupied Palestinian villages over the 1949 Armistice Line. It would appear that only Israeli-Palestinian towns in Israel proper that closely hug the Green Line are afforded this peculiar Narnia-like magical portal, a borderless and apparently security-free entrance. Relatively large Palestinian cities, located close to but east of the Green Line in the occupied West Bank, such as Qalqilya and Tulkarm, are practically hermetically sealed. These cities are separated from Israel proper by the Israeli-built separation wall or fence and by heavily fortified crossing points. The city of Qalqilya is surrounded on three sides by the separation barrier, most of which takes the form of an 8m-high concrete wall. Israeli (Jewish) towns or suburbs that are situated close to, but directly west of the Green Line, such as Kokhav Ya'ir, are equally sealed off.

There are no visible Israeli checkpoints at the 'back door' of the Green Line. This back door, however, only brings you so far. It's a back door or portal that permits entrance to a political twilight space. This is known locally as the Seam Zone. The Seam Zone is the area of the West Bank that lies east of the Green Line but west of the Israeli separation barrier. In some places the Seam Zone is a few kilometres deep; in others just a few metres wide. In many locations the separation barrier runs exactly along the route of the Green Line.

It is estimated that the Seam Zone is home to 57,000 stateless Palestinians trapped between the Green Line and the Israeli separation barrier.[1] For these Palestinians it is physically possible, but not legally permissible, to walk westward through the 'back door' across the Green Line into Israel proper, and legal, but generally not possible, to travel eastward across the separation barrier into the rest of the West Bank.

Perhaps nowhere is this surreal Narnia-like twilight zone so acutely felt than in the Palestinian town of Barta'a. Barta'a straddles the Green Line itself. The 1949 armistice border runs invisibly through the middle of the town. The western side of the town lies in Israel proper, its residents citizens of Israel who vote in the Knesset; the eastern side of the town lies in the West Bank, its inhabitants stateless and under 50 years of occupation. There is little or no visible Israeli security in the town itself. The eastern side of the town lies within the Seam Zone. There are perhaps few residents in all of Israel-Palestine which inhabit such a Kafkaesque reality as the town of Barta'a – a town that since 1948 has been superficially physically unified but administratively, politically and legally truncated.

_____

A pick-up truck parked on the town centre roundabout in Barta'a. The Green Line runs right through the roundabout.

opposite – A private property fence close to the 'imaginary' border of the invisible Green Line

Wrong side of the tracks: Palestinian and Jewish suburbs in the 'mixed' Israeli city of Lod, 15km south-east of Tel Aviv

There are few 'mixed' and perhaps really no socially integrated Jewish and Palestinian towns or cities in Israel. Only Akko (66% Jewish), Haifa (81.2% Jewish), Jerusalem (63.1% Jewish), Lod (67.4% Jewish), Nazareth Ilit (73.4% Jewish) and Ramla (75.6% Jewish) have substantial Palestinian minorities.

4.4 – Seamless Segregation and Greater Tel Aviv

Our perceptions of segregation and separation elsewhere are partially informed by how we live, where we live, the extent to which we ourselves live in segregated neighbourhoods and communities. So how segregated is Israeli geographic space? Just how homogeneous are Israeli towns and villages? How likely are you to find Jewish and Palestinians living side by side in the same neighbourhoods, and how might that inform Israeli attitudes to the Israeli Occupation?

The Israeli census is a good place to start to answer some of those questions. According to the 2008 Israeli Census of Population, there are a total of 430 'Israeli' communities with populations of 500 people or less.[1] The census subdivides these communities or villages into six settlement classifications as follows; 'Kibbutz', 'Moshav' 'Collective Moshav', 'Community locality', 'Jewish Other Rural Locality' and 'Non-Jewish Other Rural Locality'. Palestinians, Druze, Christian, Muslim or Bedouin are grouped in the negative as 'Non-Jewish'.[2] The census also tells us that 44 of these small communities can be found dotted across, what the Israeli census enumerators calls 'Judea Samaria' (Judea Samaria is the historical Jewish biblical name for the occupied West Bank). 'Israeli' communities in Judea Samaria are not uncommonly referred to – in international political discourse at least – as Israeli 'settlements' in the Israeli-occupied Palestinian Territories. The ethno-religious composition of these Israeli settlements in the occupied territories is overwhelmingly, and in places almost exclusively, Jewish in their make-up. The average percentage of Jews across these 44 communities is 97.8%, with 23 of these 44 communities having a Jewish population in excess of 99%. The tiny non-Jewish population is not likely to be Palestinian, but ex-Soviet immigrants and their families who are not recognised as Jews by the Rabbinical courts.[3]

Homogeneous or highly segregated communities are also very common west of the Green Line, in Israel proper. The census tells us that there are 49 small communities of 500 persons or less located in the 'Central District' area – in effect, the metropolitan suburbs and exurbs of Tel Aviv. The census further reveals that these 49 small communities of Greater Tel Aviv are as equally homogenous as the settlement communities inside the West Bank. They are, in fact, fractionally more so. The average percentage of the Jewish population across these 49 small communities in Greater Tel Aviv is 98.2%, with 27 of them having a Jewish population in excess of 99%. Ethno-religious segregation in small villages and settlements (in the broadest sense of the word) would thus appear to be the norm either side of the Green Line.[4]

The extent to which these small villages, communities, *moshavim* or *kibbutzim* in Israel are either almost exclusively Jewish or Palestinian may surprise very few. The reasons for such segregation are complex and varied. They include everything from the historic evolution of Palestinian villages, their later destruction post-1948, early Zionist 'Jewish only' collectivist settlement practices, Israeli state land policy, and the contemporary practices of the quasi-state-sanctioned discriminatory, and thus segregationist, 'welcoming committees' of many *moshavim* and *kibbutzim*. These so-called welcoming committees have recently been afforded greater legal protection.[5] A personal preference to dwell amongst family and friends including those of the same religious or ethnic makeup is also a factor. In addition, there is negligible inter marriage between Jews and Palestinians in Israel.

What is perhaps less understood or overtly acknowledged is how this subliminally 'known' patchwork pattern of 'Jewish only' or 'Palestinian only' villages and towns within Israel proper may partially inform the perception and, thus, possibly a residual passive acceptance of the continuation of the Occupation in the West Bank amongst many Israeli Jews. If acute segregation, whatever the reason, inside Israel proper is the norm, then segregation in the West Bank (notwithstanding a very different and meaningful administrative and legalistic context) begins to look, well, rather normal too. Nothing perpetuates the status quo more than a general and commonly held perception of normalcy.

The Greater Tel Aviv suburban settlement of Alfe Menashe was established in 1983. Alfe Menashe is 3km across the Green Line (population in 2008 of 6,800) and is overwhelmingly Jewish (98.1% to be exact).[6] The settlements of Oranit (pop. 5,700) and Elkana (pop. 3,400), just south of Alfe Menashe, are 99.2% and 99.6% Jewish respectively. Across the Green Line in Israel proper, however, the 'religious-ethnic' homogeneity of towns, villages and neighbourhoods is remarkably similar to that of the West Bank.[7]

The 'city' of Kfar Saba, with a population 83,000, lies just 6km west of Alfe Menashe and is 96.2% Jewish. Israeli (Jewish) suburban settlements, in the broadest sense of that word, look remarkably similar. The Israeli town of Rosh HaAyin (pop. 37,900) with its rows of red-tiled suburban houses, a typology common to the settlement suburbs of Alfe Menashe or Oranit just 2km away, is 98.8% Jewish.[8] The Israeli-Arab or Palestinian town of Jaljulia (pop. 8,400) located just 2km south-east of Kfar Saba and 5km south-west of Alfe Menashe, is 99.6% Muslim. Kfar Kassem is commonly identified as the largest 'Israeli-Arab' or Palestinian town or city closest to downtown Tel Aviv. With a population of just over 18,000. Kfar Kassem is 99.9% Muslim.[9]

The scale of a settlement or its 'typology' or 'ideological' affinity would appear to matter little. Four small *moshavim* (Neve Yamin, Tsofit, Elishama and Hagor), all located inside Israel proper and scattered between the larger towns above, each with a population of around 1,000 residents, are 97%, 98.4%, 98.8%and 99.1% Jewish respectively.[10] Put another way, if the Israeli settled exurban or rural segregated landscape doesn't perceptively look or feel that different to the pattern of Jewish settlements or 'Palestinian only' towns and suburbs in the West Bank, might that not inform how the average (Jewish) Israeli perceives the normalcy of the overtly segregated landscape of the Occupation, and the land and housing policy that informs or regulates it? In other words, in the mind's eye of the average Jewish Israeli, does the overwhelmingly Jewish Kfar Saba and the almost exclusively Palestinian Kfar Kassem in Israel proper 'look' so different from the Israeli settlement of Alfe Menashe and the Palestinian city of Qalqilya across the Green Line in the West Bank? All four, whether functioning as dormitory suburbs of Tel Aviv, self-contained or severed cities, are located within 4km of each other. All four are visible from Route 6 which runs between them. Two of these 'towns/suburbs' are readily known as being Jewish; two are readily known or self-identify as Palestinian. The fact that Palestinian Israeli residents of Kfar Kassem are citizens of Israel and free to travel anywhere within Israel (including much of the West Bank) whereas the Palestinian residents of Qalqilya are not permitted to do so (as they not citizens of Israel) may not ordinarily impinge upon the consciousness of your average Jewish Israeli.

The difference in the relative 'legal status' of Palestinian citizens of Israel and stateless Palestinians living under occupation is, of course, known by Israeli Jews, but for the most part it is peripheral to their daily lives. The difference between the 'legal' status of the cities of Qalqilya and Kfar Kassem is understood by most Israelis. Kfar Kassem lies west of the Green Line inside Israel proper, Qalqilya lies east of it in the West Bank. Both are nevertheless essentially perceived as Palestinian or Arab cities. The former is simply a city no longer permissible to visit, the latter a Palestinian or Arab city that one is unlikely to want to visit. Both exist as peripheral, almost parallel geographies.

This is a seamless landscape of segregation and separation. It is, however, a segregation of choice for Israeli Jews. For most Israeli Jews it is a segregation that is primarily seen through the prism of cultural ethnography or national identity. Citizenship and legal status are secondary. In this sense we would argue that the separation and segregation for most Israeli Jews living in this exurban periphery of Greater Tel Aviv is perceived and experienced as a difference between Jewish and Palestinian cities and villages as opposed to a difference between cities and villages inside Israel proper and those over the Green Line. It is this subtlety of perception of the seamlessness of segregation that we suggest assists in sustaining Israel's occupation of the West Bank.

Missing Palestinian villages

The 2008 census also tells us that of the 430 small villages or communities comprising 500 people or less in all of Israel proper, remarkably just seven of them are Palestinian; [11] six of the seven (Ein Hod, pop. 110; Al Aryan, 180; Khawaled, 350; Al Azy, 140; Demeide, 370; Sawa'id (Hamriy ye), 130) are overwhelming Muslim, with their average Muslim population some 99.7%. The remaining Palestinian or Israel Arab 'village' has a small Christian majority (50.9%). There are no remaining Israeli-Palestinian communities with populations of less than 500 people in the Central District. [12] The total population of the six Muslim Palestinian villages is just 1,280.

Looked at from a different perspective, just 0.09% of Israeli-Palestinian citizens of Israel live in Palestinian villages in the Israeli 'countryside'. This compares with 2.5% of all Jewish Israelis (137,000 out of total Israeli Jewish population of six million). In other words, despite hundreds of years of continued Palestinian settlement in historic Palestine (Palestinians made up 92.5% of the population as late as 1914) you are 28 times more likely as a Jew than a Palestinian to live in a small village in the Israeli countryside.

The same holds for larger towns. Of the 479 communities with a population of 501 to 1,999, just 22 are not Jewish (19 Muslim, two Druze and one other). [13] There are potentially many reasons for this. The destruction of small rural Palestinian villages during and shortly after the 1948 Arab-Israeli war is the obvious explanation. It is estimated that 400

Palestinian villages were erased between 1948 and 1949.[14]

The construction of new Israeli settlements (inside Israel proper) since 1948 has also played a significant role. The Israeli census also tells us of that of the 232 small Jewish communities (population less than 500), some 166 of them were founded since 1948. All Jewish towns and villages are given the year of their foundation; none of the Muslim settlements have a foundation date (all are simply noted as 'historical'). It would appear then that census shows that no new Muslim settlements have been constructed in Israel since 1948. The 2008 census states that the then most recent Jewish settlement was founded in 2007.

What is the true settler population?

The estimated settler population living in the West Bank and annexed occupied east Jerusalem ranges from an upper figure of 780,000 [15] to a low of 547,000,[16] the latter from the Human Rights organisation Btselem, 2015.

Somewhat peculiarly, there would appear to be greater consensus on the numbers living across the West Bank than east Jerusalem. In late 2015, the Israeli Central Bureau of Statistics (CBS) gave a figure of 386,000 for the number of settlers living in the West Bank outside of annexed east Jerusalem.[17] With reported 4% annual growth rate (much of it, natural increase as opposed to new home construction), it is not unreasonable to assume a figure of 417,000 by the end of 2017. The 2015 CBS figure is widely quoted by other organisations with diverse political perspectives. A report in early 2016 put the figure at 406,000.[18]

The numbers for east Jerusalem are more varied. The Yesha Council (the political voice of the settlers) estimates a figure of 300,000.[19] A report in the *Jerusalem Post* in 2014, quoting the then Minister for Construction and Housing, Uri Ariel, put the figure between 300,000 and 350,000.[20] The Jerusalem Institute for Israel Studies put the population of the Jewish neighbourhoods in annexed east Jerusalem at 197,700 at the end of 2012. Human Rights organisation Btselem also quotes the same modest figure of 197,000 on its website today.[21] Assuming an across-the-board 4% growth rate, the Btselem figure of 197,000 at the end of 2012 would 'only' be 240,000 by the end of 2017.

Combining the above estimates, the settler population is likely to reach somewhere between 657,000 (240,000 east Jerusalem; 417,000 West Bank) and 742,000 (325,000 east Jerusalem; 417,000 West Bank). A midway estimate would put the number of settlers at 700,000 by the end of 2017. June 2017 marked 50 years of Israeli occupation. Combining the above calculations with an Israeli population of 8.7 million in May 2017 (CBS figure that includes all Israeli citizens and non-Israeli-Palestinian population of east Jerusalem), we estimate that 8.3% of all Israeli citizens are now settlers, or 1 in 12.[22]

Given that Palestinians make up over 20% of the Israeli population, with Jews making up 74% of the population, and the fact that there are few Palestinian citizens of Israel residing in the settlements, we also calculate that 1 in 9 Israeli Jews are now settlers. Put another way, there are now nearly twice as many Jews living in the occupied territories as there are living in Tel Aviv-Yafo. There are 430,000 residents in Tel Aviv, 92% of whom the census tells us are Jews; that's a total of 395,000 Jews. With a settler population of 700,000, of which more than 99% are Jews, that's almost a 2:1 ratio of Jewish settlers versus Jewish Tel Avivians.

A NOTE ON OUR ASSUMPTIONS

In *'Constituency Geography'* (chapter 5.5) we assume a settler population figure of 660,000 at the time of the 2015 Knesset elections. This is made up of 386,000 in the West Bank and an estimated 274,000 in east Jerusalem. The population of Israel was estimated by the CBS to be 8.3 million in 2015. This includes the Palestinian residents of municipal annexed and occupied east Jerusalem. With 120 Knesset seats, this works out at 69,000 residents per Knesset seat (this includes Palestinians of annexed east Jerusalem). In *'Settling for Less'* (chapter 5.7), we use a slightly lower figure of 617,000 for the settler population. This slightly lower 2015 population estimate is derived from the most recent reliable estimate totals for each individual settlement, and those individual figures are critical to the analysis of that chapter. In *'An unsettling map of settler seats'* (page 250) we employ the estimated 700,000 settler population for 2017. With an Israeli population estimated to be 8.5m in 2017 (Israeli citizens only), this means that 8.25% of Israelis are settlers, or 1 in 12.

The 'old' Palestinian city centre in the 'mixed' Palestinian and Jewish Israeli city of Lod, 15km south-east of Tel Aviv
In mixed cities the level of segregation is deceptive. Area 4 (population 14,300) in Lod is 67.6% Jewish, but drilling down reveals that three of its sub-areas 41, 42 and 43 are 87.2%, 90.6% and 89.4% Jewish and the fourth sub-area 44 is 98.6% Muslim.

The Dead Sea Drive ... or day-trip occupation?

4.5 – The Tel Avivian Dead Sea Drive

The drive to the Dead Sea along Route 1 east of Jerusalem operates in a third dimension of occupying space. This is a day-trip occupation whose geography is familiar to Tel Avivans, most of whom are likely to have taken this journey by car many times. This is a quintessential desert drive, a desert drive into open and empty and endless space, a kind of frontier geography evocative of American popular culture and US desert landscapes. This is more imaginary Arizona and *Easy Rider* than occupied Palestinian West Bank.

Ten kilometres east of Jerusalem, beyond the vast suburban hilltop settlement of Ma'ale Adumim, begins the slow curving descent into open desert landscape. Thus begins a journey that can be characterised as a form of leisurely drive-thru occupation. The recuperative properties of the Dead Sea ahead is reinforced with playful, informative, fun tourism signage. The side of the roadway is dotted every few kilometres with reminders of the quick drop below sea level. The little blue mosaic tiles affixed to rocky outcrops appear with increasingly regularity – '250 Metres below Sea Level', '350 Metres below Sea Level', '450 Metres below Sea Level'. The few Bedouin encampments that dot the landscape, their goats an odd camel, add a nomadic, pastoral, almost biblical backdrop.

Beyond the Lido junction where Route 1 intersects with Route 90, the remaining 50km southward journey settles into a kind of relaxed carefree occupation drive. This is a 50km drive of empty geography, free of obvious or any discernible interfering political reference. There are no Palestinians, at least no visible Palestinian towns, no minarets popping up over distant hills. Even the Bedouin have vanished. This is like no other drive across the West Bank. Unlike Route 5 to Ariel, there is no barbed wire rolling along the side of the motorway. There is no motorway as such. The two-lane highway gently winds and bends, hugging the hilly and rocky terrain. This is a rugged, natural, desert mountain landscape.

The open desert road is imbued with a sense of freedom – free of obligation, free of association, detached, a never-ending horizon. The road and drive ahead is slowly purged of any awkward memories and associations of a Jerusalem left behind, a Jerusalem of visible walls and barriers, conflict and segregation. It's as if having passed through the real and metaphorical 'pinch point' of Jerusalem, whether having driven around or through the city, over or under the maze of flyovers, past the segregating walls and barriers, you have somehow escaped the oppressiveness of Israeli political geography.

Perhaps it is the thought of the curative Dead Sea experience ahead, the anticipation of cleansing, bathing, purifying, that dissolves or absolves the political context. This is after all a life affirming, skin nourishing, chemical dissolving pleasure trip. The irony, of course, is that having escaped the overtly visible political landscape of segregation in the rear-view mirror, it is only in east Jerusalem that one enters the expanse of occupied terri-

tory. The Dead Sea Drive east of Jerusalem is, after all, also a drive through Israeli-occupied Palestinian West Bank.

The illusion of 'anywhere-ness' is served by a subtle but complex sense of both absence and presence. The absence of a visible occupation, whether it be Israeli settlements or Palestinian towns, conveniently erases the underlying political landscape. This is a landscape of the great outdoors, desert holiday geography. The presence of 'the familiar', the comfort of 'the known' exerts a powerful subliminal sense in striping this landscape of the Occupation. This is a desert drive inside occupied territory, but also an everyday holiday drive that is ordinary. This comfort of the familiar in a desert landscape is found in simple everyday objects in that landscape – the presence of the isolated but commonplace Israeli bus shelter; the ordinary and routine road signage in Hebrew. The road signage guides and channels. The Dead Sea Drive road signs are literally directional, providing recognisable and practical support. They also provide a psychological security – the State is here guiding me.

The banal convenience of the roadside café and the road-side service station is equally important. Nothing could be more ordinary, more reassuring then stopping for ice cream or coffee at the Lido junction. The petrol station, shop and café located at the intersection of Route 1 and Route 90 plays a critical, if somewhat unasked for, normalising role in anchoring the ordinariness of the Dead Sea Drive. This is the last petrol station before the 50km drive south along the shores of the Dead Sea. Stopping at the Lido junction is almost ritualistic. It is synonymous with refreshments, the last chance for a restroom pit-stop or stocking up on snacks for the road ahead. This is a safe place, a normal space, just like any other big roadside café-petrol station in Israel, and therein lays its peculiarity and odd familiarity. The Lido shop and garage is, of course, not located in Israel proper. This is the occupied West Bank. There are few, if any, other unsecured 'open' petrol stations or roadside cafés of this scale located 30km inside the Green Line, and none that feels so utterly devoid and detached of the reality of its location.

This is day-trip geography, day-trip occupation. The Tel Avivian Dead Sea Drive is temporary; one's presence in the West Bank is almost fleeting, a few hours perhaps just a few times over a number of years. Yet it's the very ease of the ordinariness of taking the Dead Sea Drive that gives it a peculiar sense of detachment. For many day-tripping Tel Avivians, this isn't political, it isn't an exercise in occupation, and perhaps many would think it perverse to even consider it so. A drive to the Dead Sea through the occupied West Bank is not of course the equivalent of a conscious decision to choose to live in a settlement. It nevertheless forms part of a complex reality that informs the ordinariness of the seamlessness of the Israeli Occupation. It is this very ordinariness and seamlessness of the lived experience of the Israeli Occupation that we would argue psychologically anaesthetizes many Israelis, including many Tel Avivians, understanding of the Occupation itself.

––––––

On the road to the Dead Sea

opposite – The banality and (arguably) invisibility of the Occupation: buying ice cream at the Lido junction, intersection of Route 1 / Route 90, 25km east of the Green Line in the West Bank

Drive-thru occupation

Whilst a drive through the occupied West Bank to the Dead Sea may be viewed by many Israelis as a non-political act, for some, in particular many Tel Avivians, a decision to avoid travel into or across the occupied West Bank is considered a small solitary act of resistance, a boycott even, a refusal to participate in the settlement enterprise. There is not an uncommon attitude that even to travel there as a witness or as a demonstrator is seen as a form of Occupation voyeurism.

To drive from Tel Aviv to Jerusalem along Route 443 across the West Bank as opposed to driving along Route 1 (inside Israel proper) would, in the eyes of many Tel Avivians, be considered a deliberate political act. It would be viewed as a political act that is, in effect, normalising the seamlessness of the occupation. Such a choice of route would readily qualify as a 'drive-thru occupation'. For others it may simply be the quicker route on a given day with little or no thought given to its political context.

Perhaps there is nowhere in all of Israel-Palestine that the phrase 'drive-thru occupation' has as much searing relevance than inside the Palestinian city of Hebron. Hebron,
located deep inside the West Bank, is home to 160,000 Palestinians and 700 settlers, the
latter heavily protected by a permanent presence of Israeli soldiers. The city has been divided into two sectors – H1 and H2. The H1 sector, home to around 120,000 Palestinians,
remains under the control of the Palestinian Authority. The smaller eastern side of the city,
the H2 sector, and the historic core of the city, is home to the remaining 40,000 Palestinians
and 700 Jewish settlers. This sector of the city has a complex set of rules governing
Palestinian movement on its network of city-centre streets. Palestinians are not permitted
to drive on certain streets; on others only local Palestinian families are permitted to access
by foot. Palestinians are permitted to walk but forbidden to drive along this Palestinian
street in the heart of the city.

The front seat view of a settler/Israeli-only driveable road in the Palestinian city of Hebron, West Bank

4.6 – Up the Road: the Semi-Detached City

If Tel Aviv has a somewhat unspoken detached relationship with some of its suburbs, then this Mediterranean beach city has a decidedly semi-detached relationship with the Israeli capital Jerusalem, just 40 minutes up the road. It's not uncommon in nation states for an intense rivalry to exist between its two largest cities: think Madrid and Barcelona, Rotterdam and Amsterdam, Rio de Janeiro and São Paulo, Milan and Rome, and so on. Tel Aviv and Jerusalem rivalry is particularly special, charged even. This isn't a mere difference of political opinion, a divergence of outlook, but arguably a profound clash of culture, a battle between the secular and religious for the future political direction of the state of Israel.

If Tel Aviv aspires to 'Global City' status, Jerusalem goes one better: Jerusalem has a 'direct link to God'. This city has both historic godly connections and future celestial aspirations, handed to it of course by none other than God. *'Then I saw a new heaven and a new earth, for the first heaven and earth had passed away, and the sea was no more. I saw the holy city, the new Jerusalem, coming down out of heaven from God, prepared as a bride adorned for her husband.'*[1]

Back to earthlier matters, both cities share the trappings of Israeli state power. The official capital, Jerusalem, is home to the Knesset, but Tel Aviv plays host to all of Israel's foreign embassies.[2] Government ministries are located in Jerusalem, but the Israeli Defence Forces headquarters (Hakirya) remains firmly rooted and is highly visible in central Tel Aviv.

Despite the Trump administration's recognition of Jerusalem as the capital of Israel in December 2017, this is a capital city that in early 2018 continued to host no foreign embassies. But just how detached is the city of Jerusalem from itself? Jerusalem is the 'capital city' of Israel. It is commonly understood by most Israelis as the 'largest' city in Israel. The city is also widely referred to – by the mainstream political establishment – as the 'eternal', and 'indivisible' city of Israel. 'Largest', 'eternal', 'indivisible' and 'capital' are each impugned with varying degrees of status, religious, symbolic or political meaning in any Jewish Israeli discussion of the city of Jerusalem. Yet this is a 'capital city' that is home to no foreign embassies.[3] This is an 'indivisible' city scarred by the construction of an 8m-high concrete barrier that severs east Jerusalem from the rest of the city. This is the 'largest city' in Israel in which 60% of its municipal territory (annexed east Jerusalem) – under international law – lies outside the state of Israel. In addition, a third of its municipal citizens are permanently precluded from travelling freely within or voting in the national elections of that same state.

---

opposite – The Muslim quarter in the Old City of Jerusalem. Advertising imagery of women on billboards and public buses is generally banned in Jewish west Jerusalem.

overleaf – Praying at the Western Wall, Old City of Jerusalem

Eternal is perhaps harder to evaluate. The city can boast 3,000 years of continuous urban settlement. Tel Aviv can't compete with that urban genealogy; excluding the port city of Jaffa, the city is just 109 years old.

The 2008 Israeli Census of Population states the official area and population of Municipal Jerusalem as 125.2km² and home to 760,000 residents. Today the city's population is estimated to be greater than 850,000.[4] The city of Tel Aviv-Yafo has an area of 52km² and an estimated population of 430,000 today.[5] Going on these figures Jerusalem is certainly larger – more than twice the area with double the population of Tel Aviv. Jerusalem's 850,000 population, however, includes an estimated 300,000 municipal Palestinian residents living in annexed east Jerusalem. These residents are not citizens of the Israeli state.

That 2008 census tells us that the population of Municipal Jerusalem, Palestinian and Jewish, residing outside or beyond the Green Line was 456,000.[6] This is a city where approximately a third of its municipal citizens are not citizens of the State (Israel) of which the city is the official capital.[7] A further 195,000 municipal citizens live outside the internationally recognised borders of the Israeli state – the Jewish settler population in primarily north Jerusalem in the occupied West Bank. It is estimated that the settler population has since risen to an estimated 250,000.[8] That means that 2 in 5 municipal citizens of Jerusalem do not actually reside inside the internationally recognised borders of the Israeli state. In addition, over half (70km² to be precise) of the municipal territory of the capital city is not located inside those same borders.[9]

On these figures, the city of Jerusalem inside Israel proper is similar in size (55km² versus a 52km² Tel Aviv-Yafo), but considerably smaller in population, than the city of Tel Aviv-Yafo. Tel Aviv-Yafo, in terms of population, is approximately a third bigger than 'Israeli' Jerusalem.[10] In any event, the Tel Aviv regional authority area has a population of 1.2 million. Metropolitan Tel Aviv is home to 3.6 million Israelis.

As for the delusion of an indivisible city, today metropolitan Jerusalem is scarred by a network of walls and barriers that divide Palestinian east Jerusalem from the rest of the city. In east Jerusalem, Palestinian neighbourhoods are severed by the 8m-high concrete wall that snakes across the city. The city of Bethlehem, just a 10-minute drive from the heart of the of city of Jerusalem, is surrounded on three sides by the separation barrier. In addition, the multiple military checkpoints prevent the free movement of Palestinians living in Greater Jerusalem from travelling into or across Municipal Jerusalem. The Palestinian residents of east Jerusalem who reside west of the wall, who are not citizens of Israel but can vote in municipal elections, overwhelmingly choose not to do so.[11] Perhaps uniquely, Jerusalem is the only capital city of a nation where the historic or indigenous residents of the city are 'legal' municipal citizens of the capital of the state they live in, but are not citizens of that same state. Jerusalem is many things to many people, but as a city it cannot reasonably be described as either united or indivisible.

Jerusalem is of course the official capital of Israel, a status which is implicitly disputed by the international community following the passing of the 1980 'Jerusalem Law', which in effect annexed the occupied eastern part of the city. Following the passing of the Jerusalem Law, and the passing of Resolution 478 at the United Nations the same year which condemned the law, the international community began to move their embassies outside the city, primarily to Tel Aviv.

Today Jerusalem is an increasingly religious city. The census tells us 26.6% of Jewish men aged 15 and over studied in a *yeshiva* or Religious Orthodox school. In over a third of the neighbourhood districts identified in the Israeli census this figure rises above 50%. The comparable figure for Israel is 6.8% and for Tel Aviv-Yafo just 1.1%.[12] The religiosity was reflected in the 2015 Knesset voting in the city, when 50.9% voted for the Religious Orthodox or radical right-wing parties, including both the Haredi (Shas, UTJ) and the hard right (Yisrael Beiteinu) and settler parties (Habayit Hayehudi).

The Israeli census tells us that just 63.1% of Jerusalem is Jewish but, oddly, lists no sub-district (out of 33) as less than 76.2% Jewish. Of those 33 sub-districts, in fact, the Jewish population is greater than 90% in 31 of them. Somehow the Palestinian population, approximately one third of the city, has gone missing.[13]

Jerusalem is one of the poorest cities in Israel. The city is ranked as the 61st poorest or socio-economically vulnerable of 255 Israeli local authorities. All but 10 of those 60 towns or cities ranked poorer are Palestinian, Bedouin or Druze communities. The city has a lowly ranking score of 3/10. Tel Aviv scores 8/10.[14]

Jerusalem has many other earthly problems, including an increasing number of so-called 'ghost apartments' – homes left vacant for extended periods of the year by their overseas owners. It is estimated that there are 10,000 such homes in the city.[15] In a city with a chronic housing shortage for all, this is understandably seen as a problem. With 34% of its population under the age of 14, compared to just 16.7% in Tel Aviv, that housing pressure is likely to dramatically escalate in future years.[16]

In addition to its 'ghost apartments', Jerusalem has ghost parliamentarians. The Israeli Knesset is located in Jerusalem, yet Jerusalem is home to just 1 in 9 Knesset members. Some 6% of Israelis citizens live in Jerusalem (including occupied annexed east and north Jerusalem). There are no local electoral constituencies in Israel; the state is a single constituency. With no local or territorial constituency to take care of, it might be expected that Jerusalem would be home to far more Knesset members. Tel Aviv-Yafo is home to just 5.2% of the Israeli population but to 18.6% of Knesset members. Add the Tel Aviv District and those figures rise to 16.4% of the Israeli population and 29.1% of Knesset members.[17] Israeli parliamentarians evidently prefer, despite the geographical inconvenience of commuting, to live in Tel Aviv over Jerusalem. Despite near universal clamouring that foreign embassies should relocate from Tel Aviv to Jerusalem, it would appear that Israeli (Zionist) Knesset members aren't themselves too bothered to actually live there.

Jerusalem is clearly a capital city in some trouble, detached (at the time of writing) from all 'its' embassies,[18] legally detached – internationally at least – from more than half of its territory and 60% of its municipal citizens. It is a city where 10,000 home-owners and over 100 Knesset members (out of 120) choose not to live in the city (see '*The Knesset lives in Tel Aviv*', page 252). It is a city where 300,000 citizens choose to boycott their own municipal elections. It would appear demographically, electorally and geographically that Jerusalem is a city in danger of becoming increasingly detached from its own realities. Is the 'eternal' and 'indivisible' city at risk of unintentionally adopting an additional and unwelcome moniker – that of the 'semi-detached city'?

Seminarians in the Christian quarter of the Old City of Jerusalem

Jerusalem Political Wallpaper

Jerusalem Municipal
1923-1947
British Mandate
19,517,642m²

In 'Jerusalem Political Wallpaper' we print five political or historic Jerusalems (north-south axis tilted 90° west), which include:

– west Jerusalem and annexed east Jerusalem (dark blue)
– Jerusalem west of the Green Line or the 1949 armistice border (green)
– Municipal Jerusalem, 1949 to 1967 (pale blue)
– 'Jordanian' Arab Jerusalem Municipality 1950 to 1967 (red)
– British Mandate Municipal Jerusalem, 1923 to 1947 (orange)

East Jerusalem Municip
1952-1967
6,096,168m²

West Jerusalem Municip
1949-1967
36,124,883m²

West Jerusalem Municip
today
51,143,931m²

Municipal Jerusalem
today
116,386,786m²

_____

Jerusalem over time

Palestinian and Jewish passengers travelling on the light rail tram, Jerusalem

4.7 – Tram Space

Jerusalem Light Rail, the electrified urban tram network, opened in 2011. This is a 14km tram line that runs north to south from the settlement of Pisgat Ze'ev, through the Palestinian refugee camp of Shuafat in annexed east Jerusalem, terminating in Mount Herzl in west Jerusalem. The construction and geography of Jerusalem's light train has been widely criticised outside of Israel as an attempt to consolidate Israeli control over annexed Palestinian occupied east Jerusalem. The State has, in effect, co-opted a municipal public transit system to establish new geopolitical facts on the ground.

The exact choice of the route of the Jerusalem light rail is likely to have been determined with many factors in mind. Perhaps not unlike many other cities, population density, commuting patterns, land use and landscape gradient were all critical in informing that decision. Another likely factor to have determined the exact location of the tram route was concerns over security. Between 2002 and 2004, at the height of the Second Intifada, there were seven separate suicide attacks on Jerusalem buses, killing 88 people.[1]

Whatever the benefits to the local Palestinian residents, the decision to route the train through the Palestinian neighbourhood of Shuafat is commonly accepted as significantly decreasing the likelihood of Palestinian suicide bomb-attacks on the tram. There are likely to be few publicly available documents suggesting that such overt security considerations informed the decision of the geography of the route. But whatever the transportation or geo-political motivations informing the choice of route, the Jerusalem Municipality, the tram operators, indeed the State, may have unwittingly unleashed both a giant mobile sociological laboratory and a cinematic view of the Occupation.

There are few bus routes in Jerusalem which embrace the diversity of the religious-ethnic geography of the city in the same way the tram does. In any case, travelling on buses is simply different. On buses, passengers mostly face the same direction. Eye contact is minimal. But the internal configuration of trams operates as a kind of mobile people-watching public space. Seats face in all directions; standing is common; space is intimate.

The choice of the route for the tram has also generated an entirely new and alternative visual perspective on the physical realities of the political built landscape of Jerusalem. The landscape literally opens up when riding the tram; we are both a passenger and an observer of a built geography of a political panorama. The physical landscape of east Jerusalem is intrinsically connected to the political landscape of the city. This is a vast, complex system of natural and man-made geography, motorway flyovers, bridges, walls, barriers and hilltop housing. Almost nothing is devoid of political meaning.

The hilly and dramatic contours of the geography of east Jerusalem add to the interest on this tram journey. The vastness of the Occupation becomes more naked. As a

The light rail tram provides for unexpected panoramic views of the man-made geography and hilly contours of occupied and annexed east Jerusalem

Travelling on the light rail tram, Jerusalem – the language may differ but the destination is a shared one.

Travelling on the light rail tram, Jerusalem

passenger on the tram, we glide along in a glassy bauble, simultaneously looking up and looking down at the constructed built landscape. The outdoors becomes a cinematic experience, the journey an oddly disconcerting Disney-like funfair ride of the geography of Jerusalem occupation – all visually consumed from the safety of the moving transit system. For less than seven shekels (€1.70) you can experience a 20-minute ride with a unique view of the Occupation.

Inside the tram, people become observers of the landscape in a way that just isn't the same as in a car. When driving, the driver tends not to fully visually embrace the almost cinematic 360-degree landscape outside, naturally focusing instead on the rules of the road. When travelling in a car, whether driving or as a passenger, we are an active participant in the surrounding landscape. The driver engages in a series of autonomous acts of movement in this landscape: left or right, straight ahead, we choose where to go.

In Jerusalem there are places where Jews or Palestinians, even if permitted to do so, instinctively never drive. In this superficially personally autonomous and mobile world, ironically it is harder to detach yourself from participating in the local rules governing movement. In this way, depending on national identity, religion or legal status, each individual becomes a willing or unwilling participant in the local geography of separation and segregation. In the 'overt' political landscape beyond and close to the fringes of Municipal Jerusalem, such stark realities become ever more acute. This is a landscape of control, checkpoints, settler-only roads (a shared military checkpoint is quite obviously a different experience for Israeli Jews and Palestinians). We become less an observer and more a player in that landscape.

On the tram, everyone temporarily shares if not the same perspective of the journey, then the experience in navigating the journey. You get on where you like and sit where you like. Everyone is subject to the same rules of movement. The shared space of the tram is fundamentally a more democratic space than a vehicular checkpoint. The tram is an intimate social space in movement in a way the car simply is not. There are strangers sitting beside you, rubbing shoulders; eye contact is very often inevitable.

The geography of the tram allows us to engage in a way that sitting back to back in a bus doesn't. We see more. Our eye wanders. Natural human curiosity is given a stage that is different from a bus. Who is carrying what, wearing that, who's with whom, what do they have in that supermarket bag, where are they going to, coming from? We can become more than curious or inquisitive; we can become nosey.

Place names can take on a new meaning. From the perspective of Israeli Jews, Shuafat and Beit Hanina are Palestinian refugee camps that, for most Israeli Jews, are perceived as forbidden, exotic and potentially dangerous. They are places that are invisible; you doesn't go there or travel through them. Their names on road signs have little directional meaning (except in the subtle subconscious sense that they are to be avoided). The names of these places occupy a kind of 'background' information noise or signage role. They are there, but they are largely ignored. Buses in annexed east Jerusalem, whilst not segregated, tend to have very specific destinations and routes that accidently or otherwise result in relatively homogeneous passengers – Haredi, Palestinian, etc.

On the tram, however, Shuafat and Beit Hanina are normalised. They become part of your journey. 'Beit Hanina' or 'Shuafat', when announced by the automated tram info-sound-system, become just another tram stop on your journey. Previously understood simply as Palestinian places, names of Palestinian refugee camps, they now become fused with a different, ordinary experience of daily life. For Israeli Jews, they now become part of the mental mapping of tram travelling. 'Shuafat – one, two, three, five stops from home', 'Beit Hanina, six stops to go before I get off'. These places become part of the daily commute; they have a direct link to the journey home or to work; they become familiar and connected. They begin become part of a shared space. The significance of this shared space cannot be underestimated particularly in the context of Jerusalem or, indeed, Israeli civic or public space. This is not to imply that the tram itself is an engine of coexistence; politically charged violence on or against the tram is not uncommon. Yet the Jerusalem light rail perversely superficially normalises the Occupation; Shuafat becomes just another residential suburban stop along the tram route. Both the 'Green Line and the annexation is erased. The different legal status of its passengers becomes, however temporary, invisible in the tram space.

The Shuafat refugee camp and west Anata, inside the municipality borders of Jerusalem
Shuafat is surrounded by a 8m-high wall on three sides, physically preventing access to the local authority. This island outpost is the size of the 'Old City' of Jerusalem (0.9km²). With a population of 40,000, it has one of the highest urban densities in the world. With little municipal planning oversight, the camp has witnessed a laissez-faire explosion of development, with unauthorised 12-storey towers mushrooming inside this walled no-man's-land island city.

5 – Invisible Geographies

5.1 – The Road to Ariel

The seamless, uninterrupted journey along the Route 5 motorway from the beach of Tel Aviv to the settlement city of Ariel takes no more than 30 minutes. This motorway connects, if not blends, the Israeli metropolis with the occupied West Bank's fourth largest settlement.[1] This is a journey of invisible geography, a high-speed, rarely congested, almost endlessly straight motorway connecting Israel proper with Ariel which lies 17km inside the Green Line (almost halfway across the West Bank)

There are few distractions from points of interest once inside the Green Line; a Green Line that is itself 'invisible' on the ground without the aid of satellite navigation. In the not-too-far distance, on either side of the motorway, are the visible minarets of the local Palestinian towns and villages of the West Bank. There are, however, no signposts along the motorway to tell you the names of these towns and villages. There are no motorway exit signs to these villages because there are no motorway exits to access them. They lie in forbidden territory. The motorway is deliberately designed not to connect you to this invisible geography.

With no service stations along the 20-minute journey east of the Green Line and no motorway exits, there is no reason to slow down, let alone to stop. The journey is designed for constant movement; the landscape is engineered to be blurred, to be momentarily and safely consumed. If you look carefully (it passes by in a rapidly moving blur), you will notice the motorway's edge is lined with hundreds of metres of coiled razor wire. For some this may appear an almost invisible boundary. To others, perhaps – at least those who take the journey regularly – it communicates a subconscious zone of protection.

The official and altogether more impenetrable Israeli separation barrier can be glimpsed on occasion in the middle distance, snaking across the landscape. The barrier in the distance looks deceptively anodyne, pastoral even. One could be forgiven for mistaking the it as an agricultural or property boundary fence. In open, rolling countryside in this part of the West Bank, there is no wall. Up close, this is in fact a 3m-high fence, separated by two continuous rolls of barbed wire and trenches, with a paved military road running down the middle. Israel has designed the commuting journey to suburban settlements to ensure it is as seamless and secure as possible, a continuous uninterrupted expansion of Israeli living space. This is engineered, Israeli frontier geography that seeks to strip itself of an irrefutable Palestinian reality.

Travelling westwards from the West Bank, a large motorway toll-like security structure generates a sense of 'here versus there', Israel proper versus 'the territories'. The

Settlement-only exit signs on the drive from Tel Aviv to Ariel along Route 5

toll-like barrier is not intended to signify a political or national border (it isn't, after all, built on or close to the Green Line), but rather a security roadblock. This is a watchful Israeli state that perpetuates the narrative that all Israelis are living this vulnerability together. Tel Aviv, Ariel, Israel proper, the settlements are one continuous Israeli space under constant and necessary vigilance. The invisible Palestinian villages and their inhabitants, unseen, with 'no names' and no apparent means of access or exit, simply hover in the distance in a landscape of invisible and guarded geography.

This is a form of landscape design analogous to the concept of the design of 'negative space' in photography. These negative spaces exist as residual landscapes of occupation, are arguably incidental or peripheral, but in many ways they are fundamental in shaping the consumption and defining the boundaries of how Israelis, Tel Avivians, perceive the Occupation itself. They do not just complete the totality of the picture, they shape it, inform it. Essentially they allow it to continue to effectively function. In doing so they also shape and inform the story Tel Aviv tells itself.

––––––

The seamless and uninterrupted drive to the settlement city of Ariel (pop. 18,000), 17km east of the Green Line
There are no petrol stations, no motorway exits and therefore no exit signs to 'nameless' Palestinian villages. This is a journey designed to be as seamless as possible with Israel proper.

Invisible Cities

The city of Tulkarm, a Palestinian city of 60,000 people located just tens of metres east of the Green Line is hidden in full view.[2] For Israelis driving along motorway Route 6, Tulkarm is clearly visible, its houses and minarets discernible to the naked eye. Yet this city is made invisible by the simple fact that there are no motorway exits signs for Tulkarm. It is legally forbidden for Israelis to visit to Tulkarm as it is under Palestinian Authority administrative control (Area A under the Oslo Accords). If forbidden to visit, it is unnecessary to provide access and, thus, information as to how to get there. A city of 60,000 people just 200m from the Yizak Rabin motorway in Israel becomes just another nameless place in inaccessible space, a city for Israelis to be momentarily visually consumed from the side window of the car at speeds of up to 100km an hour.

Qalqilya, a Palestinian city of 45,000 residents, is located just east of the Green Line dividing Israel from the West Bank.[3] Qalqilya is also a city surrounded on three sides by the Israeli separation barrier. A significant length of that separation barrier takes the form of an 8m-high concrete wall, built close to or exactly on the Green Line. The wall however is masked from view on the Israeli side by a landscaped mound designed as a typical motorway sound buffer, and Qalqilya is made partially invisible by it.

If some Palestinian cities in the West Bank have been made invisible, many others in Israel proper are now being silenced. Draft legislation in March 2017 approved by the

Government will make it illegal for minarets to broadcast a call to prayer late at night and early in the morning. This controversial legislation, colloquially known as the 'Muzein bill', is presented as a noise-nuisance bill but is widely accepted as targeting mosques in mixed Jewish and Palestinian towns and cities.[4] In addition to the silencing of Arabic, there is a risk that the visibility of Arabic on the street may be significantly lessened. The necessity of trilingual road signage (Hebrew, Arabic and English) may soon be a thing of the past. In May 2017 the Government approved the 'nation state bill' which will remove Arabic as one of Israel's official languages.[5]

The Palestinian city of Tulkarm (pop. 50,000) in the West Bank as viewed from the Route 6 motorway in Israel proper. There are no exit signs for Tulkarm because there are no exits for Tulkarm.

Buffers and Barriers

Distinguishing between the diversity of military roadside security barriers and municipal motorway sound buffers across Israel and the West Bank can be challenging. For many Israelis, such barriers or buffers simply blend and merge both physically and perceptually. They are co-opted willingly or unwittingly into a blurred landscape of occupation. For Palestinians residing inside the West Bank this network of barriers, buffers, blockades, screens, walls or shields can each have a very different meaning.

barrier *noun*, plural noun: barriers – 1. fence or other obstacle that prevents movement or access; *synonyms:* fence, railing, barricade, hurdle, bar, blockade, roadblock; fencing – 'police erected barriers to control the crowd' / 2. a gate at a car park or railway station that controls access by being raised or lowered. / 3. a circumstance or obstacle that keeps people or things apart or prevents communication or progress. 'a language barrier'; *synonyms:* obstacle, obstruction, hurdle, stumbling block, bar, block, impediment, hindrance

buffer *noun*. a person or thing that reduces a shock or that forms a barrier between incompatible or antagonistic people or things – 'family and friends can provide a buffer against stress'; *synonyms:* cushion, bulwark; *verb*. lessen or moderate the impact of (something). 'the massage helped to buffer the strain'; *synonyms:* cushion, absorb, soften, lessen, diminish, moderate, mitigate, allay, stifle, shield, deaden – 'the aromatherapy massage was helping to buffer some of the strain'

השטח שלפניך הינו שטח
פלסטינאי A, אין כניסה
לישראלים – כניסה לשטח
זה מהווה עבירה על החוק

أمامك منطقة فلسطينية A
ممنوع دخول الإسرائيليين
دخول الإسرائيليين إلى هذه
المنطقة يُعتبر خرقاً للقانون

PALESTINIAN AUTHORITY TERRITORY
AREA ◆ AHEAD
NO ENTRY FOR ISRAELIS
ENTRY ILLEGAL BY ISRAELI LAW

Area A, West Bank – entrance forbidden to Israelis

Buffers and barriers
Driving along Route 443 in the West Bank between Tel Aviv and Jerusalem
— a sound buffer, security barrier or segregation wall?

Barriers and buffers on the outskirts of Jerusalem.

צא"ת

במערכת הביטחון התייחסו לצו
מדובר בכרש עתידי לצו ● במל"ג
צה"ל בקבינט מלא עם משרד ה
בתיאום יעלון: "התנגדתי
לשעבר יעלון:

ליליך שובל, שלמה צזנה,
מתי טוכפלד ושלומי דיאז

◆ עיסקת הצוללות החדשות לסוגיית
הצפרד שיתייעשנו, חייבג בקבינט. על
צוללות דובר צה"ל, "עמודיבר ברכש
פי הודעת של שלוש צוללות צה"ל יותר
עתידי ישל שהובאג על ידי צה"ל לשיח
מעישוד, לאחרונה, בדרגים השונים
בקבינט הממתקיים בבישחון, דיוני ד
השוטף הממתקיים בבישחון, דייני ד
ובהם רה"מ, שר הבישחון
בינט וזעדות חוץ והבישחון. לב
נוסף על כך, המועצה היי
לאומי פירסמה אתמול גם הי
עה שבה פורט הליך הרכישד
"לנוכח הטגענות הנמשכות ב
שודרת, נבהיר כי מערכת הרד
מעודרבת בכל שלבי הרכיד
והליך הרכש היה תקיד
מנגד, שר הבישחון אתמו
יעלון התייחס אתמי
ואמר כי "אבן, התי
דלת צי הצוללות
צוללות נוספר

רה"

5.2 – The Shifting Ideology of a Simple Map

To draw Israel, to literally 'draw' the contours or shape of the Israeli state, is a profoundly political act. It is an inescapable and overtly conscious exercise in political geography. Nation state map-making probably doesn't come with more caveats, explanatory footnotes or justifying annotates than the simple 'making' of the map of Israel. Perhaps this is not surprising. Israel is somewhat unique as a nation state in possessing for the most of its political life 'internationally' disputed, at times indeterminable, and sometimes hugely shifting borders. On at least a half-dozen separate occasions, Israel's borders substantially shifted between 1949 and 1980s.[1] Following the Yom Kippur War and the conquest of neighbouring Arab and Palestinians lands in 1973, the territory under Israeli control swelled to 329% the size of Israel proper – a case of temporary bloated occupation.[2] Navigating the 'realpolitik' of Israel's borders is thus a potential cartographic quagmire.

Notwithstanding this unstable fluidity, the state of Israel is – in the eyes of a majority of the international community of nation states – commonly understood as having a total area of 20,770km². This excludes both the Golan Heights, which Israel has occupied since 1967 and which it 'unofficially annexed' in 1981, and Israeli-occupied Palestinian east and north Jerusalem, an area of some 70km², which Israel 'officially annexed' in 1980. No other nation state, including the United States of America, currently recognises either annexation as territorially legitimate. The West Bank, some additional 5,800km², is by common international consensus accepted as Israeli-occupied Palestinian Territory, and is also excluded from both our calculation of Israeli land area and our initial cartographic drafting of the Israeli state.

Ask your average (Jewish) Israeli high school student, however, to draw a map of Israel and few are likely to consciously or unconsciously omit the West Bank. This is perhaps understandable. It is, frankly, simpler to delineate Israel's eastern border by drawing a relatively 'straight line' from north (the Golan) to south (the Red Sea) than to recreate from memory the tortuous contours of the 1949 Green Line. High school students of course learn their geography for the most part at school. Israeli schoolchildren are no different. Israeli geography schoolbooks have something of a schizophrenic attitude to the Green Line. It appears and disappears at apparent random from page to page. This simpler version of Israel is also the one most commonly used in the mainstream Israeli media. Every major daily national newspaper and all major national TV channels employ this map of Israel – devoid of any problematic Green Line border – in their daily or evening weather forecasts.

The missing Palestinian cities and the invisible Green Line in a daily Israeli newspaper Israel Hayom (Israel Today) *weather map*

Weather forecasters and the maps they use can often provide interesting insights into the local narrative of accepted political geography. Whether consciously deliberate or sloppily indifferent, the various cartographic omissions or inclusions in the daily evening news weather maps across the world can be strikingly revealing. Israeli weather forecasters are, once again, no different.

In *Yedioth Ahronoth*, Israel's largest selling daily newspaper, all major Palestinian population centres (apart from the mixed city of Jerusalem) in the West Bank are omitted from the weather map. This omission, one could argue, is reasonable, as these Palestinian cities are technically not inside Israel, nor have they been officially annexed by the Israeli state. The same, however, is also true of the Israeli settlement city of Ariel, whose residents are almost exclusively Jewish and are citizens of the state of Israel. Ariel is just 15km from the Palestinian city of Nablus. The population of Nablus (120,000) is six times greater than that of Ariel (pop. 18,000). Nablus is also invisible on Channel 1, the Israeli public broadcaster's nightly news weather map.[3] Similarly, the Channel 10 nightly weather forecast and *Israel Hayom* (Israel's largest freebie newspaper) do not show (other than the mixed city of Jerusalem) any Palestinian cities or the Green Line in their weather maps

The Israeli weather forecast map of choice is also sometimes referred to as 'Greater' or 'Eretz' Israel. This is an Israel that views the Green Line as nothing more than an artificial, temporary, and man-made armistice border. It is the preferred map of choice of the Yesha Council.[4] The Yesha Council – a political wing of the settler movement – does not pay much deference to the Green Line. For the Yesha Council, Judea and Samaria (the historical Jewish religious name for the West Bank) are both historically and politically a de facto part of Israel. In their eyes this may be disputed territory; it is territory that may not have been officially annexed (yet), but historical Judea and Samaria are understood as being an integral and indeed seamless part of contemporary political geography of Israel. Put simply the 'Eretz' Israel map is the choice of the Israeli right.

Those who are likely to self-identify as being on the mainstream or establishment left, who seek an end to the Israeli Occupation and who favour instead the creation of a two-state solution, prefer a very different Israeli map. A map of Israel that omits the West Bank is perceived or understood – historically at least – as identifying with this narrative. This is an Israel that adheres to the validity of the 1949 Armistice Line as primarily informing the delineation of the future Israeli border with a Palestinian state. To draw this map of Israel is to deliberately and self-consciously withdraw from the occupied territories. It is as if at the (albeit tortuous) stroke of a pen, the map-maker carefully but wishfully liberates all Israeli-occupied West Bank. In drawing a map that omits the occupied West Bank, separation and withdrawal is somehow made real.

The reality is that there is and has been, since 1967, only one state between the Jordan River and Mediterranean Sea; that state is Israel and it currently denies 2.7 million Palestinians in the West Bank the right to vote in the state in which they live. A new left perspective is beginning to cleverly use that obvious fact and employ the one-state Israeli map as a vehicle for advancement of universal suffrage in all of Israel and the West Bank. The final destination may be unknown (two-state solution, single state, bi-national state), but in some ways it's irrelevant to a more important narrative of highlighting the existence of a single state (and map) that denies the vote to 25% of its (indigenous) inhabitants because of their ethnicity, nationality or religion. Ironically, as such a narrative potentially gains momentum ('one man, one vote' across Israel-Palestine), the radical or Neo-Zionist right requires the necessary pretence of resurrecting the Green Line as a thin veil to disguise a long-term aspiration of a single Jewish state (without voting rights for Palestinians) between the Jordan and the Mediterranean.

The Israeli occupation of the West Bank entered its 50th year in 2017. The Israeli state came into existence in 1948. The so-called 'Occupation' – a linguistic term long infused with an intangible temporality – has now existed for almost three-quarters of the lifetime

"The state of Israel and its borders with its neighbours 2008"
Headline and map from an Israeli high school geography book, with a Palestinian West Bank made invisible. The black dotted lines indicate 'Palestinian territory confines (Area A)'. This is Palestinian national geography reduced to the language and mapping of reservations surrounded by a seamless Israel.

פרק מבוא: גבולות ישראל

לבנון

סוריה

ירדן

מצרים

ארץ ישראל היא מולדתו של העם היהודי, ממנה
ה ואליה נשא את נפשו אלפי שנים. בחלק מארץ
ראל הוקמה בשנת תש"ח (1948) מדינת ישראל,
דינת לאום של העם היהודי. מדינת ישראל
זה מתון מאבק עם הערבים, ומכיוון שהמאבק
ך עד עצם היום הזה אין הסכמה על גבולותיה
מדינת ישראל, ולא אחת מתרחשים סביבם
ורתים קשים.

ותיה של ארץ ישראל השתנו פעמים רבות
ך ההיסטוריה – בעקבות מלחמות, או בהתאם
כמים ולתמורות מדיניות שהתחוללו באזור.
ך ההיסטורית הייתה הארץ מוקד למאבק בין
זות שונות, אשר רבות מהן שלטו בה לתקופה
זת ואחר כך פינו את מקומן למעצמה אחרת.
זעצמות והעמים ששלטו בארץ היו הפרסים,
ם, הרומים, הביזנטים, הערבים, הצלבנים,
כים, העות'מאנים והבריטים.

שראל נמצאת באזור המגע בין יבשות
ו ואסיה. היא גם שוכנת לחופי הים התיכון
אזור מוצא מיבשת אסיה אל הים התיכון,
ל אירופה ואל האוקיינוס האטלנטי. שטחה
ישראל משמש גם כגשר יבשתי בין הים
בין ים סוף, ודרכו אל האוקיינוס ההודי
ס השקט ואל מזרח יבשת אסיה. מיקום
חשוב זה, הוא שהפך אותה לבעלת גורם
ק למעצמות הגדולות.

ההתפתחות הטכנולוגית של אמצעי
והתחבורה, ובעיקר עם התפתחותה של
אווירית, ירדה חשיבותה הגאופוליטית
ראל, אך עדיין יש למיקומה חשיבות
הסיבות המרכזיות לחשיבותה היא
השחור, שמאגריו הגדולים בעולם
ימי מדינות המזרח התיכון השוכנות
ץ הפרסי. ביקוש גובר למשאב זה
המדינות המתועשות – ובראשן

of that state. If we view the Occupation neither as a temporary aberration, nor as a semi-detached extension of Israel proper, but rather as an integral part of a 'permanent norm' (does three-quarters of the lifetime of a state qualify as temporary or an aberration?), then our circumscribed 1967 map of Israel is somewhat dishonest or delusional or both.

Any political desire to reinstate the 1967 border to facilitate the creation of two states should not be confused with the responsibility of present day map-makers – whatever their political persuasion – to call it as it is. Aspirational geography should not be substituted or confused for territorial reality. We cannot subcontract our present-day known geography for a virtuous or virtual mental map of an unknown future. Wishing away or detaching the West Bank from Israel proper doesn't make it so. To do so distorts our perception and understanding. It exaggerates the difference of the 'here' and the 'over there'. It absolves us of the responsibilities of the now. For many Israeli (Jewish) citizens there is no meaningful border. The Green Line simply doesn't exist. The Green Line is invisible in Greater Jerusalem, it's invisible when crossing Route 443 (Tel Aviv to Jerusalem), Route 5 (Tel Aviv to Ariel) or Route 55 (Kfar Saba to Alfe Menashe).

At present there is just one nation state that controls all of the territory between the Mediterranean Sea and the Jordan river. Currently that state is home to 2.7 million Palestinians who reside on the West Bank, and these 2.7 million Palestinians have no right to vote in the state in which they live in. The reality of the Palestinian Authority administration and quasi-government apparatus muddies somewhat that perception. The Palestinian Authority perpetuates a sense of two states (one unborn). It ironically serves to obscure the reality of a single state, a single Israeli state, and assists in perpetuating a myth of a democratic and undemocratic Israel sitting side by side.

A whole generation of Israelis who are now retiring today (aged 65) were still in high school (aged 15) when the Occupation began in 1967. They have spent their entire working lives (and army service) living in an occupying Israel state. It is not surprising that their children (aged 40) and grandchildren (aged 15), who have been born into and have since come of age in an occupying Israeli state, should view the Occupation not as a temporary arrangement but as a permanent norm, a fixed geographic and political reality. It would thus be naïve not to conclude that the collective or consensus mental map of Israel, what territory actually constitutes Israel, where exactly is Israel, what are where are its borders, etc, would not have mutated or blurred during the past 50 years.[5]

Images and maps of Israel that includes all of Israel-Palestine devoid of the Green Line are ubiquitous. Whether in weather forecasting maps, high school geography books, online census information, government websites, or even left-wing satirical TV programmes, a singular Israel comprising all of Israel-Palestine with no Green Line border is everywhere.

It is not uncommon for self-identified leftist Tel Avivians to believe they have divorced themselves from a certain type of politicised Israeli Geography. They nevertheless voluntarily or involuntarily consume it every day in multiple ways.

---

top – Channel 10 nightly weather forecast and the invisible Palestinian cities

bottom – The weekly left-wing satirical show on Channel 10, Gav HaUma (Back the Nation), *and its borderless Israel*

ערי הצפון 14°-9°

חיפה 19°-13°

הכינרת 22°-13°

תל אביב 20°-13°

אריאל 17°-9°

השפלה 21°-12°

ירושלים 17°-9°

מחאת
סיבות לסיום

ילדי גן מחופשים לחיילים

האומה

את בית המקדש,

227

What's missing in Mini Israel?
A six-hectare miniaturised representation of the state of Israel, 25km south-east of Tel Aviv

5.3 – Mini Israel

There are no borders, no settlements and no West Bank. The separation barrier is conspic-uous by its absence. The geography is not particularly faithful. The southern coastal city of Eilat is too close to the city of Tel Aviv. Jerusalem is far too big. The invisible geography of the Israeli Occupation is nevertheless somewhat unsettling. Welcome to Mini Israel.

Mini Israel is a six-hectare, miniaturised toy-like representation of the state of Israel, 25km south-east of Tel Aviv. This is a fun park for getting to know more about your country and an opportunity to walk the length and breadth of it in less than an hour. Mini Israel is arranged in a comfortable and rather functional series of pathways in the shape of Magen David (Star of David). Sometimes national symbols are curiously a perfect fit for the needs of fun park pathway geography; Mini Israel is political kitsch meets Noddy-land Zionism. Despite the glaring absence of places – no overtly visible settlements or (apart from Jerusalem) Palestinian cities in the West Bank – there is something oddly familiar about the missing geography of the Occupation in Mini Israel. Tempting as it is to imagine, this isn't a fun park geography designed by some ideological state censor at the Ministry of Toys. Mini Israel geography is a simple reflection of how many ordinary Israelis tend to 'see' the 'borders' and 'boundaries' of their state. They are in many places simply invisible.

Few Israeli Jews, perhaps contrary to popular perception outside of Israel, are daily witnesses to the built security apparatus of the Occupation for the simple reason that much those built-security geographies are made invisible to them. In many locations it is impossible for Israelis to readily or easily identify when they are crossing the Green Line. The 8m-high concrete wall that makes up the Israeli separation barrier surrounding the Palestinian city of Qalqilya (just 15km from Tel Aviv) is 'disguised' as a landscaped embank-ment when viewed from the adjoining Route 6 motorway which runs immediately west of the city. Other security geographies are hidden in full view, including the settlements them-selves and the Israeli-built West Bank motorway network which, in many locations, prevent access to Palestinian villages. This vast patchwork of settlements and the motorway net-work that serves them are very often simply perceived as just Israeli roads and Israeli homes.

There is no Green Line in Mini Israel. To be fair to the model-makers, in Mini Israel identifying on the ground where the contours of the Green Line run between east and west Jerusalem is near impossible. It is equally impossible to tell in many places when you are crossing the boundaries of the multiple political geographies of the city of Jerusalem. It is decidedly unclear to the motorist in the vast motorway and flyover network around Jerusalem where exactly Israeli west Jerusalem, annexed Israeli-controlled east Jerusalem (the boundaries of Municipal Jerusalem) and Occupied Palestinian east Jerusalem begin and end. The very clearly visible 8m-high concrete Israeli separation barrier that severs the landscape serves only to confuse. In Jerusalem the Israeli barrier bears no geographic relationship to the Green Line whatsoever. There is, of course, no Israeli separation barrier in Mini Israel. There is no miniaturised 8m-high concrete or plastic wall snaking across the miniaturised hilly landscape. The built geography of Palestinians and Jewish settlers in the West Bank is also absent in the toy town that is Mini-Israel.

Not unlike in Mini Israel, the physical geography east of Greater Jerusalem is an equally obscure place for most Jewish Israelis, a place that seems to vanish off the edge of some imaginary end-of-the-world like map. Life simply ends east of Jerusalem (or at least east of the settlement Ma'ale Adumim and Route 90 to the Dead Sea). A barren desert of knowledge, a forbidden and dangerous expanse of Palestinian, then Arab lands extends seamless beyond. In Mini Israel this is mirrored in the borderless area of hilly overgrown grass that ill-defines the edge of the fun park behind a miniaturised Mount of Olives. There is no West Bank west of Jerusalem in Mini Israel.

A miniaturised mechanical ski-lifts sits atop the 3m-high Mount Hermon in the Mini Israel Golan Heights. Mount Hermon is the highest point 'in Israel'. The Golan has been occupied by Israeli since the 1967 war with Syria. The Golan presents fewer problems for the map-makers of Min Israel. It was unofficially annexed by Israel in 1981. Most Israelis are also very familiar with the small ski resort in Mount Hermon in the Golan; many will have visited it at least once in their lives. The Golan Heights is arguably, for Israelis at least, an acceptable face and, more importantly, a safely accessible place of occupation.

Every nation state perpetuates territorial myths, their own myths, through map-making. Few perhaps are afforded the luxury or opportunity of designing myths of the scale of Minister Israel, a scale of 1:125 to be precise, spread over 35,000m², housing 350 individual large-scale models and buildings. Perhaps the oddest thing about Mini Israel is that few Israelis know that it is not actually located in Israel proper at all, but in a surreal, contested (legally, at least) no-man's land, trapped between two 1949 armistice Green Lines.[1]

———

The Israeli separation barrier that divides the Palestinian town of Baqa el-Garbiya in Israel from the Palestinian town of Baqa al-Gharbiyye in the West Bank

Israeli separation barrier in Baqa al-Gharbiyye

opposite – There are no mini walls in Mini Israel
... but the paths form the Star of David

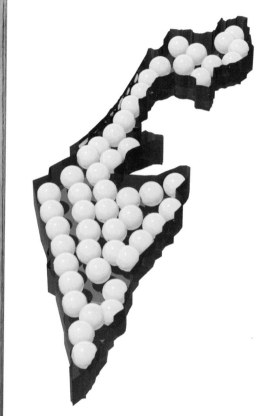

Who's counting whom?

5.4 – Invisible Geography and the Census

The Israeli census, like many national censuses, has its own reasons for its particular and peculiar interests: 'the percentage of Jewish men aged 15 and over who studied in a *yeshiva* (college devoted to full-time study of the Torah) is unlikely to appear in many other national censuses. But there is clearly something very unusual about District Code 7 in the census. This district, according to the 2008 census, is home to 281,000 Israelis but has no calculable population density simply because the region has no stated area. Its territorial geography is apparently incalculable or somehow invisible. Yet the census tells us that 97.7% of the population who reside here are Jewish.[1]

District Code 7 has a name. The census calls it the 'Judea and Samaria Area' (the Jewish biblical name for the occupied West Bank). The West Bank is currently home to 2.7 million Palestinians. The Israeli census enumerators have chosen to make these 2.7 million people invisible. The census actually goes as far as stating that the Muslim population of Judea and Samaria is 0.1%.[2] This is an invisible parallel geography in the sense that two groups sharing the same (but for the most part segregated) space are counted or not depending on the ethno-religious identity ascribed to them.

One can argue that this is after all an Israeli census of Israeli citizens. The Israeli census enumerators don't count stateless 'Palestinians' for the simple reason they are not citizens of Israel. Palestinians living inside Israel proper with full Israeli citizenship – also known as Israeli-Arabs – are of course included in the census enumeration.[3] The census enumerators faced with the reality that they count only Israeli citizens in Judea and Samaria (also known as Israeli settlers living is Israeli-controlled settlements in the occupied West Bank), in theory at least had three potential options. The first option was simply to state the geographic area of Judea and Samaria in its entirety (including or excluding annexed east Jerusalem). The area of Judea Samaria or West Bank is 5,640km². To have chosen this option may have risked the not unreasonable accusations of census-segregation. The second option was to try to actually calculate, no matter how tortuous and fragmented, that proportion or area of the West Bank under direct Israeli administration and security control – in effect Area C under the Oslo Accords (this is approximately 61% of the West Bank), home to 280,000 Israeli settlers.[4] For Israeli census enumerators to have chosen this option would have quantifiably and very visible eradicated the historic and political understanding of biblical Judea and Samaria, and in effect politically solidified the Oslo Accords and territorial acknowledgement of Palestinian geography inside the Israeli census. The third option was to simply fudge the issue by not stating any quantifiable geographical area for the territory of Judea and Samaria, to simply avoid calculating the area of occupation, and at a stroke make invisible 2.7 million people. This is what the census publication chose to do.

Invisible
but watched

Israeli security towers,
Route 60 and Route 443 West Bank

No settlement in the West Bank (unlike every other city, town or local municipality in Israel proper) is given a local geographical area or a population density by the census (Table 2a). The irony is that few Israelis would instinctively know when they are crossing municipal boundaries in Israel proper, particularly in the greater Tel Aviv area where 'cities' seamlessly merge into one another. All Israeli settlements in the West Bank, however, have security entrance gates, most are permanently manned with armed guards, and all are surrounded by security fences. Yet these clearly demarcated settlements apparently have no calculable area for the census enumerators.

235

Israeli security tower, West Bank

5.5 – Constituency Geography

The 2013 local municipal elections for the city of Tel Aviv-Yafo were pretty unremarkable in many respects. Turnout was very low at just 28.7%.[1] A multitude of bewildering and fragmented grassroots and party groupings emerged with council seats.[2] Typical local elections issues such as transport, affordable housing and municipal services dominated the political debate. There was, however, one striking and locally unremarked-upon peculiarity: there are no 'locally' elected councillors in the local elections of Tel Aviv-Yafo because there are no local constituencies, or local area-based geographical representation. The entire city area, some 52km[2] comprising all of its 430,000 residents, is treated as just one constituency. For a municipal or local election, the absence of area-based representation in City Hall politics is (outside Israel) rather unique. The absence of a local area-based or territorial link to local elected councillors may not strike Tel Avivians as peculiar for the simple reason there isn't one at national level either. In Israeli national elections, the electorate also votes in a single electoral constituency. This may not be unique to Israel, but it is extraordinarily rare.[3]

In the first Knesset elections in 1949, and in every subsequent election thereafter, the entire country of Israel has been treated as one single constituency to elect its 120 national parliamentary members.[4] It seems reasonable to conclude that the absence of multiple or area-based constituencies at national level informs, perhaps sustains, the apparent lack of appetite or interest in a local area-based or constituency representation in Tel Aviv-Yafo municipal politics.

But what explains this rather unique national Israeli electoral geography, a geography devoid of any local or regional area based political representation? It has been suggested that the relative small size of the new Israeli state explained the reluctance to put in place local or area-based Knesset representation.[5] This seems, in isolation at least, a rather unconvincing argument. The geographic size of the Israeli state as far as the 1949 Armistice Line is 73%, 53% and 51% the size of Belgium, the Netherlands and Denmark respectively – small but not so small. The population of the state in 1949 was, however, very small – just 800,000. By 1955 this had already risen to 1.8 million. By 1965, following massive Jewish immigration, it had climbed to 2.6 million. Anticipated rapid but unpredictable levels of immigration may explain a reluctance to draw and constantly radically redraw constituency boundaries. A tripling of the population in 15 years would have inevitably wreaked havoc on the stability of constituency boundaries.[6]

It has also been suggested that a party list system, with no area-based representation, allowed the party elites to keep tight control of the names entering the Knesset.[7]

Voting in the (2015) Israeli Knesset elections (pick a party but not the person)

Unstable international borders or the constant threat of shifting territory would also perhaps have dampened any local appetite to entertain the complexity of multiple constituencies.

Israel as a nation state has lived with unstable or indeterminate borders for almost its entire 70 years of independence. Whether through annexation, occupation, defensive or offensive war, the state of Israel has had remarkably fluid borders since its declaration of independence in 1948.[8] While these shifting borders could not have been foreseen as such, they nevertheless may have been anticipated. The 1947 UN resolution of the partition of historic Palestine, if an anathema to Palestinians and the wider Arab world, it has been argued was equally viewed by many critical players in the pre-state or Mandatory Palestine Jewish resistance as both unacceptable and unsustainable for the long-term viability of a Jewish state.[9] The proposed partition of historic Palestine was of course a huge victory for Zionism, and greeted as such. The location of those borders, the territorial division itself, was rejected out of hand by all Arab states. War followed. It is a difficult job to draw and maintain internal electoral constituency boundaries if the very borders of the state itself keep shifting. The need to have to constantly redraw constituency boundaries is unlikely to have been a priority of a state born under such political uncertainty.

Today the boundaries of the single national constituency itself remain unclear for the very simple reason that Israel has (multiple) internationally disputed borders. The definition of what even constitutes an international border is contentious. The Golan Heights (occupied Syrian territory since 1967), 'unofficially' annexed by Israel (1981 Golan Heights Law), is one such border.[10] The 1949 armistice border, Israel's contested boundary with the Palestinian territories, is perhaps the most challenging. Some 70km^2 of east Jerusalem was incorporated into municipal west Jerusalem by the state of Israel in 1967 following the 1967 Arab-Israeli war. The passing of the Jerusalem Law in 1980 gave it further legitimacy in the eyes of the Israeli state, but it provoked an international backlash. This annexation is not recognised under international law, nor is it recognised by any other foreign state, including the United States of America.[11]

One further possible explanation for the absence of an electoral geography with multiple member or single-seat area-based representation is that it would have starkly revealed the territorial extent of the concentration of the Israeli-Arab or Palestinian minority population within Israel. A national constituency-based electoral system that nakedly exposed the regional territorial divisions of Israeli political geography potentially risked undermining a nascent national Israeli (Jewish) narrative of a unified (Jewish) state. More importantly, it may have been viewed as potentially nourishing quasi-territorial secession. A multiple constituency-based electoral geography where Palestinian parties might succeed in gaining 10 or 15 Knesset seats risks visible regional territorial expression on election night. If not entirely erased, the demographic reality or political visibility of this secessionist geography is certainly masked by a single national constituency.

There is, however, little consensus on this. It has been argued that a single constituency not only makes sense in the context of the emerging Israeli state because Israel is a very small country geographically, but also that Israel did not have strong 'regional distinctions at its birth'.[12] But Israeli certainly did have acute regional distinctions the time of its birth. Following the 1948 Arab-Israeli war, and despite an estimated expulsion and fleeing of some 700,000 Palestinians from the newly created Israeli state, some 156,000 Palestinians remained. The vast majority of those remaining, some 18% of the fledgling Israeli state, were geographically concentrated in the northern Galilee region of Israel.[13] That historic concentration has continued to the present.

Today the Palestinian population makes up just over 22% of the Israeli state and is predominately located in what is known colloquially in Israel as the 'The Triangle' in the Galilee region of northern Israel.[14] In an area stretching from the Lebanese border to the Jezreel Valley in north central Israel, the indigenous Palestinian communities constitute a majority of the region's population.[15] Majority concentrations of Palestinian communities also dominate the hills hugging the West Bank, stretching from the cities and towns of Umm al-Fahm, through Baka el-Garbiya, to Taibe. In addition, a substantial proportion of the northern Negev has a majority Arab (Bedouin) population.

It seems unlikely that in a region of fiercely contested national political space, the preference of the Israeli state for a single national constituency for Knesset elections would not have been indifferent to the reality or challenges of the Palestinian population concentration. A singular electoral constituency had, and has, the effect of geographically neutralising the Palestinian voting public and the political parties that have historically represented them in the Knesset. They, in effect, became and remain significantly aspatial. They are aspatial in the sense that the Palestinian voting bloc, like all Israeli political groupings, are, whether by design or otherwise, 'geographically invisible' on election night.

In a national single-seat constituency of 120 Knesset members (MKs), there are no maps on Israeli election night. What is often central to television audiences on election night in other countries simply doesn't exist in Israel. There are no 'swing states', constituency 'swingometers' or maps of colourful flipping seats. There is no 'blue' or 'red' states, no 'blue', 'red' or 'green' constituencies. Election night analysis is for the most part restricted to the declaration of overall national 'winners' and 'losers' and the perennial Israeli challenge of coalition formation. There is little or no analysis of regional or local swings in the popular vote. For the Israeli television audience, in a country and region torn by territorial division and segregation, Knesset elections are, ironically, aspatial. The Knesset is conveniently or accidentally stripped of all geography. It's as if the indigenous Palestinians and the political parties that represent them almost float detached from their territorial roots. They are electorally severed from their geographical and historical connection to the land. Territorial constituencies are, by definition, rooted in territory in the soil of the state itself.

A further potential explanation for the lack of a constituency-based electoral system is that it would also have revealed, geographically at least, the deep ethno, religious and social economic cleavages that exist within Israeli *Jewish* society itself. This includes the historic and long controversial State policy to settle newly arrived Jews from the Arab and Muslim world to peripheral, politically vulnerable and environmentally inhospitable corners of the new state (Negev Desert, etc). An area-based constituency approach would have given additional acute geographical expression to an already emerging political division in Israeli society.[16] Existing classic 'centre-periphery' political cleavages or tensions would have been visibly exacerbated.

Israel as a nation state is not particularly unusual in this regard. It is a relatively young nation state and one that was forged out of a unique set of historical and geopolitical circumstances. Any electoral system that unnecessarily accentuated or magnified internal

Israeli-Palestinian city of Umm al-Fahm (pop. 52,000), Israel

Jewish divisions risked disrupting the forging of a unifying Zionist national narrative. It is not unreasonable to presume that the forging of that unifying national Jewish narrative was considered critical. That constructed story inevitably sought to promote symbols of national (Jewish) unity. These included the national anthem, the flag, and a revitalised and immersive Hebrew language. Magnifying geographic divisions would likely have been viewed as more than a distraction. It would potentially have undermined a national narrative of Jewish unity. Despite the above, there have been spasmodic attempts to introduce constituency-based electoral reform in the Knesset.[17] All have proved unsuccessful.

Perhaps a more compelling contemporaneous reason for the current lack of multiple or area-based Knesset constituencies is the Israeli occupation of the West Bank, which entered its 50th year in 2017. Following the six-day Israeli-Arab war in 1967 and the subsequent occupation of the West Bank, the Israeli settler population grew at first quite slowly. As late as 1972, some 10,000 Israeli settlers were scattered across the West Bank. This accounted for just 0.31% of the total Israeli population (Palestinian and Jewish). By 1993 that had risen to 280,000, or 5.3% of the Israeli population. Today 7000,000 Israeli citizens (99% of whom identify as Jewish in the Israeli census) live in the occupied territory of the West Bank (including annexed east Jerusalem). Put another way, today 1 in 12 Israelis (1 in 9 Jews) are settlers living in the occupied West Bank. In 1972 the figure was just 1 in 300.

The 700,000 Israeli settler population of the West Bank who reside outside the borders of the internationally recognised Israeli state are nevertheless also eligible voters in Knesset general elections. The West Bank is also home to 2.7 million stateless Palestinians. These 700,000 Israeli citizens, who live outside Israel proper, now make up approximately 9% of the Israeli population.[18] In a multiple constituency-based electoral system, these Israeli citizens would account for 10 Knesset seats (out of 120). Another potential reason for the lack of electoral constituencies is the role a lower turnout amongst Israeli Palestinians has in diminishing voting power of Palestinian electoral block in a single national constituency. Electoral boycotts or generally lower participation rates suppresses the electoral weight of Israeli Palestinians.

A constituency-based electoral geography would, however, largely render irrelevant turnout in Palestinian communities. The reason for this is the very concentrated geography of Palestinian populations. The largely Palestinian Joint List secured 97% of the vote in Qalansawe, 96% of the vote in Taibe and Umm al-Fahm, and 95% in Tira in 2015.[19] In our single electoral constituency of 'Qalansawe-Taibe', the political block Joint List would have secured our notional seat on a 10% turnout, as it would on a 65% turnout. In fact, a constituency-based electoral geography with high concentrations of Palestinian voters but lower turnouts would disproportionately favour the power Palestinian voters who do vote. It may take just 20,000 Palestinians to elect their MK in Umm al-Fahm (with low turnout) as opposed to 40,000 Jewish Israeli voters in, say, Kfar Saba (with a much higher Jewish turnout).

The most obvious political challenge in designing electoral constituencies is how exactly would one delineate the geographic boundaries of these 10 Knesset seats? The drafting of those potential boundaries in a multiple Knesset electoral constituency is likely to prove exceedingly tricky. It presents enormous cartographic challenges with potentially profound political implications. Notwithstanding these obvious geographic and political challenges, the Israel Democracy Institute (IDI) has proposed that Israel should consider adopting a multi-seat constituency system. In a report titled *Reforming Israel's Political System: Recommendations and Action Plan*, published in 2011, the IDI proposes the very specific recommendation of 'instituting a dozen multi-member electoral districts to preserve a high level of proportionality'.[20] One of those hypothetical electoral districts is called 'Jerusalem and the Judean Hills'. Presumably this region includes all of the Israel citizens of the Jerusalem and Judea (southern West Bank).

Whatever the preference, whether it be 120 single-seat constituencies or 'a dozen multi-member electoral districts', the challenge of how, and more specifically, where, to draw those constituency borders remains the same. There is no escaping the drawing of lines on a map. There are two potential choices here. The first option would involve drawing the boundaries of the constituencies so that they included citizens (voters) of the Israeli state but excluded the non-voting Palestinians residents of the occupied West Bank. This would, in effect, follow, for the most part, the geographic contours of the Oslo Accords. We call this the 'ethno-gerrymandering option'.

Area C as defined by the Oslo Accords (approximately 61% of the area of West Bank) is under both direct Israeli administrative and military control. Area C is also home to 400,000 Israeli citizens or Jewish settlers. A further 280,000 Jewish Settlers live in annexed east Jerusalem).[21] The political geographic boundaries of these constituencies would, however, not only be cartographically visually tortuous, they would implicitly deeply embed the Oslo Accords into the political quasi-constitutional apparatus of the Knesset. It would amount to a de facto Israeli electoral withdrawal from half of the occupied territory.

The creation of such official electoral constituency maps would inevitably pose profoundly uncomfortable political questions for the Israeli state. The starkness of these necessarily ethno-gerrymandered tortuous borders would be obvious. The geographic electoral visibility of the extent of existing Jewish-Palestinian segregation and separation if not revelatory, would nevertheless be revealing. It could be argued that even these extreme gerrymandered constituencies could at least preserve a plausible narrative of a democratic and contiguous Israeli State. All those living inside the constituency border would have or be given the right to vote in the Knesset. Those living outside would remain stateless and continue to remain under Israeli occupation.

A second cartographical option is to simply divide the entire West Bank into 10 separate Knesset constituencies, their territorial or geographic size reflecting the local Israeli (almost exclusively Jewish settler population) voting population. These constituencies would thus include the 2.7 million permanent indigenous Palestinian residents of the West Bank who have no vote in the Israeli Knesset. We call this the 'electoral annexation option' Any electoral constituency whose territory included long-standing indigenous residents but simultaneously denied those same residents a right to vote would of course be viewed as problematic. The 'electoral annexation option' would be better described as 'ethno-annexation option'. There are other more familiar or appropriate words to describe that level of electoral segregation.

Whatever the choice, be it the tortuous 'gerrymandering' or electoral annexation of the entire West Bank/Judea Samaria, both would cartographically or electorally advertise the political reality that 2.7 million permanent residents are currently denied a right to vote (in the Knesset) in the state in which they reside. Perhaps this reason alone explains why

Israel since 1967 has not chosen, and is unlikely to choose, to experiment with constituency geography. Prime Minister David Ben-Gurion's musings on the relative benefits of electoral constituencies were of course prior to 1967.[22]

This may partly explain why the IDI, in proposing their 'dozen multi-member electoral districts', avoids actually putting pen to paper to draw the electoral map. The IDI conveniently absolves itself of that challenge, and instead suggests an 'overlap between electoral districts and existing administrative districts (those of the Ministry of the Interior or the regional division serving the Central Elections Committee), in keeping with common contemporary practice, to eliminate suspicion of arbitrary boundary determination and minimize potential political struggles'.[23] In suggesting multiple member constituency (in this case with 12 members) for the entire West Bank and Jerusalem, the IDI conveniently bypasses having to subdivide the West Bank into constituencies. Such convenient sidestepping of the politically problematic job of carving up territory inhabited by both Israeli citizens and stateless Palestinians does not absolve itself of the obvious challenges. To suggest that such a map would 'minimize potential political struggles' seems at best narrowly conceived, arguably politically naïve.

What if the Knesset went local?
(FIRST PAST THE POST – 120 SEATS)

In 'What if the Knesset went local?' we have mapped out our 120 theoretical single-seat constituencies in Israel.[24] These constituencies are home to all the eligible voting citizens of the state of Israel residing in 'Israel proper', the West Bank and the Golan Heights. They also include one group not currently entitled to vote in the Knesset election – the Palestinian municipal residents of east Jerusalem. The reasons for their inclusion are discussed below.

Using the Israeli census Small Area statistics to first create 120 Knesset seats, we then extrapolated the voting behaviour in those theoretical 120 single-seat Knesset constituencies using Small Area election results. Our 120 Knesset is a simple model. The party that wins a majority or plurality of the vote in each seat wins the seat. We cannot, of course, assume that voting behaviour would not change, perhaps dramatically so in such constituencies. It is highly likely that in such a 'first past the post', winner-takes-all system that voters of smaller parties would gravitate to a larger party to 'block' the election of their least preferable rival grouping. Neither, however, can we presume how that coalescing around like-minded larger groups would work. In our simple model we therefore assume no change in the first-preference vote. It's worth stressing that the 2015 Knesset election is itself just a once-off electoral snapshot.

A first-past-the-post system generally favours both larger parties and parties with concentrated or regional support. So what would a 120 single seat constituency Knesset electoral geography look like? And how would it compare to the current representation in the Knesset. Our first-past-the-post electoral model leads to a dramatically changed Knesset landscape. The Likud Party would see its seat share rise from 30 to 60 (one seat short of an overall majority). An overall majority on a relatively low plurality of the vote is not uncom-

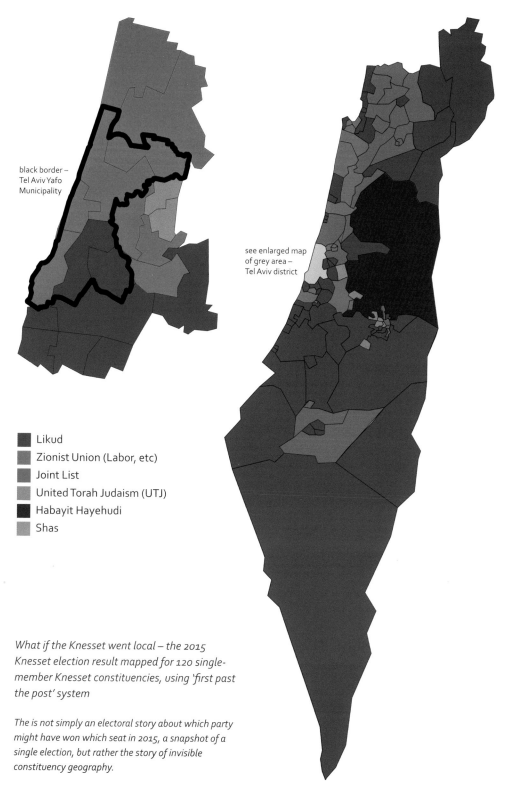

black border –
Tel Aviv Yafo
Municipality

see enlarged map
of grey area –
Tel Aviv district

- Likud
- Zionist Union (Labor, etc)
- Joint List
- United Torah Judaism (UTJ)
- Habayit Hayehudi
- Shas

*What if the Knesset went local – the 2015
Knesset election result mapped for 120 single-
member Knesset constituencies, using 'first past
the post' system*

*The is not simply an electoral story about which party
might have won which seat in 2015, a snapshot of a
single election, but rather the story of invisible
constituency geography.*

mon in first-past-the-post systems. In 2005 the British Labour party secured a 66 seat overall majority (55% of the parliamentary seats) on just 35.2% of the national vote.[25] In 1993 the Progressive Conservative Party of Canada famously lost 154 of its 156 seats despite winning 16% of the national vote. In the same election Bloc Québécois with its vote concentrated in Quebec secured 38 seats on just 13.5% of the national vote.[26]

In our first-past-the-post model, the small and medium-sized parties with evenly spread voting support – Yisrael Beiteinu, Kulanu, Meretz, Yesh Atid – would vanish altogether. The Joint List, a party with concentrated regional support in the Palestinian population centres of the Galilee and Bedouin Negev (potentially in east Jerusalem in our model) would see its seat share rise from 13 to 25, equalling that of the official opposition Zionist Union, which would gain just one additional seat putting the party on 25. United Torah Judaism, with concentrated support in Religious Orthodox cities, would gain eight seats compared to just six in 2015 Knesset elections under the existing electoral system.

A second dramatic change would be the emergence of a new electoral landscape. Israel would be confronted for the first time with a spatial and very visual electoral geography. The map shows a nation of Likud blue, urban concentrations of Labour in and around Tel Aviv and Haifa, with isolated pockets of religious and right-wing parties clustered in and around Jerusalem. The real dramatic visual impact would be the extent of regional concentration of Joint List in Palestinian areas of the north and south of the country. Habayit Hayehudi would secure the large sprawling seat of Samaria-North West Bank.

What if the Palestinians of east Jerusalem could vote?

Our 120 Knesset constituencies include all those Israeli citizens who were entitled to vote in Knesset elections in 2015. This included an estimated 660,000 Israeli settlers living in the West Bank and annexed east Jerusalem, and the Israeli citizens living in the occupied Golan Heights. It does not include the 2.7 million stateless Palestinians living in the occupied West Bank.[27] We have deviated from current Israeli Knesset voting eligibility by including the 300,000 or so Palestinian residents of annexed east Jerusalem and the 18,000 or so Druze residents of annexed Golan Heights. We have included these populations for three reasons.

Firstly, these Palestinian residents of east Jerusalem, along with the 18,000 residents but non-Israeli citizens of the Golan Heights (largely made up of local Druze population), are the only Israeli non-citizen residents included in the Israeli census headcount. Our 120-seat constituencies simply include all those counted in the Israeli census. Foreign workers, as non-citizens, are not entitled to vote. They are however, irrespective of legal status or length of residency, *not* included in the Israeli census.[28] Secondly, the Palestinian residents of annexed east Jerusalem are entitled to vote in municipal elections in Jerusalem. They are not, however, afforded the same right in the Knesset. By including them we wish simply to draw attention to this electoral fact. Similarly, the Druze population of the Golan are entitled to vote in municipal elections. Thirdly, in choosing to include these 300,000 Palestinians in our 120-seat constituency geography, it gives a small geographical electoral glimpse of the demographic electoral power a further 2.7 million Palestinians would have in a one-man one-vote single state, 120-seat Knesset constituency geography.[29]

The Palestinian population of annexed east Jerusalem constitutes about 12% of the overall Palestinian population of the West Bank. If given a vote in the Knesset, and in the absence of electoral gerrymandering, they would likely dominate and win four single-seat Knesset constituencies. If all the Palestinians in the West Bank were given the right to vote in an Israeli election, they would likely win 26 seats in the 120 seated Knesset.[30]

The Palestinian residents of east Jerusalem have historically and overwhelmingly boycotted the local Municipal Jerusalem elections, but they are unlikely to boycott a vote in the Knesset. We have therefore allocated these four seats to the Joint List.

An unsettling map of settler seats

The settler population of the West Bank, including annexed east Jerusalem, is now approaching 700,000 Israelis citizens.[31] As citizens, those of 18 years and older are entitled to vote in Israeli national or Knesset elections. In the 19th elections to the Knesset in 2015, these voters, then estimated to be 660,000 strong, would have determined the allocation

Inside a home of the West Bank Haredi settlement of Beitar Illit (pop. 49,000 in 2015).
The official Knesset website lists seven members whose homes are in the West Bank (Judea and Samaria).

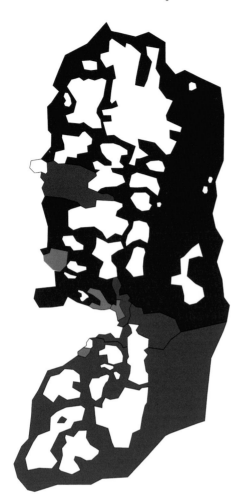

potential 2015 Knesset seats

■ Habayit Hayehudi (1)

■ Likud (5)

■ United Torah Judaism (UTJ) (4)

□ disenfranchised non-voting
  Palestinians (0)
  (Areas A and B Oslo Accords)

An unsettling map of settler seats?
If Israel and the occupied West Bank had electoral
constituencies, the settler population would justify 10
seats in the Israeli Knesset (Israeli voting areas only)

opposite – Ynet mapping of the 2015 Knesset
election results
The absence of constituencies obscures electoral ethno
gerrymandering. The 'empty' grey space has no voters
but it is home to 2.7 million Palestinians living in the
West Bank.

of approximately 10 Knesset seats.

In '*An unsettling map of settler seats*' we map out these 10 electoral constituencies. In electoral constituency geography, seats are usually allocated according to the total population and not the voting age population. Each of our Knesset constituencies has on average approximately 67,000 Israeli residents. We then 'apportioned' a single party electoral winner by aggregating each party support across the various cities, towns, Jerusalem suburbs and isolated outposts in each constituency. The party that secured a majority or plurality of the vote was deemed the winner of the seat. Our 10 West Bank or Judea and Samaria constituencies, their major population centres and their respective winning party are listed in the References (page 330).[32] The Likud Party wins five seats, the Haredi United Torah Judaism (UTJ) wins the Haredi cities of Modi'in Ilit, Beitar Illit and seats in (annexed) north and north-west Jerusalem. Habayit Hayehudi wins a single, but geographically sprawling seat of Samaria-North-West Bank, which includes the settlements of Beit El, Geva Binyamin, Eli, Kedumin, Har Adar and Talmon amongst others.

The white areas on our map correspond to Areas A and B under the Oslo Peace Accords. These areas (including parts of Area C) are home to 2.7 million stateless Palestinians, living under Israeli control since 1967 but who are not entitled to vote in Israeli Knesset elections. There is only one sovereign in control of Israel Palestine since 1967. That state is Israel. The Knesset is its democratically, and undeniably unrepresentative elected parliament. Should all of Israel and the West Bank have a vote in the Knesset (excluding the Gaza Strip), each 120 single-seat constituency would have a population of approximately 90,000 residents. The West Bank would thus have around 33 seats in the Knesset.

Joining the dots with Ynet

The Israeli news agency Ynet has mapped out the 2015 Knesset results. In the absence of constituencies, the maps identify the voting preference (via a pie chart) of all the major Israel population centres – cities, towns, villages, *kibbutzim* and *moshavim*, etc. This includes the vast majority of Israeli settlements of the West Bank.[33]

The map delineates the Green Line by a grey dotted line. The map, cartographically at least, suggests a comparable electoral geography both west (Israel proper) and east of the Green Line (West Bank). The empty grey space between the cities and towns and villages imply there are no residents and thus no voters. In Israel proper this is essentially true. This grey space may include a tiny number of isolated single homes or farmsteads. Rural settlement geography in Israel tends to be in the form of clustered, relatively homogenous communities. These are shown on the map.

This is not the case in the West Bank. In the vast, empty grey space in the West Bank between the Jewish settlements and isolated outposts there are residents but no voters. Here reside 2.7 million stateless Palestinian residents who are not entitled to vote in the state (Israel) which controls their lives. The map inevitably, perhaps conveniently, obscures the political reality of the lack of voting rights for the Palestinian population of the West Bank.

The Knesset lives in Tel Aviv

So where do members of the Knesset actually live? The official Knesset website reveals, if not the street address, the cities, towns, *kibbutzim* and *moshavim* of 71% of all Knesset members (86 out of 120).[34] Approximately 8.6% of Israeli population now live in settlements in the occupied West Bank. The West Bank is also home to 8.1% of MKs. A full 62% (5 out of 8) MKs from Habayit Hayehudi live in settlements. Put another way, 71% of all MKs who are settlers are from Habayit Hayehudi.[35]

Tel Aviv-Yafo is home to just 5.2% of the Israeli population but is home to 18.6% of (stated) Knesset members. Add the Tel Aviv District and those figures rise to 16.4% of Israeli population and 29.1% of Knesset members.[36] Jerusalem is also (slightly) over represented. Some 6% of Israelis citizens live in Jerusalem (including occupied annexed east and north Jerusalem); 1 in 9 or 11.6% of Knesset members live there.[37] The Knesset is, after all, in Jerusalem. With no constituency home base to take care of, one might have expected Jerusalem to be the home of many more Knesset members. Somewhat surprisingly even the majority of the MKs of United Torah Judaism give Jerusalem a miss, preferring instead to live in the Tel Aviv District (albeit the religious Haredi city of Bnei Brak). Shas, the ostensibly Haredi party of the Mizrahi has no (stated) MKs living in Jerusalem at all. Some 40% of the MKs of the Zionist Union live in Tel Aviv-Yafo, with just 10% favouring Jerusalem.[38]

The Israeli political elite clearly favour Tel Aviv over Jerusalem. If Israel cannot convince its parliamentarians to live in Jerusalem over Tel Aviv, then perhaps the protestations of the decision by international community to locate their embassies in Tel Aviv and not Jerusalem rings somewhat hollow. Despite its Tel Avivian image, just one of the five Meretz MKs live in Tel Aviv-Yafo.

So if Tel Aviv-Yafo, and to a lesser extent, Jerusalem, is over represented, which region is politically geographically short changed? The answer – the periphery, both north and south. Some 43.9% of the population of Israel lives in the north (Northern District), including Haifa or the south (Southern District), yet these peripheral regions are home to just 25.6% of the (stated) homes of MKs. Some 80% of Shas MKs live in the north or south.[39]

Kulanu MKs are geographically invisible. A full 90% of their MKs do not state their home town. The party that ran primarily on a platform to reduce house prices is ironically geographically homeless.

Electoral geography and Greater Jerusalem

In '*Electoral geography and Greater Jerusalem*', we first map out the ethno or religious identity of those neighbourhoods and communities in the greater Jerusalem area that are either eligible or not eligible to vote in the Israeli Knesset elections. In our '*Knesset geography and Greater Jerusalem*' map, we deliberately strip away or erase the geography of artificial administration – the Green Line and the municipal boundary of the city of Jerusalem – to reveal a stark and scattered patchwork of electoral discrimination.

All of the neighbourhoods, suburbs, satellite towns or exurban commuting communities of Greater Jerusalem are either overwhelmingly, often almost exclusively Palestinian or Jewish. Our map reveals a scattered patchwork of Palestinian communities (green), with concentrations in Ramallah to the north, east Jerusalem in the centre, and Bethlehem to the south, none of which are eligible to vote in the Knesset. All Jewish neighbourhoods, without exception, in Greater Jerusalem, irrespective of location, are eligible to vote in the Knesset. The solitary Palestinian community in greater Jerusalem permitted to vote in the Knesset (because they are citizens of Israel) is the town of Abu Gosh, located 12km west of downtown Jerusalem. Irrespective of their eligibility to vote in Knesset elections, all of these residential neighbourhoods are subject to either the application of Israeli civilian of military law since 1967.

In our second map, '*Knesset and Municipal Electoral Geography*', we further disaggregate the greater Jerusalem patchwork of voting rights. Overwhelmingly Jewish west Jerusalem and the finger dormitory suburbs extending northward, Pisgat Ze'ev and Neve Yaakov, are eligible to vote in both the country that governs them (Israel) in Knesset elections and in the municipal elections of the city of Jerusalem (yellow). The Palestinian communities (blue) and suburbs further to the north, south and east of downtown Jerusalem are not permitted to vote in either Knesset nor Jerusalem municipal elections. The almost exclusively Jewish neighbourhoods, including those scattered amongst these Palestinian communities, are all permitted to vote in Knesset elections (green). Palestinian east Jerusalem (red) is permitted to vote in Jerusalem municipal elections but excluded from voting in national Knesset elections. Finally, the Palestinian town of Abu Gosh (dark blue), west of downtown Jerusalem, is permitted to vote in Knesset elections but not Jerusalem municipal elections.

Voters

Note: the 2008 Israeli Census of Population tells us that the Palestinian town of Abu Gosh in Israel (pop. 5,800), located west of Jerusalem is 99.3% Muslim. The settlement of Beitar illit, located south-west of Jerusalem in the West Bank (pop. 32,900), is 100% Jewish, and west Jerusalem itself (pop. 244,300; Areas 8, 9, 10, 11, 12) is 97.2% Jewish. That 2.8% non-Jewish population of west Jerusalem is more likely to be made up of ex-soviet 'Jewish' immigrants not officially recognised as Jewish by Rabbinical Courts than it is by Palestinian citizens of Israel.

page 254 – Knesset Geography and Greater Jerusalem – Who votes where? Who can vote in the Knesset?

Yes, votes in Knesset (Jewish)

No, doesn't vote in Knesset (Palestinian)

Yes, votes in Knesset (Palestinian)

page 255 – Knesset and Municipal Electoral Geography – Who votes where? Who can vote in the Knesset and the local elections in Jerusalem?

Both Knesset and Jerusalem vote (Jewish overwhelmingly)

No vote (Palestinian)

Jerusalem vote only (Palestinian)

Knesset vote only (Jewish)

Knesset vote only (Palestinian)

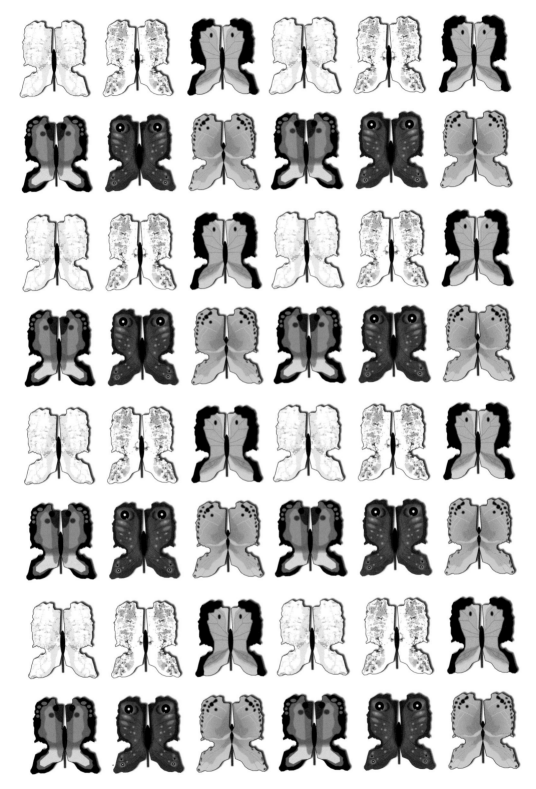

5.6 – Butterfly State

In '*Butterfly State*' we pin down six varieties of butterfly to be found locally in Israel-Palestine. The butterfly is a universal symbol of freedom, beauty and fragility, possessing a tragic elusiveness almost impossible to catch, yet doomed and trapped by in its temporal destiny. The apparent random curiosity of the flight of the butterfly is a journey that is both an escape into space and a prisoner of time.

Our butterfly images are both ugly and beautiful at the same time. In mixing the natural and the man-made we construct very different but equally real states of the Palestinian butterfly. '*Butterfly State*' seeks to create a visual appetite to look again, to look harder, to question our assumptions, to open our minds. Which are real or imagined, natural or man-made? What can we see? What do we choose to see and not see, and can temporal beauty reveal the tragedy of spatial stories and journeys we have chosen not to navigate?

Our capacity to see new geographies, other geographies, more specifically other people's geographies, is in part determined by our own capacity to escape our learned or received and accepted spatial narratives. What are we permitted to look at? When do we avert out gaze? When do we choose to look or not to look, and what do we choose to see when we occasionally choose to glimpse over the fence at the other side?

'*Butterfly State*' is not simply a game of fantasy geography. The increasing invisibility of the Green Line for many Israelis serves to erode or erase the geography of a future Palestinian state. Yet simultaneously, and somewhat paradoxically, the emergence of an increasing visible proto-Palestinian state serves to reinforce a belief that a Palestinian state exists somewhere, somewhere over there, not quite geographically knowable.

It is this vague sense of 'somewhere-ness', we argue, that assists in muffling or masking a comprehension of the reality of the contours of the geography of the Occupation. This proto-Palestinian state is a member of UNESCO and has its own parliament in Ramallah. It operates a separate vehicular license-plate system to Israel. Its quasi-citizens have their own Palestinian passports issued by the state of Israel – a make-belief delusion of freedom of flight or travel. It's as if the reality of more than a hundred disconnected archipelago islands that make up the Palestinian Authority has somehow emerged magically into a fantasy state, occupied, simultaneously illusory but nevertheless real. An unborn state of both mind and place.

And yet, an additional paradoxical and simultaneous process is also at work. This quasi-Palestinian state, with a titular Prime Minister, a national flag and a national parliament exacerbates what we call the 'separatist delusion'. The separatist delusion is the narrative that the Palestinians are equivalent to other oppressed national minorities who have campaigned for but have failed to secure an independent state. The equivalence is decep-

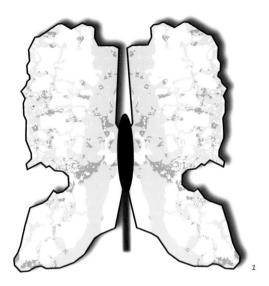

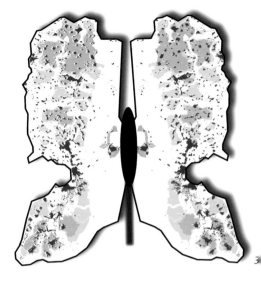

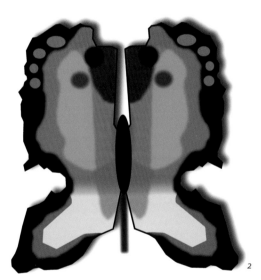

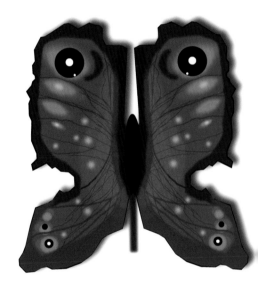

Butterfly State

1. *Speckled Settler*
   (Varia Colonus)
   distribution: throughout West Bank
   flight: all year round

2. *Blue Spotted Arab*
   (Colotis Phisadia)
   distribution: throughout Israel-Palestine
   flight: May to November2

3. *Oslo Spotted Arab*
   (Colotis Oslo)
   distribution: throughout West Bank
   flight: all year round

4. *Large Brown Wall*
   (Lasiommata megera)
   distribution: throughout Israel-Palestine
   flight: May to November

tively convincing.

Palestinians, like Basques and Kurds, are a self-identifying minority that have historically been oppressed by a dominant nationalism (Castilian Spain, Turkish-speaking Turkey, Zionist Israel). They seek an independent nation state (a Basque Homeland, a Kurdish state in eastern Turkey or northern Iraq, a Palestinian state in the West Bank and Gaza). They have, at times, resorted to political terrorism to achieve their goals (ETA, PKK, PLO/Hamas/PFLP).

This comparative equivalence ignores a simple but important difference. Palestinians, unlike the Kurds or Basques, cannot vote in the state they reside in. As a national minority, the Kurds and Basques may not have a state of their own, but they are not stateless; they are citizens of the state they live in, the state that controls their lives. This may appear blindly obvious, but it is a distinction that has become partially obscured in Israel. With the Occupation 50 years old, the increasing erasure of the Green Line, and an Israeli settlement population approaching 700,000 (20% of the population of the West Bank), Palestinian nationalism (a desire for a separate state) is in danger of being erroneously viewed through the prism of a 'separatist' movement, a region or a people that wishes to beak away from a (single) nation state.

A recent study found that 60% of young (18-29) Israelis believed that Israel had already annexed the West Bank.[1] It seems, that the 50 year duration of the Occupation is reinforcing not just its normalcy but ironically its invisibility. Whether an illusory unborn fantasy state or an emerging state born out of secession, 'Butterfly State' is reclaiming and mapping imagined and existing geography.

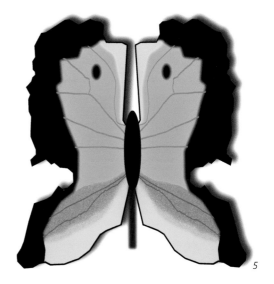

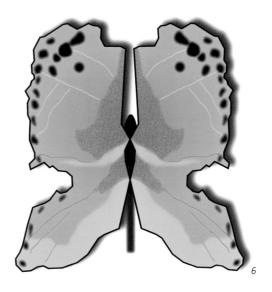

Butterfly State

5   *Large Salmon Arab*
    (Colotis Fausta)
    distribution: throughout Israel-Palestine
    flight: May to November

6   *Yellow or Small Spotted Arab*
    (Colotis Amata)
    distribution: throughout Israel-Palestine
    flight: May to November

Naming Geography

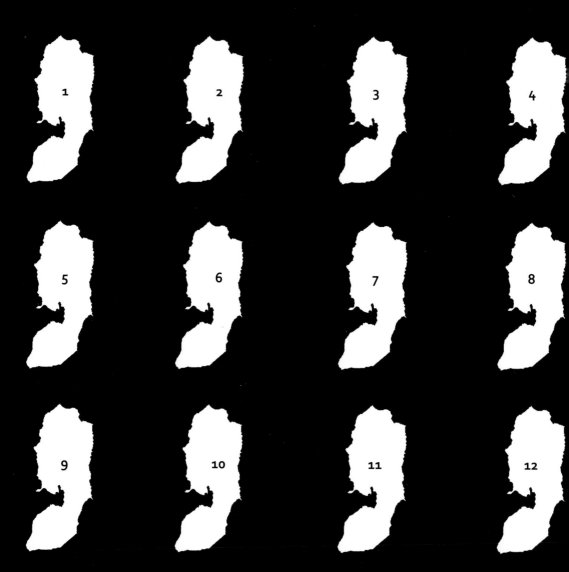

1. ad-Daffah al-Garbiyah, 2. Area A, B, C (Oslo Accords), 3. Disputed Territory, 4. Eretz Israel (Greater Israel), 5. Israel, 6. Judea and Samaria, 7. Palestinian Authority, 8. Palestinian Territory, Occupied, 9. Palestine, 10. State of Palestine, 11. Unborn State, 12. West Bank

Naming geography

It is a well-worn truism that the victors of war write its history. The victors of war, or, more specifically, the victors of contested space, also rewrite its geography.

In 'Naming Geography' we provide multiple-choice answers to identify the region generally known inside Israel as Judea and Samaria, and most commonly referred to outside of Israel as the West Bank or Israeli-occupied West Bank.

The name West Bank is a translation of the Arabic term ad-Daffah al-Garbiyah, given to the territory west of the Jordan River that fell under occupation and administration by Jordan in 1948. The term 'Palestinian Territory, Occupied' was used by the United Nations (UN) and other international organisations between 1998 and 2013 to refer to areas controlled by the Palestinian National Authority. UN secretariat communications replaced this in December 2012 with the term State of Palestine. The West Bank is also officially called Judea and Samaria in the Israeli census. Potential names, alphabetically ordered include:

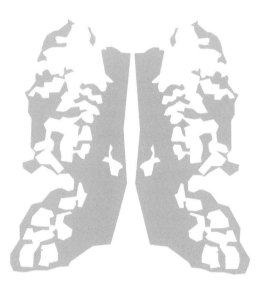

- ad-Daffah al-Garbiyah

- Area A, B, C (Oslo Accords)

- Disputed Territory

- Eretz Israel (Greater Israel)

- Israel

- Judea and Samaria

- Palestine

- Palestinian Authority

- Palestinian Territory, Occupied

- State of Palestine

- Unborn State

- West Bank

Butterfly State

Palestinian demonstration against the construction of the Israeli separation barrier, Bidu, 10km north-west of Jerusalem, West Bank

Haredi children, Beitar Illit, West Bank

5.7 – Settling for Less

There is an increasingly fashionable opinion amongst strands of both the Israeli left and right that the 'two-state solution' is now a thing of the past, that the window of opportunity has now closed. It has withered on the vine of ever-increasing settler population numbers. The so-called 'facts on the ground', Israeli man-made facts (the construction of thousands of settler homes) have all but choked any realistic possibility of creating a viable contiguous Palestinian state. Perhaps the evacuation of at least some settlements would be required. There are arguably multiple ways to identify without prejudice those Israeli settlements that are likely to find themselves on the 'wrong' side (from the settlers' perspective) of the border of any future Israeli-Palestinian two-state solution. Two are employed here.

The first is the construction of an evacuation predictor. We call this algorithm SELFIE (Settling for Less Formula for Israeli Evacuation). SELFIE is a mathematical formula for predicting the probability of which settlements will be evacuated or left behind across a new border and which are likely to be incorporated into an enlarged Israeli State. The second is the construction of evacuation maps. We call these maps 'Borderlands'. In 'Borderlands' we crunch a series of population settlement evacuation scenarios and then calculate how much territory Israel would need to retain for each settler evacuation scenario. If Israel were to retain an improbable 90% of the settlers and their homes, what would the redrawn map look like and how much of the West Bank would Israel need to annex. We repeat this exercise for 85%, 80%, 75%, 70% and 65% of the settler population.

Some facts. The Israeli settler population is conservatively estimated to be some 637,000, that's a 276,000 increase since the year 2000. That constitutes a 76% increase in just 15 years. In 1975 just 1 in 300 Israelis were settlers; today that figure is 1 in 13; some figures have it as high as 1 in 11.[1] Elsewhere in the book, we refer to the estimate of 700,000 settlers at the end of 2017.[2] In this chapter, a lower figure of 617,000 settlers, dating from 2015, is used because the 2015 estimate, unlike the 2017 estimate, provides a detailed breakdown of every settlement.[3] This detailed breakdown of population is essential to the analysis in this chapter.

It has long been accepted that larger settlements with a significant proportion of settlers living close to the Green Line, including most that are located west of the Israeli separation barrier, will be annexed as part of a land swap in a future peace treaty. Some 87,000 settlers, however, now live east of the Israeli separation barrier, almost double the 44,733 prior to its construction in the early 2000s.[4] Some 54,000 settlers also now live in settlements at a distance of 16km or greater from the Green Line. The further from the Green Line, the less likely annexation, the more likely the necessity of evacuation. The comparable number in 2000 was just 36,000.[5] The entire West Bank is just 58km at its widest point; it's just 30km wide at its Jerusalem pinch-point. Despite those daunting numbers, it could argued, the facts on the ground, relatively speaking, haven't deteriorated.

Now some different 'facts'. In the year 2000, 12.4% of all settlers lived east of the (future) separation barrier. Today, despite the quarter-million increase in settler population, that has risen to just 13.6%.[6] Of that quarter-million increase, 159,000 occurred just 2km or less from the Green Line. Just under half of all settlers today (48.9%), some 311,000 people, reside in dormitory communities less than 2km inside the West Bank. In 2000 42% of settlers lived less than 2km inside the West Bank.[7]

In 2000 just over a quarter (27.2%) of settlers lived in a narrow 1km to 2km band from the Green Line. Today almost a third do (32%). Of those 54,000 settlers who live in settlements at a distance of 16km or greater from the Green Line, a third of them live in the city of Ariel. Ariel, however, lies west of the Israeli separation barrier, and despite its location, and Palestinian protestations, is likely to be retained by Israel.[8] Today, as in the year 2000, just 1.6% of all settlers live as far away as 25km from the Green Line, deep inside the West Bank. They now however number 10,400. The Disengagement Plan carried out in Gaza in 2005 saw the Israeli state forcibly evacuate 8,000 settlers.[9]

If one excludes the settler population in the largely dormitory suburbs of annexed east Jerusalem, the figures are even more revealing. The proportion of settlers living just 2km or less from the Green Line has risen from 21% in 1999 to over 36% today. The proportion living 16km or more deep inside the West Bank has fallen from 21.1% to 14.7%.[10] This has occurred in part because of the massive increase in population of just two Religious Orthodox settlements, Modi'in Ilit and Beitar Illit, which lie less than a couple of kilometres east of the Green Line. The population of these settlements combined jumped from 25,600 in 1999 to 114,000 today. In fact, these two settlements alone account for 87,000 of the total 209,000 increase in settler population between 2000 and 2015 (excluding the settlement population in annexed east Jerusalem).[11] The geography and demography of the settler population would nevertheless require the evacuation of tens of thousands of settlers.

If all the settlements west of the barrier were annexed, and all those 5km or less from the Green Line but east of the barrier were also annexed, in addition to Kokhav Ya'akov, (the largest settlement east of barrier located 'just' 8.5km north of Green Line, but 2.5km north of annexed east Jerusalem), then some 73,000 settlers would still be required to evacuate.[12] If all settlers living east of the Israeli separation barrier (86,000) were to remain living where they currently reside, but find themselves living in a newly created Palestinian state on the West Bank, the population of that state would be approximately 3% Jewish. Today approximately 20% of the entire population of the West Bank, including annexed east Jerusalem, is Jewish.[13]

---

opposite – Our SELFIE formula

SELFIE: the evacuation formula

There are potentially many criteria informing SELFIE (Settling for Less Formula for Israeli Evacuation), a formula for predicting the probability of which settlements will get evacuated or left behind across a new border, and which are likely to be incorporated into an enlarged Israeli state. Our SELFIE formula includes just three criteria: distance from the Green Line, size (the population of the settlement), and wall location – whether the settlement is located east or west of the Israeli separation barrier. There are, of course, many more – local topography, geographical clustering, proximity to infrastructure, water resources, accessibility to motorway network, severance of Palestinian communities, and of course not least the power of settler political lobbying, including the political clout of individual settlements. We invite others to build upon our model.

The SELFIE output is the percentage chance or probability of a settlement being evacuated and therefore not being incorporated into Israel.[14] Note: the model equation applies for settlements east of the separation barrier. In order to obtain evacuation probabilities for settlements west of the separation barrier, the model simply scales down the evacuation probabilities for settlements east of the barrier by a fixed percentage. In our model this is 60%.

Probability of Evacuation

$$(1 - \frac{P}{P_m})^{(0.1 + 1.4(\frac{P}{P_m}))} \times (\frac{D}{D_m})^{(0.35 - 0.34(\frac{D}{D_m}))}$$

P_m = Maximum population of a settlement (65,000 in this model)

P = Population of a given settlement

D_m = Maximum distance of a settlement from the Separation Barrier (55km in this model)

D = Distance of a given settlement from the Separation Barrier (in kilometres)

Distance from an increasingly invisible Green Line is arguably the most important criteria. Political logic would suggest a settlement one or two kilometres from the Green Line significantly increases the chances of that settlement 'survival' and likely incorporation into the state of Israel. Those settlements 10km or 20km further east are most likely to be evacuated, unless either their inhabitants, the state of Israel and a future Palestinian state collectively decide that Jewish settlements can remain and are subsumed into and under the authority of the new Palestinian state. On the distance criteria and having regard to their small populations, the settlements of Ma'ale Efrayim and Elon Moreh, 38km and 28km respectively from the Green Line, are unlikely to be incorporated in the Israeli state. Our formula predicts a 95.6% chance of evacuation for Ma'ale Efrayim (pop. 1,200) and a 88.4% chance of evacuation for Elon Moreh (pop. 1,800).

Size matters. The scale of a settlement is not unimportant. Larger settlements, particularly those with populations in excess of 10,000 residents, are likely to punch above their relative geographic weight. The city of Ariel with a population of approximately 18,700 is particularly interesting in this regard. Excluding the settlements of greater annexed east and north Jerusalem, Ariel is the fourth largest settlement block or city in the West Bank. Ariel is also 17km east of the Green Line. Any future Israeli-Palestinian border that incorporates Ariel inside Israel will be geographically tortuous, requiring to snake deep inside the West Bank. Ariel is, however, located west of the Israeli separation barrier, which does in fact snake westwards. Our formula predicts a 37.9% chance of evacuation for Ariel. The largest settlement block, Modi'in Ilit, has a population of 64,000. The centre of Modi'in Ilit is also located just 1.5km over the Green Line. Not surprisingly our formula predicts just a 0.04% chance of evacuation of Modin Ilit, or, put another way, a 99.96% chance of retention by Israel.[15]

There are a large number of small to medium-sized settlements, with populations greater than 2,000 but less than 8,000, which are also located some distance from the Green Line, greater than 15km. Many of these are also the more ideological settlements. These include Ofra, Beit El, Shilo, Eli and Kiryat Arba. All are likely to be evacuated.[16] Ofra, with a population of 3,000 and 17.5km from Green Line, has, according to our model, a 75.2% probability of evacuation. For Shiloh (pop. 3,400), 28km east of Green Line, the evacuation probability is 87.9%.

A critically important criterion is whether an existing settlement presently finds itself on the wrong side of the Israeli separation barrier or wall – the de facto New Green Line. Having 'invested' hundreds of millions of dollars in constructing an unmissable and largely impregnable border running almost the entire length of the West Bank, logic would suggest it significantly reduces a settlement's chances of been annexed into Israel proper if that settlement finds itself east of the barrier. Complicating this criterion is the reality that a substantial part of the barrier is currently under construction; a significant, and more provocative, portion, whilst approved by the Knesset, awaits construction commencement. Other portions of the potential barrier remain as 'blueprints', awaiting planning or permit approval. The settlement of Efrat (pop. 9,200), 8km east of the Green Line, is located west of the separation barrier. SELFIE predicts Efrat has just a 32.1% likelihood of being evacuated (or a 67.9% of being retained). Beit El (pop. 6,000) is located 15km east of the Green Line but is east of the separation barrier and has a 70% probability of evacuation.

Perhaps these probabilities are not too surprising to those familiar with the geography of the settler enterprise as it reflects known geographies. The Israeli larger settlements are, with exception of Ariel, all located close to the Green Line, with many of the smaller, more ideological, isolated settlements located deep inside the territory of the West Bank. Perhaps somewhat controversially SELFIE predicts that the settlement of Ma'ale Adumim (pop. 37,000) on the outskirts of east Jerusalem, located 7km east of the Green Line, has just a 15% probability of evacuation if the settlement is considered west of the barrier and a 25% chance of evacuation if considered east of the barrier. Currently the separation does not fully encircle the settlement.

A fourth important criterion not included in our simple model is what we call 'relative clustering'. What we mean by this is the location of a settlement relative to a larger or group of settlements and, critically, whether a larger settlement lies east or west of it. A medium-sized settlement of a few thousand residents that lies east of a much larger settlement may not be incorporated into Israel. A tiny settlement, however, of just a few hundred people, if it lies west of much larger settlement likely to be incorporated into Israel, has a significantly increased chance of not being evacuated.

Probably the fifth most important criterion is political clout. Political clout is a largely unmeasurable geographic metric. It may be informed by a host of other local geographies, including those discussed above. These other local geographies could include the height of the settlement (most are built on local hills), the impact on the potential severance of a Palestinian state, and proximity to aquifers (water resources). Whether or not a member of parliament (Knesset) or a minister in government lives in a particular settlement may also be a factor.

Our SELFIE formula is capable of being infinitely mathematically calibrated to take into account a myriad of local geographies. We have modelled just three. We have suggested a few more. SELFIE is a simple algorithm that could in theory be manipulated to accommodate 100,000 or more additional pieces of geographic, political, environmental and demographic data to predict the political future. SELFIE could of course also be used to determine that political future. It could assist in make judicious investments. Any decision to expand a settlement to facilitate so-called 'natural growth' could for example be restricted to only those settlements that have an 85% or 90% chance of being retained by Israel in the event of the creation of a Palestinian state.

SELFIE could also be used to objectively evaluate political actions suspected of deliberately thwarting a two-state solution. A recent Israeli government decision to create a new settlement near Shiloh is a case in point. According to SELFIE, the settlement of Shiloh, located some 28km from the Green Line, has just a 12.2% chance of being retained by Israel if the two-state solution is to be implemented. It is not unreasonable to conclude that any further settlement expansion there is deliberately designed to undermine the two-state solution.

———

Haredi settlement of Beitar Illit (pop. 49,000), West Bank, the second largest settlement city

Borderlands

It is commonly accepted that if a two-state solution is to come into being, Israel will retain sovereignty over major settlement blocs that hug the Green Line. This will necessitate a re-drawn border and potentially 1:1 land swaps with the future Palestinian state. The proportion of the West Bank that Israel would, could or should retain in such a final agreement peace deal is of course a hotly contested subject.

It has been widely reported that during the Camp David peace negotiations between Israel (Ehud Barak) and the Palestinians (Yasser Arafat), Israel sought to retain 9% of the West Bank (plus a 12-year presence on a further 25% of the West Bank in the Jordan Valley). The Palestinians were willing to allow Israel annex 2.5%.[17] The figures apparently moved somewhat during the TABA negotiations a year later, with Israeli demanding 6% of the West Bank (plus an additional 2% on a long term lease), with the Palestinians ceding between 3% and 4.5%.[18] A decade or so later (2008), Israel, under Ehud Olmert, was reported to have 'offered' 94% of the West Bank, seeking to retain just 6%; the Palestinians (Mahmoud Abbas) apparently insisting on ceding just 2%.[19]

Few of the maps generated during these negotiations were made public. The exception was the 'non-government'-sponsored Geneva accords in 2003, whose map was ac-

------

How much of the West Bank would Israel need to retain if the following percentages of settlers remained in situ and Israel annexed the settlements into Israel proper?
(top – % West Bank land; bottom – % settler population)

tually posted to every single home in Israel.[20] The media, then and now, has tended to focus on these 'raw statistics'. In a largely territorial conflict, discussion around where the actual line on the map may go has almost become secondary. It has largely descended into a numbers game. The conflict has, at times, become peculiarly aspatial. Getting the respective parties to actually put a line on a map may have been difficult. Today, perhaps for obvious reasons, the Israeli centre-left peace camp refuses to put pen to paper and draw the potential new borders of an Israeli and Palestinian state. It would, the argument goes, pre-empt discussions, be unnecessarily divisive, and ultimately presumptuous. Perhaps.

Free of such constraints we draw the potential map(s). In 'Borderlands' we work in reverse. We first crunch a series of population settlement evacuation scenarios and then calculate the 'optimum' land bank withdrawal as a residual. If Israel were to retain an improbable 90% of the settlers and their homes, what would the redrawn map look like? If Israel were to retain just 65% of settlers, what would the redrawn map look like, and so on?

We have drawn six different scenario maps of redrawn borders that allow Israel to retain 90%, 85%, 80%, 75%, 70% and 65% respectively of the settler population. We then calculate the proportion of the West Bank that Israel would retain under each scenario or peace agreement option. In theory there are an infinite number of permutations and combinations facing such choices. In our calculations, our objectives are to maximise (settler) population, minimize annexation of (West Bank) territory, have regard to current location of barrier and minimise the severance to major Palestinian communities. Our population numbers for each settlement are from 2015.[21]

THE 90% SOLUTION

To retain 90% of all settlers, all settlements with a population over 3,000 (with the exception of Kiryat Arba (7,100), Talmon (3,700), Tekoa (3,500) and Ofra (3,200) are incorporated into Israel. No settlement with a population of 1,500 or greater and located less than 8km from the Green Line is evacuated. To retain 90% of all settlers would result in Israel annexing

5.0%

(80%)

6.4%

(85%)

7.7%

(90%)

7.7% of the West Bank. The map shows a number of unavoidable tortuous-shaped fingers extending deep into the West Bank. These would inevitably and severely compromise ease of movement between Palestinian population centres in a future Palestinian state.

THE 85% SOLUTION

At 85%, the settlements of Beit El (6,000), Shiloh (3,400), Eli (4,100), Dolev (1,300) and Halamish (1,300) are evacuated. All are located at least 9km from the Green Line. All currently contribute to the severance of Palestinian movement. The largest settlement to be evacuated is Kochav Yaakov (7,300). Kochav Yaakov and nearby Psagot (2,000) are both located north of annexed east Jerusalem. Also evacuated is Geva Binyamin (5,200). All settlements currently west of the Israeli separation barrier are retained, including three currently located east of it (Avnei Hefetz, Nili, Shavei Shomron). To retain 85% of all settlers would result in Israel annexing 6.4% of the West Bank.

THE 80% SOLUTION

At 80% the settlement fingers extending east of Alfe Menashe are all evacuated. These are all more than 9km east of the Green Line, but currently located west of the tortuously shaped route of the Israeli separation barrier. The largest are Karnei Shomron (6,900) and Kedumin (4,300) and Immanuel (3,250). The settlements of Nili (1,400), Migdal Oz (400), Kedar (1,500), Avnei Hefetz (1,700), Peduel (1,600), Alei Zahav (1,200) and Bet Arye (4,700) are also evacuated. To retain 80% of all settlers would result in Israel annexing 5% of the West Bank.

THE 75% SOLUTION

At 75%, the largest settlement to date in our incremental evacuation to be evacuated is the city of Ariel (18,700). Barkan (1,700), Revava (2,000), Kiryat Netafim (900) all west of Ariel, are also evacuated. Ariel is located 16km east of the Green Line and the largest settlement located that deep inside the West Bank. Alon Svut (3, 200), in the Gush Eminin bloc, is evacuated. The small and 'isolated' settlements of Salit (700), Hinanit (1,100) and Zufin (2,000), despite their proximity (all 3km) to the Green Line are also evacuated. The settlement of Mevon (2,500), located just 0.5km from the Green Line, is likely to be retained by Israel in any withdrawal agreement. We have chosen to evacuate it here because doing so would allow the future Palestinian state to retain the large area of the Latrun. This is not likely, however, as the main highway between Tel Aviv and Jerusalem (Route 1) actually cuts across the West Bank here. To retain 75% of all settlers would result in Israel annexing 2.9% of the West Bank.

THE 70% SOLUTION

At 70% the largest settlement in the Gush Etzion bloc is evacuated Efrat (8,300), along with Bat Ayin (1,000), Neve Daniel (2,300) Kfat Etzion (1,100) and Elazar (2,600), Elkana (3,900)

Sha'arei Tikva (5,600), Etz Efraim (1,800), all less than 6km from Green Line are also evacuated. To retain 70% of all settlers would result in Israel annexing 2.1% of the West Bank.

THE 65% SOLUTION

Finally, retaining just 65% of settlers would necessitate the evacuation of Ma'ale Adumim (37,500), the largest settlement to be evacuated. This would allow the retention of two thirds of all settlers whilst annexing just 1.9% of the West Bank. The 65% solution would include the retention of all the settlements in currently annexed east Jerusalem (excluding Atarot Airport). It would also include retaining the two largest Haredi settlements close to the Green Line, Modi'in Ilit (64,00) and Beitar Illit (49,000).

The two so-called 'quality of life' settlements of Oranit (8,500) and Alfe Menashe (7,600) would also be annexed by Israel. Both Oranit and Alfe Menashe, located just 0.5km and 3km east of the Green Line, effectively function as dormitory suburbs of Greater Tel Aviv.[22] Whilst the Likud Party topped the poll in both settlements in 2015 Knesset elections, both settlements divided their vote between the centre-left (Zionist Union, Meretz, Yesh Atid) and the religious right (Likud, Habayit Hayehudi, Israeli Beitanu, Shas, United Totah Judaism) – Oranit 46% to 44% and Alfe Menashe 43% to 44%.[23] Alfe Menashe and Oranit are also the two wealthiest communities in all of Israel proper (and the West Bank), where a plurality of voters voted for the Likud Party.[24]

So how do our 90% to 65% settler annexation scenarios compare to the apparent number-crunching of Camp David or later negotiations? Ehud Olmerts's 6% offer is closest today to our 85% settler annexation map. The Palestinians offer of 2.5% under Camp David would today be midway between our 75% and 70% settler annexation map. Of course, the absolute numbers of settlers and their spatial distribution was somewhat different in 2000 and 2007. With a potential incorporation of 90% of all settlers for 7.7% of the West Bank, the numbers perhaps give lie to the apparent fatalism of many of the doomsday merchants of the two-state solution. That 7.7% however includes tortuously shaped 'annexation fingers' that would result in acute severance of Palestinians towns and cities.

In 'Border Lands' we simply endeavour to bring the mapping debate to a wider audience, an exercise recommended for every High School Israeli geography student and, indeed, every Israeli political party.

––––

6 – The State of Tel Aviv

The Social Protest Movement – 300,000 march in Tel Aviv on 4th September 2011
The origins of the protest began with the pitching of a single tent on Rothschild Avenue in protest at soaring rents and house prices. House prices in Israel rose 35% in the five years before the protest. House prices have risen 35% in Israel in the five years since the protest (2011-2016). House prices have risen 150% in Tel Aviv since 2001.

6.1 – Bursting the Tel Aviv 'Bubble'

The perceived radical and leftist politics of the city of Tel Aviv, relative to the rest of the state of Israel, is a significant narrative in perpetuating the myth of the Tel Aviv 'Bubble'. The Tel Aviv Bubble is both an Israeli pejorative and a readily embraced local moniker for a certain Tel Avivian. This is the supposedly laid-back, introverted Mediterranean city of Tel Aviv, detached from and delusional to the realities of the local Israeli-Palestinian conflict and the wider geography political challenges of living in the Middle East.[1]

But just how left-leaning is the city of Tel Aviv? Defining what is left, progressive, or which party is leftist, centrist or rightist is a fraught task in a political analysis of any party electoral system. The Israeli theatre of politics is arguably more complex than many others. Issues of national security and (Jewish) ethnic origin do not simply cut across traditional left-right welfare-tax or social issues, they are, arguably, the primary factors in determining who votes for whom.

Tel Aviv is certainly the political spiritual home of Meretz. Meretz, depending on one's political perspective, is a progressive, liberal, gay-friendly, leftist, social democratic party committed to universal human rights and a two-state solution.[2] For others it is a privileged bastion of the Ashkenazi elite, whose origins lie in the subsidised *kibbutzim*, naïve to Middle Eastern realities, and whose members tend to snobbishly look down on the Israeli masses. Perhaps neither description or caricature is particularly inaccurate or unfair. The party has been labelled as a 'secular-leftist party' and 'proudly left-wing' in the international media.[3] Meretz received just 4% of the vote, and five seats nationwide in the 2015 Knesset election. In Tel Aviv-Yafo, Meretz (translates as 'energy') received 13.1%. The party received in excess of 25% of the vote in a contiguous small cluster of adjoining neighbourhoods in downtown Tel Aviv centred around Rothschild Avenue – home to some 44,000 people – its biggest concentration of the vote in the entire country.[4]

The Israeli Labor Party stood on a joint centrist/centre-left platform with Hatnua and the Israeli Green Movement under the umbrella of Zionist Union (in Hebrew, HaMahaneh HaTziyoni, 'Zionist camp'). The party received 34.3% of the vote in Tel Aviv and 18.7% nationwide. Combining the Labor and Meretz vote, the two centre-left and left-wing parties received 47.4% in Tel Aviv-Yafo but just 22.6% across the whole of Israel.

The nationalist right-wing Likud Party received 18.2% of the vote in Tel Aviv compared to 23.4% nationwide. Combined with the hard right-wing Habayit Hayehudi and Israeli Beitanu, the Likud Party and its right-wing sister parties got 35.2% of the vote nationally. In Tel Aviv-Yafo these three parties received 23.2%.[5] Simply number crunching, with the centre-left polling 24.2 percentage points more than the right in Tel Aviv, but 12.6% less than the right in Israel as a whole, then without a doubt Tel Aviv is certainly more left-wing.

A more accurate description of Tel Aviv isn't one of a leftist Tel Aviv versus the rest of Israel, but something altogether more subtle. It's a wealthy, disproportionately Ashkenazi north Tel Aviv that's anchored to the suburbs further north, and a southern poorer Tel Aviv that politically and socially blends almost seamlessly with adjoining suburbs further south.[6]

In the wealthy suburbs of north Tel Aviv and in the adjoining wealthy municipality of Ramat HaSharon, the Labor Party (Zionist Union) averaged 45% of the vote.[7] In the largely poorer south-west and south-east of the city, in neighbourhoods stretching from Yafo (Jaffa) in the south-west to Yad Eliyahu in the south-east, the party didn't manage to top 25%.[8] Labour fared equally poorly in the southern adjoining municipalities of Bat Yam and Holon, getting just 15.2 and 20% respectively.

In those same northern wealthy neighbourhoods where Labor dominated, Likud polled on average 12% to 18% of the vote. In the southern, largely poorer neighbourhoods Likud generally polled (outside of Palestinian Jaffa) in the mid to high 30s. In the adjoining southern municipalities of Bat Yam and Holon, Likud fared equally well with 33.3% and 31% of the vote respectively. It would appear that the relatively wealthy or economically secure in Israel vote 'left' and the poor vote 'right'. The Labor Party, in fact, did not receive a plurality of the vote in a single city, town or village in one of the top 100 poorest or socio-economically vulnerable Israeli local authority communities. The party topped the poll in 45 of the top 50 privileged towns and cities.[9]

Shas, the Religious Ultra-Orthodox party of Mizrahi (Jews of North African and Middle Eastern descent) transcends easy left/right definitions. The party is ultra-conservative on social issues, but 'welfarist' and populist on economic matters. On matters of national security, Palestinian self-determination and the two-state solution, the party has zigzagged from left to right over recent years. Shas received a fifth of the vote in many impoverished southern neighbourhoods in Tel Aviv.[10]

Labor is not just the largest party in Tel Aviv, but also the largest party in the adjoining northern suburban municipalities of Kfar Saba, Hod HaSharon, Ra'anana and Herzliya, where it secured in excess of 33% of the vote in all four cities. Arguably, Tel Aviv-Yafo is a tale of three cities. The largely Palestinian Joint List, a coalition of diverse leftist and Palestinian nationalist parties, topped the poll in Adjami and Yafo (Jaffa), securing a plurality in six adjoining neighbourhoods, topping 50% in three of them. The party received just 3% of the vote across all of Tel Aviv-Yafo.

If Tel Aviv swings left relative to the rest of Israel, then the Israeli capital Jerusalem firmly swings politically rightward. In Jerusalem the Religious Ultra-Orthodox parties, United Torah Judaism, Shas and other minor Haredi parties received 40% of the vote. These same parties received 13.7% across Israel. The six largest religious and right-wing parties were just shy of half the vote (48.9%) across the entire country, but topped 75% in Jerusalem.[11]

Of course, depending on where one draws the borders of Tel Aviv, the power or relative strength of the various voting blocs inevitably rise and fall. Greater Tel Aviv is home to 40% of Israelis. Perhaps not unexpectedly – as home to 2 out of 5 voters – Greater Tel Aviv is fairly representative of Israel as a whole.[12] Neither the city of Tel Aviv nor Jerusalem are typical of Israel. That honour falls to the city of Haifa, Israel's third largest city. Haifa is a traditional Labor city, with a significant Jewish orthodox or Haredi minority. Palestinians make up approximately 1 in 10 voters. Whilst the Palestinian population of Jerusalem is closer to the overall national average, Palestinian east Jerusalemites are not permitted to vote in Knesset elections. The Likud vote in Haifa almost matches its exact share of national vote.[13] Whilst Labor is the largest party in Haifa (25.3%), beating Likud (21.2%) into second spot, Labour and the leftist Meretz jointly polled 30.4% compared to 34.4% for Habayit Hayehudi Yisrael Beiteinu and the Likud Party combined.[14]

There is, of course, more to the politics of the Tel Aviv Bubble then simply trawling through the local Tel Avivian electoral geography of Knesset voting patterns. Some 300,000 people took to the streets in Tel Aviv in September 2011 – Israel's largest ever demonstration – to protest against the cost of living. Demonstrations against the Occupation, if not infrequent, have nevertheless, in recent years, been a tiny fraction of that. In recent years the municipal authority itself has become increasingly politically assertive. The Tel Aviv municipal authority has openly challenged the government on everything from the prosaic rules governing the opening hours of trading on Shabbat, to broader and national issues of pluralism, press freedom and a two-state solution. The city's elected mayor of 18 years is a frequent vocal and public critic of the nation's Prime Minister of 11 years. Just hours after a Palestinian terror attack in Tel Aviv in June 2016 which left four dead, its four-times elected mayor, Ron Huldai, openly (and provocatively for many Israelis) directly attributed the attack to the Israeli occupation of the West Bank.[15]

Yet this is also a city that many Israelis feel is dismissive, indifferent and occasionally hostile to the rest of Israel. Residents of Tel Aviv are mocked for failing to disguise what many Israelis suspect is their true political priority – a desire not to withdraw from the Palestinians in the West Bank, but to disengage from Israelis living outside Tel Aviv. This desire to disengage from the rest of Israel is central to the narrative of the Tel Aviv Bubble. This narrative says that Tel Aviv is both wilfully and naïvely disconnected from the social and political 'realties' of Israeli life outside Tel Aviv. By implication, Tel Aviv somehow isn't real Israel. Real Israel lies elsewhere.

This dominant and traditional prism of analysis of the narrative of the Tel Aviv Bubble is framed around the supposedly divergent political values or lifestyle of downtown Tel Avivians versus the rest of Israelis. It peddles the myth that this city and its inhabitants live inside a self-created illusion, a mirage of a fantasy of otherness. This is a city that is pejoratively seen as delighting in itself as a Mediterranean beach-city one flight away from Berlin, New York or London. This is a city that looks west not east, a city that provocatively and proudly turns its back on the politics of Jerusalem 40 minutes up the road. It is a bubble that is disconnected, indulgent, indolent even. Tel Avivians, the pejorative cliché goes, sit around in cafés all day long, they hang out on the beach, they party and generally indulge themselves. They tend to favour renting over owning homes. They are wasteful of money. They live for the moment. Yet this indulgent Tel Aviv is also the powerhouse of the Israeli economy. Disposable income per household is 35% higher in Tel Aviv-Yafo than the rest of Israel.[16] The city of Tel Aviv-Yafo, with just 5.2% of the population, accounts for 16.7% of GDP and 28% of hi-tech firms.[17] Tel Aviv-Yafo ($6,890m) dwarfs Jerusalem ($396m) 17 times over in raising seed-funding capital for hi-tech start-ups, with the Tel Avivian city-suburb of Herzylia ($806m) rasing twice that of the capital.[18] Greater Tel Aviv accounts for half the economy of Israel.

We would argue that the Tel Aviv Bubble is primarily a story of misunderstood urbanism, and that the Bubble narrative is fed unwittingly by a confusion about the hierarchy of place in metropolitan Tel Aviv. Tel Aviv is generally and erroneously viewed as just another, albeit larger, more central and wealthier city. It is viewed (by many non-Tel Avivians) as the first city of many in the metropolitan region. There are no fewer than nine 'cities' in addition to the city of Tel Aviv located inside the Tel Aviv District. These range in population from Holon (188,000) to Or Yehuda (36,000).[19] There are in fact a further 19 cities in the Central District of Israel – in effect, Greater Tel Aviv. In Israel a 'city council' is the official designation of a city under local government administration. The Interior Ministry grants city status to an urban area if that urban area has a population of just 20,000 – a relatively low urban bar to obtain city status. This all contributes to a delusional, polycentric city narrative.

This 20,000 city threshold contributes to a misunderstanding of the geography of metropolitan urbanism and suburbanism. Whilst the 'cities' of Petah Tikva, Holon, Ramat Gan, Bnei Brak, Rehovot all exceed 100,000 people, none of the centres of these 'cities' can boast of a vibrant, diverse or large-scale city-like urban centre. They effectively operate as fringe suburban communities, a significant proportion of whose residents commute to Tel Aviv to work. Their commercial downtowns are largely made up of relatively small strip malls. Culturally they are fringe players in metropolitan Tel Aviv. Holon, perhaps in recognition of this, has cleverly sought to punch above its suburban weight with the Ron Arad Design Museum of Holon. The 'city' centre however fails to match this cultural ambition. Ramat Gan is home to the Israeli stock market and the Israeli Diamond Exchange and can boast of an impressive cluster of skyscrapers, but the immediate street area below is a sea of traffic, devoid of attractive urban street life.

As 'cities' that function as suburban but administratively autonomous municipalities, they can all be best described as 'suburbalities'. A suburbality is essentially a suburb with an autonomous local government structure. Many of this suburbalities exhibit very high rates of out-commuting. Holon, in fact, has one of the highest, with some 60% of its residents leaving Holon 'city' to work.[20] Put bluntly, many of the more peripheral municipalities or suburbalities surrounding Tel Aviv suffer a delusion of 'city-ness' when in reality they are simply suburbs of varying size and complexity in a single large city, a greater Tel Aviv.

The downtown or city centre neighbourhoods of many, perhaps most, 'western cities', particularly in the last 20 or 30 years, tend to be wealthier, more liberal, younger, generally more creative, dynamic, vibrant and diverse places in the greater geography of those same cities. All those packed bars, restaurants and coffee shops are also full of the very suburban residents of Greater Tel Aviv who flock to its centre when they can or when they can afford to. It's simply how cities function.

And as for that argument that Tel Avivians spend too much time lounging on the beach, it is worth restating that Tel Aviv is, after all, a city on the beach, its own beach. This city of 52km² has 14km of coast, the vast majority of it sandy beaches. Of the larger 'cities' or metropolitan suburban municipalities that fringe Tel Aviv-Yafo – Holon, Petah Tikva, Ramat HaSharon, Rehovot, Bnei Brak, Givatayim, Ramat Sharon, Or Yehuda, Kiryat Ono, Ra'anana, Hod HaSharon and Gvat Shmuel – none have a coastline. If Tel Avivians go often to the beach, perhaps it is simply because they can.

––––––

Habima Square, Tel Aviv

Aylalon motorway, Tel Aviv

6.2 – The world's first Jewish Global City?

In the 1970s and early 1980s Tel Aviv could best be understood as the dominant if not particularly dynamic city in a polycentric cluster of somewhat disconnected small and peripheral cities (mostly towns) scattered across the wider (Gush Dan) region. The city's population had peaked at 390,000 in the 1960s, representing 16% of the country's total. A long period of steady decline followed. By the late 1980s the city's population, aging considerably, had fallen to 317,000, just 7% of a rapidly rising Israeli population.[1]

Founded as recently as 1909 as a suburban extension of the city of Jaffa, Tel Aviv witnessed a flourishing of architectural creativity in the 1920s and 1930s.[2] Tel Aviv is famed, occasionally fêted, as the world's only UNESCO-designated Bauhaus or International Style city. Notwithstanding the disputed importance of the role of prominent Bauhaus architect's contribution to that creativity, there is no doubting the importance of that architectural legacy today.[3] Equally, despite the view that this Tel Avivian modernist experiment amounted to nothing more than a grand speculative house building boom contained in a colonial town-planning framework, the fact remains that the sheer number and quality of 'Modernist' Bauhaus houses built is undisputed. Myth-making or Zionist narratives aside, the value of that urban legacy in serving a livable Tel Aviv urbanism today is incontrovertible.

By the late 1970s, however, the magnificence of this built architectural heritage had become increasingly eroded. Urban hollowing and suburbanisation, the arrival of the now ubiquitous air conditioner (many balcony spaces were enclosed, unsightly air condition boxes attached to façades), an ageing city-centre population and a high ratio of rent controlled apartments all combined to undermine Bauhaus consciousness and investment in renovating the built physical fabric. Many if not most buildings were in poor condition.[4]

Tel Aviv slowly emerged from this low-density urban patchwork as a 'proto-global city' in the making by the mid-1990s.[5] The rise of Tel Aviv is really the story of the ascent or emergence of downtown or inner urban Tel Aviv. Downtown Tel Aviv became an increasingly desirable place to live. Home prices in the city have soared 152% in 15 years.[6] The so-called 'new economy', changing tastes and recreational lifestyles rapidly increased wealth and the increasing power of proximity all combined to drive forward urban regeneration.

The international 'rise of the city' as a cultural and economic global phenomenon has been well documented since the early 1990s.[7] The forces shaping Tel Aviv during this period in many ways paralleled the emergence of cities, specifically city downtowns, as the new economic and cultural powerhouses across the western world. Assisted by a forward-thinking and ambitious mayor, Ron Huldai, Tel Aviv has consolidated its place as the undisputed and unrivalled first city of Israel.[8]

Tel Aviv may be Israel's most economically powerful city, but can it lay any claim to the status of global or world city in the making? The term 'global city' has been used, per-haps overused, and much abused in the literature and discourse on cities for some 30 years. The term refers to a city that can lay claim to having not-insignificant influence in the global economic system. It may and often can include a verifiable outsized role in one or more par-ticular, economic, social, legal or cultural networks.[9]

The criteria with which to judge the emergence of the rise of a global city are as multiple as they are diverse. The five critical factors, each with a host of subset criteria that informs the ranking of a global city according to AT Kearney, include business activity, human capital, information exchange, cultural experience, and political engagement.[10]

Tel Aviv has consistently appeared in the top 50 Global City rankings in recent years. In the AT Kearney listing, the city was ranked in the top 50 in 2008, 2010, 2012, before slipping to 62 in 2016. By 2012 Tel Aviv was ranked as a 'Beta+' city alongside 23 other cities, including Berlin, Hamburg, Rome, Copenhagen, Bangalore and Cape Town. 'Beta+' in sport-ing analogy is, in effect, division 5, with at least 44 other cities ranked higher. Only New York and London occupy a place in division 1, Alpha++. Dubai in 2012 was the only Middle East city ranked higher than Tel Aviv.[11] In 2016 the city was ranked 48 in terms of 'outlook' of 'fu-ture potential', ahead of São Paulo, Shanghai, Mexico City, Doha, Hong Kong, Kuala Lumpur and Buenos Aries.[12] In 2017 Tel Aviv jumped back up five places in the Global City rankings to be ranked 57.

As recently as 2000, Tel Aviv was ranked a lowly 'Gamma' city, along with 18 oth-ers (in effect, division 9) with at least 83 other cities ranked higher. The Middle East cities of Beirut, Cairo and Dubai were then all ranked higher, with the Saudi coastal city of Jeddah then seen as being on a par with Tel Aviv. The city was, however, recognised as an early leader in the high-tech revolution. The city region was identified as having a real chance of becoming 'Europe's' Silicon Valley.[13] Despite more mixed fortunes on the NASDAQ in re-cent years, Israel was identified as having more firms in the NASDAQ index in the early 2000s than all EU countries put together.[14] By 2015 Tel Aviv was ranked as the 25th most important financial centre in the world, ahead of such cities as Paris, São Paulo, Beijing Abu Dhabi and Amsterdam.[15]

The exact year when Tel Aviv emerged or exhibited evidence of a proto-global city in the making is disputable, if not impossible to identify. There is of course no single event, be it economic, political or physical, that can be identified as having played a critical or outsized role in the rise of Tel Aviv as an emerging global player. Many global sleepy city backwaters of different scales, for a host of diverse reasons, have witnessed urban trans-formations in the 1990s – Shanghai, Dubai, Shenzhen. A very unique local, once-off factor contributing to Tel Aviv's integration into the global economy was the massive Soviet im-migration in the early 1990s when a million immigrants arrived in Israel. Many were highly skilled in engineering and science, and provided a deep pool of talent, just as the high-tech era took off globally. The fortuitous timing of the collapse of communism and the emer-gence of the high-tech industry combined with Zionist immigration policy was a boon to Tel Aviv. The city has also seen a huge increase in wealth in the past two decades and more. Israeli GDP soared in the 1990s, with GDP per capita rising from $5,700 (31% of that of USA

The 'world's first Bauhaus tower', the Frishman Tower (2012), Tel Aviv (architects: Yossi Sivan, Rachel Feller)

GDP per capita) in 1985 to $23,000 (55% of USA) by the year 2000. Today GDP is above $36,000 per capita (67% of USA).[16]

Perhaps one of the first visible evidence of this evolutionary 'tipping point' or mutation in Tel Aviv's urban-suburban geography is the city's dramatically transformed skyline. It is difficult and perhaps a futile exercise to disaggregate those factors that drive a hitherto very low-rise city upward. Property speculation, planning policy, changing cultural tastes and perceptions of status all invariably play a role. The city of Tel Aviv was a low-rise city for the first 60 years of its existence, with the first 'tall building' – the 34-storey Shalom Meir tower – completed in 1965. Little happened after that for thirty years. Things began to change significantly by the mid-1990s. Today Tel Aviv has dozens of tall buildings, towers or skyscrapers above 100m. The city currently has 14 towers built or nearing completion above 150m, with at least a further six in advanced stages of proposal and/or approval, with many more under serious design consideration.[17]

The rise in the concentration of specialised and high-paid employment in Tel Aviv relative to its satellite city-suburbs, including an ever-increasing centre-periphery relationship, as evidenced by an expanding radial spatial commuting functional relationship confirms the rise in local pulling power, status and wealth of Tel Aviv compared to its peripheral suburban 'cities'. They do not in themselves confirm the emergence of a proto-global city. Tel Aviv, however, by the 1990s was the dominant player in Israel's economy.[18]

Arguably another seminal moment for the city was the UNESCO declaration in 2003 of Tel Aviv as a World Heritage Site.[19] The awarding of the UN designation was the culmination of a decade or more of ambitious self-promotion.[20]

Whilst generally hailed as a huge success – particularly from conservation, urban regeneration and city branding perspectives – the 'rediscovery' of the White City of Bauhaus Tel Aviv in the 1980s has not been without local critics,[21] who argue that this rediscovery is essentially a story of the Ashkenazi white tribe elite seeking redemption in a return to some nostalgic and noble form of Zionism.[22] This narrative risks overlooking the importance of the international 'rise of the city' in late 1980s and 1990s. There is no doubt that Tel Aviv's World Heritage status is as much about 21st-century marketing and contemporary urban regeneration as it is architectural conservation and 20th-century Bauhaus architecture. Today Tel Aviv's liveable urbanism however owes as much, perhaps a lot more, to the last two decades of municipal ambition as it does to 1930s architectural and planning vision.

Property prices, in particular for much-sought-after renovated and rebranded 'International Style' apartments, have soared since designation in 2003.[23] Whilst it is difficult to attribute the housing price boom primarily to the UNESCO designation (The Israeli economy has had robust growth over the past decade), what is not in doubt is that the city core has increasingly become the preserve of the well-off. 'Owning a little piece of Bauhaus Tel Aviv' is a typical marketing tool of the local real estate market. Living in the heart of the (white) city has become the default choice of the local wealthy elite.

Bauhaus marketing has been co-opted by the builders of tall buildings. A recently completed 28-storey tower designed by local architects Moore Yaski Sivan has been dubbed 'The World's First Bauhaus Tower' on account of its self-conscious curved corners, inspired, say the architects, by the tradition of local Bauhaus – some 24 storeys below.[24] 'The World's First Bauhaus Tower' may be marketing hubris par excellence, but it captures the growing sense of the showy confidence imbuing the city. The creation of a 'Tel Aviv – a Global City' department in the municipality of Tel Aviv somewhat superficially captures this emerging Tel Aviv zeitgeist. Its online Tel Aviv global city link ambitiously seeks to position Tel Aviv as a 'leading city brand worldwide' through a 'quantum leap in the global arena' transforming it from the 'center of the "Startup Nation" to a world-leading innovation hub'.[25] The fact that a city identifies itself as a global city is of course an altogether unconvincing argument for making the case for whether that city has achieved global city status.

Arguably this very self-conscious and very much publically communicated ambition of the Municipality of Tel Aviv to unashamedly position itself as a global city player has in part contributed to and been fed by the increasing appearance of Tel Aviv in both the international academic and populist comparative literature of global or world cities. For the city of Tel Aviv, this is an unapologetic self-aware branding promotional strategy. The branding of cities has itself become a huge global business in recent years.[26] There is, however, an academic body of research that identifies the vital role of local actors or agencies that seek to punch above their weight; they are also somewhat disparagingly referred to be 'Wannabe World Cities'.[27]

In recent years it has become somewhat popular to eschew the fashionable rhetoric of global city status and instead to focus on 'liveable city' or 'smart city' status. Tel Aviv very consciously adopts and promotes a positive public face in all three. They are of course not mutably exclusive. Liveability, 'a cosmopolitan ambience and liberal lifestyle' is accepted as a vital factor for global city status.[28] Tel Aviv has long championed its image as fun and liveable place to live. 'The city that never stops' is more than a decade-long municipal advertising slogan.[29]

In 2014 Tel Aviv won first prize in the World Smart Cities Award at the Smart City Expo World Congress in Barcelona (250 cities competed in the competition). Lonely Planet ranked the city the third best in the world to visit in 2010 ('a modern Sin City on the sea').[30] Tel Aviv now regularly tops global lists as diverse as world's best 'gay city', which has attracted accusations of so-called 'pinkwashing'.[31] In 2015 the city was ranked the fifth best city for global high-tech start-ups, behind New York, Boston, Silicon Valley and Los Angeles, ranking third in that global listing for start-up talent.[32] Israel, and by extension Tel Aviv, has occupied a decade-long pre-eminent position on US Nasdaq index of high tech.[33]

The ambition of Tel Aviv to gain a foothold in the ladder of international global city or status city rankings cannot be divorced from its desire to escape the perceived constraints of both local (Israeli) and regional (Middle East) political geography. That ambition and desire are inextricably linked and mutually reinforcing.

It is argued that Tel Aviv, for obvious historic and geopolitical reasons, effectively functions as an island or cul-de-sac economy in its regional Middle East geography and that this necessarily imposes regional hegemony ambitions that may be considered a prerequisite for top-tier global city status.[34] Tel Aviv may be one of wealthiest (per capita), most culturally and socially dynamic cities in the Middle East, its economy may dwarf many cities in the region with the possible exception of Cairo (the latter has a population of 9.5 million), but it has little or no functional relationships with most of them.[35] Nothing demonstrates this as sharply as the fact that there are no international flights between Tel Aviv and the cities of Beirut, Dubai, Doha, Riyadh, Damascus, Baghdad or Tehran. Israel, of course, does not have diplomatic relations with most Arab and Muslim states in the region. It is the cities that do not appear on the arrival and departure screens in Tel Aviv's Ben Gurion Airport that reveal more about the city's local regional connectedness. Of the largest 50 metropolitan conurbations within a 2,000km radius of Tel Aviv, there are direct flights from Ben Gurion Airport to just eight.[36] If regional flight connections are weak, trade links fare no better. Israel exports more to tiny Togo ($117 million) than to neighbouring Jordan ($98 million). Israel imports twice as much from faraway land-locked Paraguay ($92 million), with a population of just three million, than it does from neighbouring Egypt ($54 million) with a population of 80 million.[37]

The reality of residing (from an Israeli perspective) in an economically regional cul-de-sac has arguably spurred Tel Aviv's global ambitions to escape the limitations and constraints of its regional political geography. Tel Aviv does, however, have direct flights to both its closest Arab capital, Amman, and the largest and most important global Arab city, Cairo. And of those 44 'regional' metropolitan conurbations that Tel Aviv does not have direct flights to, few rank high in the Global City rankings. Tabriz, Kartoum, Mosul, Shiraz, Isfahan, Jeddah or Saana, despite their size, do not rank in the top 120 Global City rankings.[38] Abu Dhabi, Riyadh, Doha, Kuwait and Tehran are all ranked lower than Tel Aviv. The two highest-ranking regional, 'Middle Eastern' or Muslim global cities, both ranked higher than Tel Aviv, are Istanbul (26) and Dubai (28). Cairo fell nine places between 2016 and 2107, and at 62 is now ranked below Tel Aviv at 57.[39]

The narrative of a geopolitically isolated Tel Aviv is somewhat undermined by the fact that Tel Aviv is strategically well located to take advantage of global airport hubs. The city's global geography allows it to avail of direct non-stop flights to New York, Toronto, Johannesburg, London, Moscow, Bangkok, Beijing and Hong Kong. In addition, there are on average a dozen direct flights to Istanbul a day. Istanbul is now the world's 11th busiest airport by passenger traffic.[40] Whether or not the city of Tel Aviv has recently emerged or is soon to emerge as a major global city is ultimately a question of subjective assessment, and an assessment one imagines that is probably of little interest to the vast majority of its residents. The future economic health of the city is far more likely to be determined by the outcome of its local and increasingly bitter political struggle with the capital city of Jerusalem than its relative position in any Global City rankings. That struggle between what we have termed the 'State' of Tel Aviv and the 'State' of Jerusalem is discussed in the next chapter, *'The Looming Divorce?'*

In its 'Tel Aviv Global City' self-promotional manifesto, the municipality of Tel Aviv-Yafo goes some way to imagine this 'state' of Tel Aviv when it declares that 'Tel Aviv-Yafo is not only a city, it's a way of thinking' whose 'global standing is not dependent on [its] geographic location or [its] national affiliation'.[41] In the context of the above this can perhaps be read as a municipal mix of defiance, a not-so-coded declaration of secessionist political intent, or a subliminal scream desirous of social separation. It begs the question what next for Tel Aviv's relationship with the rest of Israel, and is Jerusalem listening?

Can Tel Aviv successfully build a global city brand surrounded by Israeli-built walls of occupation?

7 – Autonomy

Anti-Occupation demonstration Rabin Square Tel Aviv. The posters state '50 and Enough – Peace Now', referring to 50 years of occupation.

7.1 – The Looming Divorce:
the 'State' of Tel Aviv and the 'State' of Jerusalem

Tel Aviv, and Tel Avivians, have long been ridiculed by many (non-Tel Avivian) Israelis for living in a bubble, a fictional bubble of their own making. They are derided for apparently living a deluded existence vainly seeking to divorce themselves from the harsher realities of life and conflict in the Middle East. Tel Aviv is mocked as a naval-gazing Mediterranean city in denial of a threatening Middle Eastern irredentist geography lurking over its shoulder. Many Tel Avivians would argue that it is not Tel Aviv that lives in a bubble, but rather much of the rest of Israeli society, or at least those on a wide spectrum of the political and religious right. This is a city not without its own problems and prejudices, injustices and inequalities. It is a city, however, that is growing ever more uncomfortable functioning inside what it views as the straitjacket of an increasingly particularistic and assertive governing Judeo-ethno-centric Israeli bubble.

This Judeo-ethno-centric bubble finds political expression primarily through the Settler Movement and its supporters on the political right, both religious and secular in Israel. In the Israeli Knesset, its chief ideologues and cheerleaders are undoubtedly Habayit Hayehudi. The Haredi parties, United Torah Judaism and Shas who favour the primacy of Judaism in state law, and whose voters are also political champions of the settlements, are critical allies of this Judeo-ethno centric agenda.[1]

The term Neo-Zionism is perhaps the more commonly used, if somewhat elastic and occasionally opaque, term that groups the collective ideology of political and religious beliefs of Judeo-ethno centrism.[2] The governing Likud Party has, in recent years, increasingly advocated a radical Neo-Zionist agenda.[3] This agenda includes, amongst other policy platforms, creeping annexation (of the West Bank) without the granting of Knesset full voting rights to its 2.7 million Palestinians inhabitants. Government ministers are now openly calling for the annexation of the settlement city of Ma'ale Adumim (pop. 40,000), 7km east of Jerusalem.[4]

Neo-Zionists believe that the occupied West Bank is part of the historical or biblical land of Israel. They oppose the creation of a Palestinian state and tend to favour the primacy of Halacha law (Jewish law and jurisprudence based on the Talmud) over secular Israeli state law. In recent years, Neo-Zionism has been in the political ascendancy in Israel. The centre of gravity of every Israeli Government has drifted ideologically rightwards following each of the Knesset elections of 2009, 2013 and 2015.[5] The success of advancing the legislative agenda of Neo-Zionism has been steady and undisputed.[6] Neo-Zionism, as the name suggests, is an evolution on previous Zionist incarnations. It remains a work in progress. Neo-Zionism is arguably the primary, but not the exclusive, political heir of 'traditional' or 'Revisionist' Zionism of the largely secular Likud Party.[7]

Israeli Zionism is however mutating on both the right and the left. Labor Zionism, the spiritual home of the *kibbutz* movement and the driving ideology of the Israeli Labor Party, is today all but politically moribund. The Zionist state is established. Labor's brand of subsidised Ashkenazi socialism is economically and politically discredited.[8] Its voters have electorally scattered, abandoned the rhetoric of Labor Zionism, or have increasingly died off. A changing demography in the past 25 years has transformed the electorate.[9] The Israeli Labor Party which dominated every Israeli government from 1948 until 1977 has not won a plurality of the vote since 1999 when it commanded the loyalty of just 1 in 5 voters. The party and its allies (appearing under various names) has won on average just 14% of the popular vote in the five subsequent elections (2003 14.5%, 2006 15.1%, 2009 9.9%, 2013 11.5%, 2015 18.7%).

So where does Tel Aviv today fit in this mutating multiplicity of Zionism? And why is it so important to the future economic health of this city? Both the Neo-Zionist Habayit Hayehudi and the increasingly Neo-Zionist Likud Party electorally underperform in the city of Tel Aviv. The Likud Party and Habayit Hayehudi received just 21% of the vote in the city of Tel Aviv in the Knesset elections of 2015 compared to 30% nationally.

Historically the right has always underperformed in Tel Aviv. Tel Aviv votes left. This is a city that traditionally has favoured the Israeli Labor Party and its brand of Labour Zionism. The electoral picture today is more fractured and complex. Today Tel Aviv is increasingly and perhaps unwittingly evolving into a Post-Zionist city.[10] Post-Zionism has at its core a belief that Zionism fulfilled its historical mission in 1948 with the establishment of the state of Israel. It is of the opinion that the Israeli Occupation and the Neo-Zionism territorial ambition to annex the West Bank essentially put at risk the very existence of the Israeli State. Post-Zionism's tends to stress the need to prioritise and resolve the inherent, often contradictory challenge of juggling individual and collectivist human rights in a contemporary Zionist Israel. It elevates the primacy of universal values, democracy, equality before the law.

Israelis of course do not walk around as the proud card-carrying members of one or other brands of competing strands of Zionism. Few, if any, Tel Avivians (outside a tiny clique of academics) would openly identify or call themselves Post-Zionists. Many Tel Avivians, nevertheless, would articulate a not unreasonable, rational and secular fear of the growing political clout of Neo-Zionism, and the consequences such Neo-Zionism has for the future of Tel Aviv. Post-Zionism remains, however, a largely pejorative label. The Israeli left, including the small progressive Meretz Party, would not identify as Post-Zionist. The term tends to shut down debate. For this reason we coin the term 'Permissive Zionism'. Permissive Zionism shares many of the characteristics of Post-Zionism, including a belief in individual social liberty. In this way the 'Permissive' is intended to convey a sense of openness and tolerance. Permissive Zionism is supportive of LGBT rights, generally supportive of pluralistic values, it doesn't however question the core basic tenets of Zionism. If Post-Zionists can be caricatured as taking pride in pronouncing an intellectual certainty of belief in the inherent contradiction between liberal democracy and Zionism, adherents of Permissive Zionism tend to shirk that conundrum and instead muddle through by addressing the recognised tensions with messy public policy solutions.

There is a second intended meaning in the word 'Permissive'. This is a sense of acquiescence, a passivity, a permission by default. If the liberal side of Permissive Zionism can be summed up as a positive 'live and let live' attitude, the passive side manifests itself with a resigned 'shrug of the shoulders'. Permissive Zionists are opposed to the Occupation but are overwhelming passive in their opposition. Disapproval of Permissive Zionism of the increasingly religious and rightward drift of government policy is largely restricted to conversations with friends and family over dinner or watching the nighty TV news, or the obligatory four-yearly vote for the Knesset. It is the 'tut-tut' and hang-wringing passivity of Permissive Zionism which gives permission to the agenda of the radical Neo-Zionism that, we argue, compounds the undermining of the core values of the 'state' of Tel Aviv.

Permissive Zionism, in many ways, is being forced upon Tel Aviv by the emergence and success of radical Neo-Zionism at the heart of government for a decade or more. This is a Neo-Zionism that has recently outlawed criticism of the Israeli Occupation itself.[11] This is Neo-Zionism, many of whose adherents support the full annexation of the entire West Bank without granting citizenship or voting rights to Palestinians. This is a radical Neo-Zionism that, perhaps correctly, believes it can continue to expand and entrench the settlement enterprise and maintain the Israeli Occupation without incurring any consequential response from the international community. This is essentially a belief that the Occupation is a free ride devoid of any political or economic costs. Whilst a plurality of Israeli Jews favour a two-state solution, 1 in 7 Israeli Jews apparently now favour the expulsion of Palestinians from the West Bank.[12] In many ways this is an ideology that has come out of the shadows, refuses to play clever or duplicitous word games on the future possibility of a two-state solution and is unafraid of openly advocating and defending a dual electoral system in a one-state solution.[13]

If Tel Avivians admit to living in a bubble, they perhaps would characterise it, somewhat counterintuitively, as a bubble of sanity or political rationality. The Permissive Zionist Tel Aviv Bubble is internationalist and cosmopolitan, and aspires to normalise and better integrate itself as a city into universal western norms of citizenship and civic society. It is a bubble that seeks to unshackle itself from what it sees as an increasingly religious, messianic and chauvinist Israeli parochialism. The municipality of Tel Aviv-Yafo itself sums it up perfectly, if not obliquely. 'Tel Aviv-Yafo is not only a city, it's a way of thinking' whose 'global standing is not dependent on [its] geographic location or [its] national affiliation.'[14]

This is ultimately a battle for Zionism, or a battle of Zionism to determine the future of Israel to be precise. It is a battle of Zionism fought in the media, the Knesset, the courts and in the theatre of popular culture. It is also a battle with strong geographic or regional expression. The city of Tel Aviv and its (northern) suburbs are the ideological, electoral and geographic home of Permissive Zionism. The city of Jerusalem and its satellite religious and settler suburbs are the spiritual, electoral and geographic home of Neo-Zionism.[15] We have called these two territorial and competing visions of Zionism, the Permissive Zionist 'State of Tel Aviv' and the Neo-Zionist 'State of Jerusalem'.

The geography of regional Zionism has been significantly underplayed in Israeli political discourse, primarily because the state of Israeli itself is treated as a single electoral constituency in Knesset elections ('*Constituency Geography*', page 239). Historically, social division and political polarisation inside Israel proper, including the electoral or legislative battles of Neo-Zionism, Permissive Zionist and, critically, Anti-Zionism has primarily been viewed through a sectoral as opposed to a geographical prism. The geography of regional Zionism is a story of competing geographies. An increasingly globalised, Permissive Zionist Tel Aviv is broadly outward-looking and connected to international markets. The geography of Neo-Zionism is the politics of nativism, insularity and driven forward by the resurrection of imagined biblical heroism of the ancient past. This is also a nativist Neo-Zionism that, ironically, is disproportionately championed by recent or newly arrived Jewish immigrants.[16] Some 6.6% of the non-Israeli born Jewish population arrived after the year 2000. They would appear to disproportionately favour the more ideological and geographically isolated settlements: Ofra 43%, Shiloh 13.3%, Beit El 17.9%, Eli 15.8%. All four settlements voted overwhelmingly for Habayit Hayehudi in 2015.

The divergence of our 'state' of Tel Aviv and 'state' of Jerusalem is magnified by two powerful socio-economic forces that have combined to accelerate social and political polarisation, a polarisation that has real spatial expression. The first is the role Israel, and in particular the city of Tel Aviv, has played, is playing, in the global high-tech economy. The second, perhaps less well known outside of Israel, is the Religious Ultra-Orthodox or Haredi fertility rate and its impact on Israeli society.

Israel is an acknowledged global leader in high tech, driven in part and sustained by massive government R&D in the Israeli military and security industries. Israelis invented or pioneered Instant Messaging, USB flash drive, GPS technology (WAZE), and nano-medical visual technology (PillCam), amongst others. Israel hosts more NASDAQ-listed companies per citizen than any country in the world.[17] Many of these start-up firms are clustered in and around Tel Aviv. Tel Aviv as a city acts as laboratory in nurturing this creative dynamic.

The second force or trend is the exceptionally high fertility rate amongst the Religious Ultra-Orthodox or Haredi population, with families of 10 or 12 children not uncommon. The children of Haredi families are schooled separately. Many of these religious schools have increasingly opted out of the mainstream curriculum. Basic maths, English and science are losing out to religious-orientated studies. There is a significant risk of educationally embedding economic marginalisation for future generations of Haredi children. A third of the population of Jerusalem (half the Jewish population) is now Ultra-Orthodox. The Israel Census Bureau predicts that by 2059, some 40% of all Jewish children in Israel will be raised in Haredi homes.[18] Israel is in 'danger' of 'designing' a society where a tiny, wealthy, highly educated minority, dedicated to coding a high-tech future for itself, lives amidst a scientifically illiterate majority wedded to decoding the biblical text of the past. These parallel socio-economic phenomena find manifestation in real space in the 'state' of Tel Aviv and the 'state' of Jerusalem.

The seeds of this decoupling have been germinating for decades. In 1972 Israel had a lower fertility rate (3.7) than Ireland, Turkey, China, South Korea, Indonesia, Saudi Arabia, India, South Africa, Colombia, Mexico, Brazil, Peru and Costa Rica, to name but a few.[19] Today, thanks to a growing Haredi population, Israel's fertility rate at 3.1 is higher than all of these countries. In addition, very specific local conditions have spawned the rise of national-religiosity and nativist insular ideology. The 1967 Israel-Arab war set in motion a chain of events that have ultimately transformed Israeli politics – the Israeli occupation, the emergence of the messianic settler movement, the explosion in settler numbers, and the subsequent success of political Neo-Zionism.

The Israeli occupation was 50 years old in 2017. The first Israeli settlements were constructed in 1968, a year after the 1967 Israeli-Arab war. The very early settlements were built in the Jordan valley – Qalya and Argaman (both 1968), and Mehola (1969). Today these isolated settlements continue to be home to no more than a few hundred Israelis.[20] By 1972 there were 10,000 settlers living in the occupied West Bank; this included just 1,200 scattered across the entire West Bank outside east Jerusalem. By the mid-1970s just 1 in 300 Israelis lived in the settlements. Today, with a settler population of 700,000, 1 in 12 Israelis are settlers and 1 in 9 Israeli Jews are now settlers.[21]

Fifty years of Israeli occupation has unleashed and nourished the political religious elixir that has fuelled the core conviction of Neo-Zionism. This is the messianic belief in the return to the Jewish biblical lands of Judea and Samaria (West Bank) and the intoxicating belief (with very much earthly consequences) in God's promise to Abraham – the handing over of the 'Promised Land' (or the real estate of the West Bank to be exact) to the Jewish people. Intoxicating or toxic, the 'state' of Jerusalem on the floor of the Knesset is duly obliging in facilitating this transfer of the promised land from Palestinians to Israeli Jews. Recent legislation passed by the Knesset has retrospectively legalised the 'appropriation' of private Palestinian land by Israeli settlers.[22]

If the 'state' of Jerusalem and the 'state' of Tel Aviv are never likely to agree as to who inhabits a political bubble, it is in part because they do not share a common framework of language. A Tel Avivian open-market economy of ideas cannot compete with a Jerusalemite inward-looking closed mind on a mission to fulfil God's will. The 'state' of Tel Aviv' and the 'state' of Jerusalem and the overwhelming majority of their respective citizens are playing out arguments on different fields of debate. These two cities and the politics they represent have probably passed the point of meaningful understanding of each other.

Economically, at least, there can be no argument as to who inhabits a bubble of delusion. Tel Aviv is the economic, singular powerhouse of Israel.[23] This is a city that sustains the rest of Israel economically. Given the size of its economy, Tel Aviv ultimately provides the funding to subsidise the Haredi lifestyle, and essentially foots the bill for the settler enterprise. It is a city that is mocked, without any irony, by the 'state' of Jerusalem for its apparent sloth and laid back lifestyle.

Just a 40-minute drive separates Tel Aviv and Jerusalem. These two cities are hitched together by both history and geography. Their political and urban trajectories now seem destined more than ever toward a political, cultural, almost existential battle. Politically, socially and culturally they have become to barely tolerate each other. A messy divorce is probably inevitable. The challenges of a successful divorce are perhaps insurmountable. Divorces are always complicated. Separation is invariably difficult for both partners. Tel Aviv is as an emerging global city that simply cannot afford to operate under the shadow of an increasing vocal and global Boycott Disinvestment and Sanctions (BDS) movement that seeks to de-legitimise Israel because of the political choices of the 'state' of Jerusalem'. An outward-looking globalist, albeit arguably economically self-interested, Tel Aviv is evermore fearful of an inward-looking Jerusalem that risks dragging Israel to a South African like tipping point in the BDS movement.

Divorce, as in an agreed separation that takes the form of some sort of regional or devolved federalism, is theoretically possible, but as of 2018 politically improbable. There

Which direction? Sitting and waiting in Magen David Square, Tel Aviv

are, on occasion, popular and populists calls, in particular from Tel Avivian liberals, for greater regional autonomy in Israel.[24] This would include giving the city of Tel Aviv, or a Greater Tel Aviv, civil or secular control over the certification of marriage and divorce. Currently the Orthodox Rabbinical courts have full control over all Jewish marriages and divorce in Israel. A substantial level of devolved power already exists at the sectoral level in the educational realm, with separate Palestinian, Jewish and Haredi schooling systems. For the 'state' of Tel Aviv, federalism would facilitate further separation of religion and state.

There are powerful political and territorial reasons why a devolved form of regional autonomy is likely to prove an unattractive solution, in particular to the 'state' of Jerusalem. Geography is key, but it is not size that matters. The relatively small size of Israel is not the challenge. The smallest seven cantons in Switzerland are each less than 300skm² in size. The singular most powerful reason in preventing the emergent of any type of Zionist federalism is Palestinian geography. Federalism would at a stroke of a geographical pen significantly increase the risk of Palestinian territorial secession. A fear of magnifying the Palestinian and Bedouin Arab electoral majorities in Galilee and the Negev is why Israel is almost unique amongst democracies in not having a multi-constituency-based electoral geography. (see 'Constituency Geography', page 239)

In addition, the patchwork of Palestinian, Jewish and Religious Orthodox settlements certainly represents a real but not insurmountable challenge for effective sectoral territorial devolved government. The Haredi city of Bnei Barak is a Religious Orthodox island city of 180,000 people, surrounded by relatively secular Greater Tel Aviv. The Galilee region is a speckled mosaic of Palestinian and Jewish villages, towns and cities. We map out these territorial divisions as devolved possibilities in *'The Geography of Regional Zionism'* (page 305). If meaningful devolved regionalism or further sectoral autonomy remains unlikely, then ultimately one vision in the battle of polarised Zionism will emerge politically victorious.

Whether the 'state' of Tel Aviv and the 'state' of Jerusalem emerges the political victor will largely depend on which city or vision attracts and retains a greater share of loyalty of the wider Israeli electoral city geography. While it remains uncertain which city is likely to emerge the victor, the stakes couldn't be higher. The victor is not only likely to determine the allocation of the state's resources, but also prioritise the expenditure of Israeli political capital. The choices are stark. The 'two-state solution' versus 'annexation'; democracy versus a quasi-theocracy; the consolidation of secular, civic democracy or the prioritisation of the Judaisation of Israeli state law. The battle will ultimately be played out on the floor of the Israeli Knesset.

The political divergence of the 'state' of Tel Aviv and the 'state' of Jerusalem is perhaps best exemplified by the recent Knesset elections in 2015. Political parties with a centrist and avowedly secular outlook (Labor, Yesh Atid, Meretz), at times openly hostile to both the Haredi or Religious Orthodox community and the settler movement, received 58.8% of the vote in Tel Aviv. The religious right including both the Harridim (Shas, UTJ) and the hard right (Yisrael Beiteinu) and Settler party Habayit Hayehudi received just 11.6% of the vote in Tel Aviv. The vote in Jerusalem was almost reversed, with the centrists and secular parties receiving just 17.9%, and the religious and settler right 50.9%. Add in the Likud Party in Jerusalem and the right-wing share of the vote rises to 75%.[25]

A traditional but increasingly 'Squeezed Zionism' in the rest of Israel looks on, co-opted by either visions as the referee or political arbiters in deciding the direction and fate of the country. In recent years, the 'state' of Jerusalem has been by far the more successful in convincing the cities of 'middle Israel' that its vision is more deserving of electoral support. The Israeli electoral party system largely transcends socioeconomic issues, attitudes to the Palestinian conflict and intra ethno Jewish identity has been a greater predictor or electoral loyalty in Israel.

Of the nine largest 'middle Israel' cities, outside the Tel Aviv District, eight (Rishon LeZion, Rehovot, Petah Tikva, Ashdod, Netanya, Be'er Sheva, Ashkelon and Beit Shemesh) voted for the nationalist or religious right in the Knesset elections of 2015, the latter six doing so by overwhelming margins, ranging from 24 percentage points (Petah Tikva) up to 62 percentage points (Ashdod). Only the city of Haifa came close to splitting its vote between left and right. The largely Religious Orthodox city of Beit Shemesh plumped for the religious right over the left by a thumping 82% to 6%.[26]

The division goes beyond electoral polarisation or partisan party politics. There is probably no comparable nation state in the 'western world' where its two largest cities hold politically diametrically opposed visions for the future of the state that they share. This isn't a mere difference of political opinion, a divergence of outlook, but arguably a looming clash of cultural political survival. Their large size relative to the population of Israel magnifies the polarisation. Greater Tel Aviv (with a centre-left majority) and Greater Jerusalem, with populations of more than two million and one million respectively, together account for some 40% of the population of Israel.[27]

Perhaps no single and peculiar statistic sums up the different ethos between Tel Aviv and Jerusalem than the relative proportion of men who have studied full time in a *yeshiva* (college devoted to full-time study of the Torah) versus those who have completed a university degree. In Jerusalem you are more than twice as likely to have studied or study in a *yeshiva* (26.6%) than study in a university (11.4%). In Tel Aviv you are 22 times more likely to have studied at a university (23.1%) than in a *yeshiva* (1.1%). The figures for Israel as a whole are 13.1% (university) and 6.8% (*yeshiva*).[28]

The fact that you are 2.5 times more likely to study in a *yeshiva* than a university in Jerusalem is a worrying omen for the future economic health of Israel's capital city. One quarter of young and old Jewish men in Jerusalem now dedicate their full-time 'working' lives to the study of theology. In almost half of the residential neighbourhoods in Jerusalem, the number of Jewish men who studied in a *yeshiva* is greater than 2 in 5; in some neighbourhoods the figure rises to 3 in 4 Jewish male adults committed to full-time study of the Torah.[29] With significantly higher birth rates amongst the Religious Orthodox or Harridim, those figures will only rise. Some 31% of Jerusalem households have four or more children (up to the age of 17). In some neighbourhoods this figure is as high as 50%. This compares to just 4.4% for Tel Aviv.[30] The future of Israeli scientific research that aspires to build upon the legacy of the 'start-up nation' is unlikely to be nourished by the educational priorities or scientific curiosity of the city of Jerusalem.[31]

Jerusalem is an economically subsidised city. It is heavily reliant on the public sector, with some 25.8% working in education or public administration compared to just 11.5% in Tel Aviv.[32] Just 2.4% of Jerusalemites work in 'banking, insurance or financial institutions' and a further 11.7% in 'real estate and business activities', compared to a combined 29.1% in Tel Aviv. Jerusalem, 'technically' Israel's largest city, is also one of the poorest cities in Israel. There are perhaps few 'western' capital cities that are, relative to the rest of the state, as poor as the city of Jerusalem. Of the largest 20 cities in Israel, only two are poorer than Jerusalem – Beit Shemesh and Beitar Illit. Bet Shemesh is an overwhelming Religious Orthodox city; Beitar Illit is almost an exclusively Haredi or Religious Orthodox settlement city in the West Bank. Jerusalem is ranked the 61st poorest or socio-economically most vulnerable out of 255 Israeli local authorities. All but 10 of those 60 towns or cities ranked poorer are Palestinian, Bedouin or Druze communities. The city has a lowly ranking score of 3/10. Tel Aviv scores 8/10.[33] Jerusalem is also getting poorer, having slipped 38 places since 2008. In 2008 it was ranked 99 poorest with an overall socio-economic score of 3.[34]

With different economies, very different educational structures and demographic trajectories, and decidedly different political values (evident in Knesset elections), Israel's two largest cities are increasingly growing apart. Each city represents the different values and aspirations of a deepening and polarised Israel.

Tel Aviv is also increasingly a global player in the international high-tech industry, and has recently been ranked the fifth city for start-ups, behind New York, LA, Silicon Valley and Boston.[35] There are likely to be far fewer mobile (non-Jewish), highly skilled tech, finance or creative workers attracted to permanently live in the city of Jerusalem. The 'city of God' doesn't score highly on 'technology' or 'tolerance', and is likely to remain challenged in attracting 'talent'. Some 17,000, primarily young Jerusalemites left the city in 2014 alone. The city, unusual for a capital city, has the highest net out-migration of any city in Israel.[36]

Jerusalem has some successful high-tech stories.[37] Isolated high-tech parks that operate as introverted islands surrounded by a vast sea of non-employable local Haredi and Palestinian communities do not qualify geographically, at least, as local urban innovation hubs. They are effectively aspatial, disconnected from the city. Palestinians are disconnected and disadvantaged if not by walls, barriers or checkpoints, by acute educational underinvestment. Haredi are unlikely to have the necessary advanced technological skills. Jerusalem has also one of the lowest household internet penetration rates in Israel.[38] Jerusalem's power rests not on future innovation, but on cementing historic biblical myth-making.

Jerusalem is not the only religious city in Israel that has 'tolerated' gender segregation on certain public bus routes serving the Ultra-Orthodox.[39] It must, however, be one of the few capital cities in the 'western' world where advertisement images of women are not permitted on public bus routes for fear of inciting violence from religious extremists.[49] Perhaps conscious of its image of social divisiveness and intolerance, the city of Jerusalem is building an ambitious and monumental 'Museum of Tolerance'. The proposed site for the museum, however, has attracted considerable controversy because it is proposed to build it on a Muslim graveyard.[41]

Jerusalem as a city is long synonymous with division, separation and segregation. The Jerusalem municipality has been repeatedly accused of discrimination in the provision of municipal services to the Palestinian neighbourhoods of east Jerusalem. These accusations are not restricted to leftist international organisations. The city was publically rebuked by the State Comptroller of Israel, no less, in 2016 for its discriminatory building practices

Making a wish, Habima Square, Tel Aviv

against the same Palestinians in east Jerusalem.[42]

If this is a clash of urban culture, a test of each city's resolve to dominate, a battle for the future of the direction of the state of Israel, then demography at least favours Jerusalem: 2 in 5 residents (39.8%) of Jerusalem are under 17 years of age – twice that of Tel Aviv, where just 19.3% of the city is 17 years old or less.[43]

Tel Aviv does not, of course, have a monopoly on Israeli values of internationalism, cosmopolitanism and secularism, no more than Greater Jerusalem has a monopoly on the brand of Settler-Judeo nationalism. But this is a battle of two cities for the soul and future direction of the Israeli state. Tel Aviv's relative liberalism and pluralism will survive not because it is essential to the commerce or functioning of Tel Aviv as Israel's economic powerhouse. Relatively authoritarian or socially illiberal regimes governing cities can of course successfully compete in the new globalised city, economically liberal order. Think Beijing, Singapore, Dubai, or Moscow. Tel Aviv's liberalism may survive because the alternative is not illiberalism or authoritarian nationalism, but instead a risk of expulsion from western global markets arising from any extensive expansion of Israeli annexation of the West Bank. Currently the hotbed of international BDS (Boycott Disinvestment Sanctions) activism is largely restricted to university campuses in the United States. There is always a risk that the BDS movement will reach an unexpected tipping point. An international (western, Arab and Muslim) consensus in favour of cultural, academic or trade boycott could emerge rapidly. In 2017, China insisted in a bilateral agreement with Israel that the 10,000 expected immigrant Chinese construction workers would not work in the settlements. In January 2018 the Danish parliament voted to exclude Jewish settlements in the West Bank from bilateral agreements with Israel. The UN in January 2018 apparently drew up (as of then unpublished) a list of companies with commercial interests in Israeli settlements in the West Bank.[44]

A dynamic open economy can happily co-exist with an assertive Judo-ethno nationalism. Global commerce and global city status, however, won't survive a powerful and sustained international BDS onslaught, nor in the long term a significant rise in local scientific Illiteracy (arising from unreformed Haredi education). The economic self-interest of the 'state' of Tel Aviv's commerce may accidently protect the values of Tel Avivian social liberalism.

If the self-interest of global commerce doesn't tilt the balance in favour of Tel Aviv, and in the unlikely event of a significant realignment in Israeli politics, the victor in this battle of world views between the 'state' of Tel Aviv and the 'state' of Jerusalem will probably be determined by demography. The victors of demography will ultimately reap their reward in a simple electoral headcount at the Knesset ballot box across Israel. Whilst demography is not destiny, both demography and geography will certainly play an outsized role in shaping the outcome of that electoral battle. The 'state' of Tel Aviv political representatives on the centre-left have now lost the last five Knesset elections.[45] This is not simply a case of the centre-left loosing power, but the right moving steadily rightwards. There is clear evidence of 'asymmetric polarisation' of the left and right. The centre of gravity of each of the last three right-wing governments has also shifted decidedly to the right.[46]

With 1 in 12 Israeli citizens now living in the occupied West Bank and an Israeli census projection that by 2059 between a third and half of all Jewish children in Israel will be Ultra-Orthodox, the numbers battle looks challenging for the 'state' of Tel Aviv.[47]

It is perhaps Zionism's most supreme irony that one of the greatest challenges threatening the nascent success of the world's first 'global Jewish city' is the local Israeli (Ultra-Orthodox) Jewish birth rate. But perhaps the Haredi do not constitute the greatest challenge. The year 2059 is some time away. Long-term demographic projections are always couched in great uncertainty. Greater labour-force participation for Haredi women may dramatically reduce the fertility rate of the Haredi population. Educational policy for Haredi children that currently undervalues the teaching of English, mathematics and science, may yet be transformed.

The success of the settler political agenda is more likely to threaten the Post-Zionism of the 'state' of Tel Aviv. The construction of thousands of additional settler homes can take mere months. In March 2017 the Israeli government announced the establishment of a new settlement, the first in 20 years. It is not so much its creation, or indeed its potential size, but its location (near the existing settlement of Shiloh), 45km north of Jerusalem, deep inside the West Bank, that undermines the two-state solution.

The passage in the Knesset of the hugely controversial 'Regularisation' law just four months out from the 50th anniversary of the Occupation is a defiantly provocative act of the 'state' of Jerusalem.[48] The legislation has in effect, and for the first time, 'regularised' or state-sanctioned the retro-active expropriation of private Palestinian land by existing settlers and settlements. International condemnation was swift and damning, particularly from nation states previously very close to 'Jerusalem'.[49]

Recently passed legislation to ban BDS advocates (including banning those who restrict those calls for boycotts and sanctions to settlements only) from entering Israel has an aura of the King Canute legend of the 'state' of Jerusalem trying to wish away the inevitable and unceasing tide of criticism from the seat of a passport-control desk. A rubicon has been passed. Irrespective of whether the Regularisation legislation is subsequently overturned in the Israeli Supreme Court, a clear intent has been signalled by the 'state' of Jerusalem. Politically in the ascendant for a decade or more, in passing the BDS law, the Regularisation law and in sanctioning new settlements, the 'state' of Jerusalem has elevated a radical Neo-Zionist ideology to state policy.[50]

The core voting bloc of messianic Neo-Zionism of the 'state' of Jerusalem may today constitute an Israeli voting electoral minority. This bloc is comprised of a loose alliance of national religious, Haredi, settler and hawkish secular ultra-nationalists. As a bloc it may hold incoherent and often contradictory policy objectives. Few however would deny it's political success in recent years in shaping Israeli national policy, in thwarting a two state solution and in solidifying the Occupation.

Perhaps the Neo-Zionist Israeli critics of Tel Aviv were right all along. There is an irredentist, immediate and very proximate Middle Eastern reality lurking over its shoulder that threatens to burst its cosmopolitan bubble. That irredentist threat is, however, more multifaceted than they are ever likely to admit. The spectre of another 50 years of occupation or further annexation (of the West Bank) without the adoption of universal suffrage is arguably the greatest political or economic threat facing the city of Tel Aviv today.[51]

———

In 2012 the Israeli Central Bureau of Statistics (CBS) projected that by 2059 the children of Haredi families (those 0-19 years of age) will come close to equalling the percentage of non-Haredi Jewish children – 38% versus 40%. Some 20% of children will be Palestinian.[52] The CBS projects that the proportion of Palestinian children will fall from 26% to 20% between 2009 and 2059. The proportion of children from Haredi families will rise from 15% to 38%.[53]

We extrapolated these projections, year by year, to provide the corresponding figure for non-Haredi, Haredi and Palestinian children for each year from 2009 to 2059. We then identified some demographic milestones for the Israeli state. It should be noted the base projection figures come from the Israeli CBS itself. Its figures do not include the Palestinian population of the West Bank or the Gaza Strip.

In its customary Israeli independence celebrations, the CBS announced in May 2017 that the Israeli population had reached 8.7 million.[54] Israeli fertility rates at 3.1 children per woman are now the highest in the OECD and a basket of other countries analysed by the OECD (OECD average 1.7). Fertility rates in Israel overtook South Africa and Peru in 2000, India in 2006, and Saudi Arabia in 2010. Whilst the proportion of young people of the population (under 15 years) has fallen across the OECD in recent decades, in Israel it has fallen less, and at 28.3% is now the highest in the OECD (average 18.4%), having overtaken Turkey in 2003, Colombia in 2011 and Mexico in 2013.

The CBS classified Israeli Jews as follows: secular 44%, traditional 24%, traditional religious 12%, religious 11%, Haredi 9%. (We refer to all non-Haredi Jewish children as 'non-Haredi').[55] In 2016 a quarter of all Jewish children were Haredi. By 2028 non-Haredi Jewish children as a percentage of all children will have become a minority in the Israeli state. A year later, in 2029, Haredi children will outnumber Palestinian children. Another year later, in 2030, 1 in 3 Jewish children will be Haredi. In 2032 Haredi children will comprise a quarter of all children in Israel. In 2044, 2 in 5 Jewish children will be Haredi.

A rising Haredi population translates as Israel today having the lowest percentage of adults in the workforce (61.2%) in the OECD (average 66.3%). As workforce participation has generally risen internationally (in many countries, substantially), Israel's workforce participation has stagnated, and has fallen behind Ireland, New Zealand, Iceland, Turkey, Colombia, Mexico, Korea, Turkey and Brazil since 1970.[56] Without a radical change in Haredi children's education, which currently undervalues English, mathematics and science, the impact of such demographic changes on the labour force, the knowledge economy and the political direction of the State is likely to be transformative. The long-term economic challenges or political implications of a Haredi lifestyle or value system for the State are often glossed over, and instead it is the immediate fiscal or taxation cost of state subsidies that arouses most political attention. There is a widespread political narrative in Israel that the Haredi are a fiscal drain on the 'hard-working, middle-class' Israeli tax-payer, primarily because of the State's generous child benefits to large Haredi families. This narrative is not backed up by facts. Child benefit in Israel, by OECD standards, even taking into account differential GDP per capita, is relatively ungenerous. Standard child benefit in Israel is 150 NIS (€28) per child per month, compared to €105 in the United Kingdom, €140 in Ireland, €14

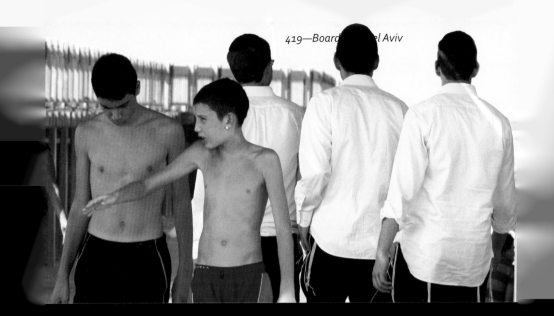

n Denmark, and €190 in Germany.[57] Social spending, as a percentage of GDP ('cash benefits direct in kind provision of goods and services, and tax breaks with social purposes') is 16.1% n Israel compared to an average of 21% in the OECD. Only three countries rank lower – France 31.5%, Denmark 29% and Germany 24.3% – and 25 rank higher.[58] Israeli public spending on 'family benefits – financial support that is exclusively for families and children health and housing not included) is again not particularly generous. Israel has a middle ranking expenditure of 2% of GDP in 2013, compared to the UK 3.8%, France 2.9%, and an average OECD of 2.2%.[59] Israel is also a low-tax economy. Tax on personal income as a percentage of GDP is low by OECD standards – 5.8% versus 8.4% (2014); 25 nations in the OECD have a higher tax take; only nine nations take less (none in western Europe.[60]

Given the current fiscal and social priorities of the Israeli state, the medium-term challenges to the projected rise in the Haredi population aren't likely to be fiscal, but political. In the absence of a broad and meaningful alliance between progressive Jews and Palestinians who wish to radically transform, as opposed to overthrow, current broad Zionist consensus that informs Israeli administrations, Israel is likely to drift further to the right to become an increasingly religious and theocratic state. There is currently little evidence of any electorally substantive meaningful alliance between secular Palestinian and centre-left Jewish political blocs. The tiny Jewish-Palestinian left-wing secular Hadash party Democratic Front for Peace and Equality) has been subsumed into the broader Palestinian alliance of Joint List. Hadash received just three seats in the 2012 Knesset election.

Demography is neither fiscal nor political destiny. Political destiny is shaped by the choices of all Israelis, not just the Haredi. A substantial number of all Israeli Jews (47% n a recent EU-funded opinion poll continues to favour a two-state solution over 'One State with equal rights for all, 12%), 'Apartheid' (15%) or 'Expulsion of Palestinians' (15%). The me opinion poll found that of Ultra-Orthodox jews, 31% favoured Expulsion and a further % Apartheid (one state with institutional discrimination, including right to vote).[61]

7.2 – The Geography of Regional Zionism

'*The Geography of Regional Zionism*' maps out the geographic contours of our Permissive Zionist 'state' of Tel Aviv and our Neo-Zionist 'state' of Jerusalem. We have also identified and geographically constructed three additional Zionisms and mapped them out accordingly.

The 2015 Knesset elections provides the electoral data for the geographic delineation of our five regional Zionisms. This election, of course, represents just one snapshot of political opinion. Political allegiances and party electoral fortunes, just like the definitions and potential multiplicity of Zionisms, remain fluid. We have allocated the largest 73 cities in Israel (including Israeli settlement cities in the West Bank) to our five different political Zionism. All of these 73 'Israeli' cities can vote in the Israel Knesset elections.

Within the Israeli system of local government, an urban municipality is granted City Council status by the Israeli Interior Ministry when its population exceeds 20,000.[1] There are 73 officially designated 'Israeli' cities in Israel and the West Bank with a population greater than 20,000. The list includes three 'Israeli' settlements inside the occupied West Bank, Modi'in Ilit (pop. 64,000), Beitar Illit (pop. 49,000) and Ma'ale Adumim (pop. 38,000). The settlement of Ariel, despite its population of 18,000, also has city status.

Some 74.2% of the Israeli population live in these 73 municipal 'Israeli cities'.[2] In addition, there are a further 30 Palestinian cities in the West Bank and Gaza Strip, each with a population greater than 20,000.[3] Palestinian cities in Gaza and the West Bank are not entitled to vote in the Israeli Knesset elections.

PERMISSIVE ZIONISM AND THE GEOGRAPHY OF THE 'STATE' OF TEL AVIV

To qualify to join the 'state' of Tel Aviv we have imposed two simple electoral thresholds on our 73 'Israeli' voting cities. The first is that a respective city needs to have given the centre and centre-left parties (Yesh Atid, Labor and Meretz) a minimum of 50% of the vote.[4] The second threshold is that this centre, centre-left vote had to have a minimum of a 10 percentage point lead over the nationalist and religious Zionist parties of the right (Likud, Yisrael Beiteinu, UTJ, Habayit Hayehudi and Shas).

Using those two simple electoral thresholds, the 'state' of Tel Aviv stretches north from Tel Aviv-Yafo to include the cities of Ramat HaSharon, Herzliya, Ra'anana, Hod HaSharon, Kfar Saba. It extends east to include Givatayim, Ramat Gan and Kiryat Ono. Our

---

Family seder *(feast), Petah Tikva*

'state' of Tel Aviv includes 11 of Israel's 73 cities. Collectively these cities had a total population of some 1.2 million in 2015.[5] That amounts to 18.9% of the total urban population of Israel. To secure the geographic status of an outpost or island of Permissive Zionism or 'state' of Tel Aviv, that outpost or city must adhere to both of the above two electoral thresholds and have a minimum population of 20,000 (city status).

Contrary, perhaps, to expectation, Haifa does not qualify as a liberal Permissive Zionist outpost of the 'state' of Tel Aviv. The centre-left, inclusive of the Joint List (Palestinian alliance of parties) did not secure more than 50% of the vote.[6] There are, in fact, just two outposts – the city of Ness Ziona and the city of Modi'in – outside our single contiguous 'state' of Tel Aviv. Both are just a 30-minute drive from Tel Aviv-Yafo.

Towns and villages with a population less than 20,000 and who do not adhere to the 'state' of Tel Aviv voting criteria outlined above are, for the purposes of our map, simply 'subsumed' into the 'state' of Tel Aviv region. We estimate the entire population of our 'state' of Tel Aviv is 1.3 million, and therefore elects 18 members to the Israeli Knesset.

Having identified the territorial geography of the 11 cities that qualify as Permissive Zionist, we then assessed their collective socio-economic status or strength using the Central Bureau of Statistics socio-economic analysis which ranks and scores the socio-economic health of all 255 Israeli cities and local authorities. A score of 10 is the highest and a score of 1 the lowest.[7] Just two communities in Israel were given a ranking of 10; these were Savyon and Kfar Shmaryahu. Our 10 Permissive Zionist cities of the 'state' of Tel Aviv have an average ranking of 8.1 (not weighted for relative population of each city). The 'state' of Tel Aviv is clearly relatively wealthy.[8]

NEO-ZIONISM AND THE GEOGRAPHY OF THE 'STATE' OF JERUSALEM

Our 'state' of Jerusalem includes Municipal Jerusalem (exclusive of the main Palestinian towns and suburbs of east Jerusalem). To qualify to join the 'state' of Jerusalem, we have imposed one simple electoral threshold. A city needs to have given the Religious Orthodox or Haredi parties – United Torah Judaism, Shas and the Religious Neo-Zionist party Habayit Hayehudi – collectively a minimum of 40% of the vote. The three parties received 17.5% of the vote across Israel in the 2015 Knesset elections.[9]

Our 'state' of Jerusalem extends westwards along the Jerusalem corridor to include the settlement Haredi city of Beitar Illit in the West Bank and the substantially Haredi city of Beit Shemesh. It extends north-west to the settlement Haredi city of Modi'in Ilit, expanding further northwards to include the city of El'ad on the exurban fringes of Tel Aviv in Israel proper. The city of Bnei Brak is the single outpost of the 'state' of Jerusalem.

Our six Neo Zionist cities of the 'state' of Jerusalem have an average socioeconomic ranking of just 1.8 (not weighted for population). The 'state' of Jerusalem is clearly, economically at least, relatively impoverished.[10] Our 'state' of Jerusalem, including the single outpost Bnei Brak, currently elects 17 seats to the Israel Knesset. Towns and villages with a population less than 20,000 and who do not adhere to the 'state' of Jerusalem voting criteria outlined above are, for the purposes of our map, simply 'subsumed' in the 'state' of Jerusalem region.

A significant real-life fault line in the tectonic political tension that divides the Zionist Geography of the 'state' of Jerusalem and the 'state' of Tel Aviv can be traced to the small strip of land that divides the cites of Modi'in and Modi'in Ilit. Modi'in (pop. 89,000) and Modi'in Ilit (pop. 64,000) may share a common name and proximity of geography but the similarity ends there. The city of Modi'in gave the 'Permissive Zionist' or centre-left parties 52% of its vote and just 13% to the religious Zionist and Haredi parties. Modi'in Ilit gave 94% of its vote to the religious right with the vote for the centre-left registering zero percent.[11] These cities are not just separated by electoral geography. They are located either side of the Green Line. Modi'in is located 1km south-west of the Green Line inside Israel proper, whilst Modi'in Ilit is located 2km to the north-east, inside the West Bank.

Our *Geography of Regional Zionism* includes three other territorial Zionisms – 'Non-Zionism', 'Squeezed Zionism' and 'Exurban Zionism'.

THE GEOGRAPHY OF NON-ZIONISM

Our *Geography of Non-Zionism* is essentially a map of Palestinian (and Bedouin) electoral geography inside Israel proper, as represented by the electoral strength of the Joint List. Joint List is an informal alliance of four Palestinian-dominated parties and secured 13 seats in the 2015 Knesset elections. To qualify to join the Non-Zionism state we have imposed one simple electoral threshold. A city needs to have given a Joint List party a minimum of 75% of the vote. Our map of Non-Zionism includes two distinct non-contiguous areas – Galilee to the north, and the predominately Bedouin communities in the Negev in the south.

The 'state' of Non-Zionism includes 11 cities with a total population of 436,000. These cities amount to just 6.3% of the Israeli urban population.[12] The vast majority of Palestinian Israelis live in towns and villages of less than 20,000. The 12 Non-Zionist cities have an average socioeconomic ranking of just 2.8 (not weighted for their relative population).[13] This is higher than the 'state' of Jerusalem but relatively low compared to the rest of Israel.

Towns and villages with a population less than 20,000 and who do not adhere to the 'state' of Non-Zionism voting criteria outlined above are, for the purposes of our map, simply 'subsumed' in the 'state' of Non-Zionism region. This includes dozens of small left voting (Zionist) *kibbutzim*. Our *Geography of Non-Zionism* runs in a narrow sliver of land from Kfar Kassem, just outside Tel Aviv, northwards to include the Palestinian cities of Tira, Tayibe, Umm al-Fahm, all the way to Sakhnin to include Nazareth (Israel's largest Palestinian city). A second smaller area is clustered around the city of Rahat in the south.

THE GEOGRAPHY OF SQUEEZED ZIONISM

The fourth geography of Zionism we call 'Squeezed Zionism'. To qualify to join the 'state' of Squeezed Zionism, we have imposed one simple electoral threshold: a city needs to have given the Likud Party, Yisrael Beiteinu and Shas party collectively more than 50% of the vote. These three parties represent substantial numbers of non-Haredi lower-income Jewish

Israelis, including ex-Soviet immigrants (supporters of Yisrael Beiteinu) and Moroccan (Shas and Likud) voters.

Outside Haredi cities, there is a strong correlation between the vote of these three parties. Likud, Shas and Yisrael Beiteinu received 23.4%, 5.7% and 5.1% of the vote respectively in the 2015 Knesset elections. In our 25 cities of Squeezed Zionism (not weighted for population) each of these party's share of the vote was substantially higher: the Likud vote was 54% higher, Shas 63% higher, and Yisrael Beiteinu 105% higher (more than twice its national average).[14] The average vote share for all other parties was lower: Zionist Union -50%, Yesh Atid -30%, Habayit Hayehudi -4%, UTJ -41% and Meretz -77%. Only the Kulanu vote share rose in Squeezed Zionist cities (up 14%).

The largest cities in our 'Geography of Squeezed Zionism' are Ashdod, Netanya, Beersheba, Ashkelon and Bat Yam. The list includes 26 cities with a population of 1.7 million[15] – 27.1% of the total urban or city population of Israel. It includes the five 'mixed' Palestinian Jewish cities of Ramla, Lod, Acre (Akko), Nazareth Ilit and Ma'a lot-Tarshiha. Our 25 Squeezed Zionist cities have an average socio-economic ranking of just 4.4 (not weighted for population).[16] This is significantly higher than the 'state' of Jerusalem and Palestinian cities of the 'state' of Non-Zionism, but substantially lower than 'state' of Tel Aviv', which scores 8.1. Squeezed Zionism is economically vulnerable and geographically peripheral.

There are two main expanses of Squeezed Zionism territory. The entire northwest of the state of Israel stretching from the Mediterranean coast to the Golan Heights, and as far as the West Bank, includes nine cities of Squeezed Zionism, the largest Kiryat Ata, Nahariya and Afula. The second expanse of Squeezed Zionism stretches from Bat Yam just south of Tel Aviv, down the coast deep into the Negev. It has 13 cities, including Ashdod, Ashkelon and Be'er Sheva. Two isolated outposts are the city of Netanya, north of Tel Aviv, and the settlement city of Ma'ale Adumim, east of Jerusalem.

The 'ethno Jewish' make up of Squeezed Zionism includes a higher proportion of Jewish Israelis who trace their origin to Africa and Asia. The proportion of Israelis who trace their origin to Africa or Asia in the 2008 census is 28.3%.[17] The comparable average (not weighted) for the 12 largest cities in Squeezed Zionism is 38.9%. The cities of Squeezed Zionism have an even higher proportion of African (predominately Moroccan) population. The proportion of Israelis who trace their origin to Africa in the 2008 census is 15.8 %. In the city of Dimona it rises to 32%, and is above 28% in the Squeezed-Zionism cities of Tiberius, Afula, Kiryat Gat, Be'er Sheva and Ashkelon.[18] This relatively economically impoverished Squeezed Zionism overall heavily favours the politically parties of the right.

There is interesting evidence, globally, of economics and politics pulling in opposite directions. Analysis has revealed that the areas won by Donald Trump in the US represented just 36% of the country's economic output. Similarly, with Brexit in the United Kingdom, with some of the areas with the highest 'leave' vote were also the most deprived.[19] The economic powerhouses of London, New York, Chicago, Los Angeles or San Francisco are electorally overwhelmed by economically struggling peripheral regions. In addition, there is a new educational electoral division, with those areas with the highest proportion of graduates favouring left or centre-left parties and those areas with lowest proportion of

The Squeezed Zionist city of Be'er Sheva is 'surrounded' by a Bedouin geography of Non-Zionism

graduates (high school education or less) favouring the political parties of the right.

A similar phenomenon is happening in Israel. The 'state' of Tel Aviv' dwarfs the economic output of the 'state' of Jerusalem. Both however are home to similar populations. Co-opting the relatively socio-economically deprived cities of Squeezed Zionism, the politics of the right electorally overwhelms the economically dominate regions of the centre-left.

There are also substantial differences in the level of educational attainment between the cities of Squeezed Zionism and the cities of Permissive Zionism. In Israel as a whole, 20.8% of the population over 15 years of age has 16 or more years of full-time education; 10.3% of the population has eight years or less full-time education.[20] The Squeezed Zionist cities with the highest collective share of the vote for Shas Likud and Yisrael Beiteinu are as follows Ashkelon: (61.4%), Afula (60.4%), Dimona (63%), Netivot 60%), Kiryat Kat (62%), Sderot (63%), Tiberies (65.4%). All but two have a higher percentage of residents with eight years of education or less than those with 16 years or more. In the city of Dimona, just 7.4% of those over 15 years have 16 years education.[21] Collectively in these Squeezed Zionist cities (not weighted for population), 10.8% have 16 years of schooling and 10.7% just eight years of schooling, just a 0.1 percentage point in favour of those with 16 or more years of full-time education.[22]

The six Permissive Zionist cities where the centre-left had its highest share of the vote are Givatayim (65%), Kfar Saba (55%), Hod HaSharon (62.7%), Kiryat Ono (58.7%), Ramat HaSharon (68%) and Tel Aviv-Yafo (59.5%).[23] Collectively in these cities (not weighted for population), 34% have 16 years of schooling and 5.7% just eight years, a massive 28.3 percentage points in favour of those with 16 or more years of full-time education. In Givatayim, 38.6% of residents over the age of 15 have 16 years or more full-time education, with just 5.5% with eight.[24] Towns and villages with a population less than 20,000 and who do not adhere to the 'state' of Squeezed Zionism voting criteria outlined above are, for the purposes of our map, simply 'subsumed' in the 'state' of Squeezed Zionism.

The electorate of Squeezed Zionism strongly leans rightwards on security, defence and Palestinian issues. It tends to favour the hawkish policies of Neo-Zionism over the perceived peacenik leanings of Permissive Zionism. It does, however, have one 'internal' deeply divisive political cleavage that has for the most part lain politically dormant, that is, until it burst forward onto the streets of Ashdod in early 2018. Who decides if shops can open on the Shabbat?

The debate about the opening hours on Shabbat may, to outsiders, seems relatively trivial in the context of the wider political challenges facing Israel. The tension between the Religious Orthodox or Haredi's insistence that shops shut, and a secular Israeli desire that they remain open is, nevertheless, a hot political and polarising topic in Israel. Government legislation introduced in 2018, championed by Shas (political party), in effect takes away from local municipalities the power to decide local Shabbat opening hours.

Ashdod is the quintessential Squeezed Zionist city. An estimated third of its population are ex-Soviet immigrants or the children of those immigrants. They are overwhelmingly hostile to any form of religious coercion, particularly on matters of who can shop where and when on a Saturday. In the 2015 Knesset election, the Russian-dominated Yisrael Beiteinu was the second largest party in the city. One-fifth of the city is now, however, made up of Religious Orthodox Haredi. In the 2015, Shas was the third largest party.

The tension between the religious and secular within the rightist camp is likely to play out in this city over the next decade or more. Its a battle that has the potential to re-align Israeli politics, with secular right-wingers – if pushed too far on matters of Rabbinical coercion – shifting from the right wing camp to more centrist and avowedly anti-Haredi parties aligned with the centre-left camp.

THE GEOGRAPHY OF EXURBAN ZIONISM

Our final regional Zionism is a kind of default Zionism. It includes all those areas or cities that do not fall under any of the above four electoral thresholds. The largest cities in this regional Zionism include Haifa, Rishon LeZion, Petah Tikva, Holon, Rehovot and Hadera. Of Israel's 73 cities (population in excess of 20,000), 19 fall into this residual regional Zionism.[25] They account for 25.9% of the urban population of Israel (1.5 million).

Geographically, this residual or default Zionism is concentrated in the suburban or exurban western and southern peripheries of Greater Tel Aviv. It also includes the city of Haifa and its exurban suburbs of Kiryat Motzkin, Kiryat Balik, Nesher and Yokneam Ilit, extending southwards to Kfar Yona. In addition, it includes isolated outposts in the north (Karmiel and Akko) and in the south (Arad and Eilat). This regional Zionism we call 'Exurban Zionism'. Our 19 Exurban Zionism cities have an average socio-economic ranking of 6.7 (not weighted for population).[26] This is higher than all other regional Zionisms with the exception of the Permissive Zionism of the 'state' of Tel Aviv, which scores 8.1.

Electorally these cities neither plump for the centre-left nor the traditional or religious right. They straddle the 'left liberalism' of the 'state' of Tel Aviv and the rightist traditionalism of the electoral geography of Squeezed Zionism. No particular party or grouping dominates in Exurban Zionism. Exurban Zionism could also be called 'Consumer' or 'A la Carte Zionism'. This is a Zionism that is not wedded to any particular ideology. Those who live in Exurban Zionism are generally suspicious of ideologues. They are not religious. There are few votes for either Shas or United Torah Judaism. They tend to see themselves as centrists, middle-of-the-road Israelis. Their primary political interest is cost-of-living issues. The affordability and rise in the price of local housing is of far greater concern than the political impact or physical expansion of suburban settlement housing over the Green Line.

The future direction of Israeli Zionism is likely to be determined by whoever wins the increasingly polarised clash between the electoral supporters of Permissive Zionism of the 'state' of Tel Aviv' and the Neo-Zionism of 'state' of Jerusalem. The victor of that electoral battle will be determined by the adherents and voters of both Squeezed Zionism and Exurban Zionism.

Neither the current electoral geography of Zionism nor the future forecasts of Jewish demography looks good for 'state' of Tel Aviv. Squeezed Zionism overwhelming favours the religious right electoral coalition that underpins the politics of the 'state' of Jerusalem. All five of the largest cities of Squeezed Zionism, each with a population greater than 90,000 – Ashdod, Netanya, Beersheba, Ashkelon and Bat Yam – overwhelming voted for the right in 2015. In all five cities the margin is greater than 34% points. In Ashdod, Israel's sixth largest city and the largest city in Squeezed Zionism, the religious right of Neo-Zionism is favoured over the centre-left by 52 percentage points (69.4% to 17.8%).[27]

Exurban Zionism splits its vote more evenly with Haifa, Israel's third city, marginally favouring the 'state' of Tel Aviv over the 'state' of Jerusalem. All the other five cities of Exurban Zionism, with a population of 90,000 or greater – Rishon LeZion, Petah Tikva, Holon, Rehovot and Hadera – favour the right-wing and religious parties. They do so with margins ranging from 7% (Rishon LeZion) to 25% (Hadera).[28]

NON-VOTING OR DISENFRANCHISED CITIES

Our electoral map of regional Zionism analyses only those cities (with a population of 20,000) that are entitled to vote in the Israeli Knesset elections. In addition to these 73 'Israeli' cities, there are a further 30 Palestinian cities in the West Bank and the Gaza Strip, each with a population greater than 20,000, none of which are entitled to vote in the elections of the nation state that effectively controls their everyday lives.[29] We have mapped out these 30 Palestinian cities, calling this geography 'Non-Voting or Disenfranchised Cities' of Israel-Palestine. Once again (any Palestinian or Jewish) towns and villages with a population less than 20,000 and who do not adhere to the criteria of our Non-Voting or Disenfranchised Cities are, for the purposes of our map, simply 'subsumed' into our map of Non-Voting or Disenfranchised map. There are, of course, no Jewish cities which cannot vote in the Knesset elections, but there are dozens of Jewish settlements with populations

The Geography of Regional Zionism
Moving from:
(A) the traditional black-and-white fixed contours of the two-state solution, to
(B) locating the 103 cities of Israel-Palestine, to
(C) imagining a new geography of local city identity, to
(D) mapping the geography of regional Zionism, to
(E) designing malleable unimagined borders, generating an 11-state federalism, to
(F, overleaf) provide for a liveable multi-hierarchy of national, citizen and municipal identities.

▉ Squeezed Zionism

▨ (Non Zionism) Palestinian and Bedouin

▩ Exurban Zionism

▬ Permissive Zionism (State of Tel Aviv)

▬ (Currently non-voting Disenfranchised) Palestinian

■ Neo Zionism (State of Jerusalem)

A   B

of less than 20,000 scattered across the West Bank that are subsumed into the Non-Voting or Disenfranchised map.

THE HIERARCHY OF MULTIPLE ZIONISM IDENTITIES
– A CONCEPTUAL FRAMEWORK FOR AN 'ELEVEN-STATE SOLUTION'

In *'The hierarchy of multiple Zionism identities'* we have built upon *'The Geography of Regional Zionism'* to construct the potential territorial contours of a new regional geography of autonomy. This is a conceptual, obviously fantastical, but territorially grounded framework for a federal 11-state solution in all of Israel-Palestine. In many ways this could form the blueprint for a hierarchical and territorially overlapping layer of national, citizen and local identities.

Our new regional geography of autonomy recognises the initial primacy of five supra-national identities – Israeli, Palestinian, Bedouin, Judean and Islam. Our Judean national identity derives its spiritual guidance and politics from Neo-Zionism and the 'state' of Jerusalem. Our Israeli national identity derives its political ethos from the Permissive Zionism of the 'state' of Tel Aviv. Our Bedouin national identity derives its social character from Bedouin nomadic culture. Our Palestinian national identity derives it political and social character from historical secular Palestinian nationalism. Our fifth supra-national identity primarily adheres to the beliefs of Islam.

Below these five supra-national identities, the basic building block of citizenship

C   D   E

is a federal state. There are 11 separate federal states in our unitary country of five supra-nationalities. Our 11 federal states derive the core of their identity and delineation of their geographical borders from the electoral thresholds outlined in 'The Geography of Regional Zionism'. Each state affiliates to a supra-national Identity. All 11 states must adhere to a common and shared basic constitution that elevates the primacy of stated articles of basic human rights. The individual states control all matters governing the separation of religion and state, including total control of the education and health spheres. Below the state level, individual cities or communities would be given municipal powers or devolved authority to decide contentious but decidedly local issues, such as the commercial opening hours on the Shabbat and the operational timing of public transport.

All individuals have the right to live anywhere and identify with any federal supra-national identity. They are, however, subject to the laws of the state they are a citizen of, and are required to abide by the local residency rules of the city they reside in. In theory an individual can identify their supra-national identity as Palestinian, choose to be a citizen of the 'state' of Tel Aviv but work in the city of Jerusalem. This would allow an individual to identify with any national identity of their choosing (including the transfer of a proportion of their taxes to support cultural activities of their supra-national identity), allow them to marry whoever they wish under secular laws of the 'state' of Tel Aviv, including the option of same-sex marriage, but require them to respect not driving on the Shabbat if they are resident in the city of Jerusalem in the 'state' of Jerusalem. This is an overlapping, fluid geography of movable identity and loyalty. It is democratic, flexible and multi-layered.

A minimum population of 500,000 residents or 5% of the total population of the entire federation of states (whichever is less) can create new federal supra-national identity. A new federal supra-national identity once created cannot be erased by a subsequent declining demography. Every citizen of every state can change their affiliation to a different supra-national identity in the federation every three years if they wish. There are no examinations, tests, qualifications or entry barriers. Every citizen of each of the federal states can change their citizenship every year if they wish. Every resident can change their registered residency from any city or community to another in 24 hours. All changes will have updated in real time to generate a register of national affiliation, state citizenship and city residency. These dynamic numbers would in part determine all taxes, expenditure and public subsidy. Thus, the triangular totality of national identity, federal state citizenship and local city residence of any individual would, in part, determine both the geographic and sectoral allocation or spending of taxes raised on any individual. The example of the citizen who identifies as Palestinian, professes loyalty to the 'state' of Tel Aviv, but who is residing and working in Jerusalem, will have part of their taxes funding Palestinian arts and culture, Tel Avivan education and justice, and Jerusalem housing, parks, and roads expenditure.

This is a 'fantastical' governing geography designed to create a cross-fertilisation of multiple, potentially endless permutations and combinations of layered and individually chosen identities.[30]

This is not a 'What if'?' about one election, one data point versus the next, but a prism of perspective. There are potentially multiple alternative identities hidden and unmapped inside the electoral geography of the Knesset election of 2015.

F

Conclusion

Seamless Neighbourhood – Redrawing the City of Israel is primarily a story of looking, literally looking around, endeavouring to see landscapes afresh. It is a story of the city of Tel Aviv, a seamless and greater Tel Aviv and its inescapable place in a wider geopolitical Israeli space. We have unmasked a fraction of the myriad building blocks, be they architectural, territorial, social or political, that make up some of the stories of this Greater Tel Aviv. To truly look afresh, to see things anew, requires a capacity to see different, parallel, often hidden perspectives.

Tel Aviv-Yafo is a small Mediterranean city of 400,000 people, with a municipal territory of just 52km², smaller than the island of Manhattan. It is also the world's first Jewish 'global city', whose commuter reach extends half-way across the West Bank, home to 2 in 5 Israelis. In calculating the totality of hidden balcony space, making visible the uncounted foreign workers, mapping non-existent constituency geography, or measuring and extending an imaginary 11½ Rothschild Avenues to the West Bank, the book number-crunches to reveal the hidden urban and suburban landscapes that make up this city region. We will have succeeded if the totality of these stories of decoded, imagined, mapped and deconstructed landscapes, each overlapping and intersecting at different scales, have coalesced to paint a unified, bigger picture of the reality of the seamlessness of a Greater Tel Aviv.

We conclude by tracing the increasingly antagonistic relationship between what we call a Permissive Zionism of Greater Tel Aviv and a Neo-Zionism of Greater Jerusalem. We can only speculate about the outcome of that struggle. It is a struggle, however, that will determine not only the future of Tel Aviv, of Israel, but arguably the future of the wider Israeli-Palestinian conflict. That wider conflict is, paradoxically, both central and peripheral to the storytelling of *Seamless Neighbourhood*. This mirrors the reality of the peripherality and centrality of that conflict in the lives of most Israelis. It is this simultaneous sense of absence and presence, of visibility and invisibility, that we have sought to reveal in the landscape stories of the book. It is a seamlessness of experience that has real political impact.

The perception and experience of the seamlessness of lands either side of the Green Line anaesthetizes Israelis to the Occupation. It co-opts to advance a form of collective consciousness of creeping annexation (of the West Bank). This consciousness of seamlessness is fed by some of the most ordinary and everyday objects and experiences – motorway signage, the humble bus stop, Tel Avivian day-tripping geography to the Dead Sea along Route 90. It includes the increasing erasure of the Green Line, both in reality on the ground and in map-making, whether in the daily Israeli weather forecast or in Israeli school textbooks. This is a seamlessness that is nourished by the adoption of a banality of language when talking of suburban settlements – 'an Israeli city over the Green Line' becomes just another euphemism for dormitory suburbs. It is a seamlessness of travel for some, but an enforced curtailment of movement for others. It is a landscape of both seamlessness and severance that nevertheless combine to operate as a vast anatomised de facto one-state reality. This de facto one-state reality could be better described as a dystopian decentralised collection of semi-autonomous truncated administrative islands with varying degrees of devolved power. This is a singular seamless state housing multiple island city-states, with a sprawling Tel Aviv at is centre. Its a faulty federalism designed by default.

This is, in part, a federalism built on segregation, differential voting rights and curtailment of free movement. Yet, ironically, inside this dysfunctional patchwork of localised and severed administration lie the very seeds of a positive federalism. These include the existing autonomy of decentralised education, self-governing municipal authorities that control everything from the opening hours of businesses to rules governing public transport on Shabbat – both hot-button issues in Israeli politics.

There is a common federalist thread that weaves through the enforced isolation of Gaza, the segregating 'welcoming committees' of *moshavim* and *kibbutzim*, the autonomy of the religious school system in Haredi Bnei Brak, the self-governing municipality of Palestinian Nazareth, the compound mentality of the settlement of Beitar Illit, or the secessionist chutzpah of Tel Aviv to subvert national by-laws governing opening hours on the Shabbat. The mental leap from the reality of today to a federalism of tomorrow isn't so great if we shift our perspective away from an illusory perception of a unitary Israeli state and an adjoining detached, but occupied, West Bank. Might a reinvented federalism provide an alternative to the moribund status of the two-state solution? Recognising the reality of a dysfunctional and, for some, a seamless federalism to enact a more democratic inclusive integrated seamless space for all, a de facto federalism without one-state or two-state labels, may instead provide a framework to better navigate a path to more meaningful change. It necessitates a shift from the struggle over the terminology of the boundaries of future sovereignty to a struggle about the language of present-day indivisible civil and citizen rights. Our electoral mapping in *'Constituency Geography'* and *'The Geography of Regional Zionism'* was primarily informed by the 2015 Knesset Election. At the time of going to print (March 2018) an Israeli election seems imminent. In any event, the next Knesset Election is due by November 2019 at the very latest. Political parties inevitably rise and fall, some can suddenly disappear, while others quickly emerge. *'Constituency Geography'* and the *'The Geography of Regional Zionism'* are not simply the mapping of a single Knesset election but the visualisation of bigger underlining story telling – namely, invisible geographies in electoral systems, and unmapped but deeply embedded socio-political identities.Our *'Geography of Regional Zionism'* and the 'hierarchy of multiple Zionism identities' is just one possible framework for envisioning a 'What if?' scenario in a new seamless federalism. This may be an unknown, perhaps constantly shifting and seamless destination.

Seamless Neighbourhood is a story on that possible journey. It is both an active way of looking and a framework for affecting positive change.

MOTTI RUIMY + PAUL KEARNS
March 2018

We conclude with the Seamless Neighbourhood as viewed from 5km above the earth in a NASA photograph. The image of Greater Tel Aviv is one of a metropolitan area connected by residential density and the lights of motorway geography. This is a metropolitan region devoid of border Green Line geography, but one that shows the importance of motorway geography. This is a seamless, metropolitan Tel Aviv that extends to Ariel along the lights of a clearly visible Route 5.

Route 443 from Greater Tel Aviv to Jerusalem cuts across the West Bank. The settlement city of Modi'in Ilit lies east of the Green Line. The city of Modi'in lies west, inside Israel proper.

This is a metropolitan geography that fuses Rosh HaAyin, a city suburb of Greater Tel Aviv, with the settlement of Oranit over the Green Line.

The reality of severed Palestinian urbanism in Greater Tel Aviv is in part revealed in the contrast between the bright lights of Alfe Menashe, a settlement of just 8,000 residents, and the dimmer municipal lighting of the Palestinian city of Qakiliya, home to 40,000.

The density contours of a Greater Tel Aviv as reflected in metropolitan street and home lights capture the sense of the 'Tel Aviv strip', wedged between the northern portion of the occupied West Bank and the Mediterranean Sea. Home to 3.3m people, or 40% of the population of Israel, the Tel Aviv strip occupies just 6.8% of Israel proper.

The proximity of Jerusalem is apparent, with the lights of the northern suburbs of Greater Jerusalem clearly visible in the south-east corner of the satellite image.

Tel Aviv

_____

NASA image of the Seamless Neighbourhood of Greater Tel Aviv, taken 5km above the earth

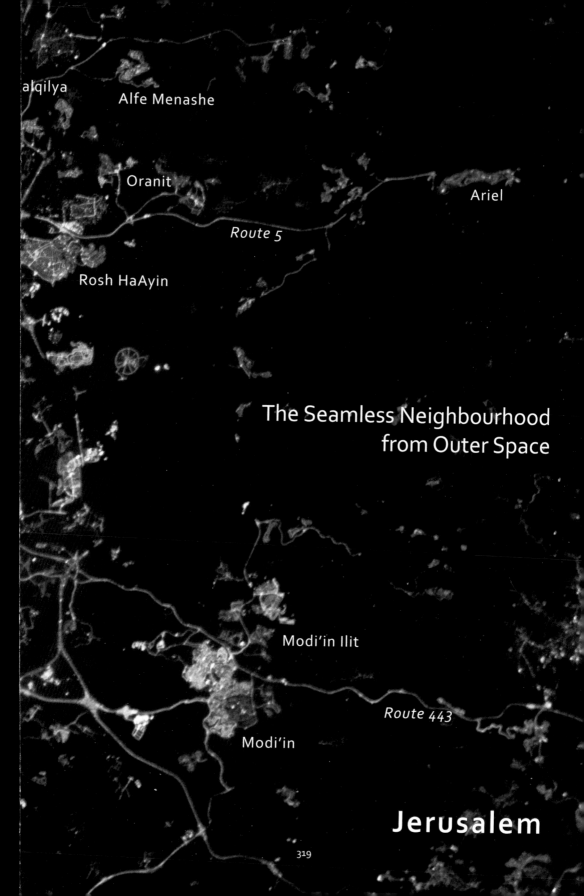

alqilya

Alfe Menashe

Oranit

Ariel

Route 5

Rosh HaAyin

The Seamless Neighbourhood
from Outer Space

Modi'in Ilit

Route 443

Modi'in

Jerusalem

The 120 single-seat member constituencies

TEL AVIV DISTRICT (19)

1   Tel Aviv North-East [census areas 12, 22, 21, 23] (Labor)
2   Tel Aviv North [census areas 11, 13, 41, 43] (Labor)
3   Tel Aviv Central [census areas 31, 32, 33, 34, 42] (Labor)
4   Tel Aviv South – Yafo [census areas 51, 52, 53, 54, 55 71, 72, 73] (Labor)
5   Tel Aviv South Central [census areas 61, 62, 81, 82, 83, 74] (Likud)
6   Tel Aviv South-East [census areas 92, 93, 94] (Labor)
7   Bat Yam North (Likud)
8   Bat Yam South (Likud)
9   Holon North-Azur (Likud)
10 Holon Central (Likud)
11 Holon South (Likud)
12 Herzylia North (Labor)
13 Herzylia South-Ramat Sharon (Labor)
14 Bnei Brak North Central (United Torah Judaism)
15 Bnei Brak South (United Torah Judaism)
16 Ramat Gan North (Labor)
17 Givatayim-Ramat Gan Central (Labor)
18 Ramat Gan South (Labor)
19 Kiryat Ono-Or Yehuda (Likud)

CENTRAL DISTRICT (29)

(note: population figures are given for constituencies that are geographically spread; otherwise they are 100% urban)

1   Kfar Yona – Mishmar HaSharon: Emek Hefer pop. 40,000 / Kfar Yona 21,000 / Zemer 6,000 (Labor)
2   Netanya North (Likud)
3   Netanya Central (Likud)
4   Netanya South (Likud)
5   Qalansawe-Taibe: Qalansawe 21,000 / Taibe 41,000 / Kohav Yair 9,000 (Joint List)
6   Kadima Zoran: Tira 25,000 / Kadima Zoran 20,000 / Even Yehuda 13,000 / Tel Mond 11,900
7   Ra'anna (Labor)
8   Kfar Saba (Labor)
9   Kfar Saba South-Hod HaSharon (Labor)
10 Petah Tikva North (Likud)
11 Petah Tikva Central (Likud)
12 Petah Tikva South (Likud)
13 Yehud – Givat Shmuel: Yehud 29,000 / Givat Shmuel 25,000 / Ganei Tikva 16,000 (Likud)
14 Rosh HaAyin – Kfar Kassem: Rosh HaAyin 42,000 / Kfar Kassem 21,000 / Jaljulia 9,000 (Joint List)
15 El'ad: El'ad 45,000 (Shas)
16 Rishon LeTsiyon North (Likud)
17 Rishon LeTsiyon West (Likud)
18 Rishon LeTsiyon South (Labor)
19 Rishon LeTsiyon East (Likud)
20 Lod (Likud)
21 Ramla (Likud)
22 Shoham-Modi'in North (Labor)
23 Modi'in Central (Labor)
24 Rehovot North (Labor)
25 Rehovot Central (Likud)
26 Rehovot South – Kiryat Ekron: South Rehovot 12,000 / Mazkeret Batya 12,000 / Kiryat Ekron 10,000 (Likud)
27 Ness Ziona: Ness Ziona 47,000 (Labor)
28 Yavne: Yavne 42,000 (Likud)
29 Gan Yavne – Gadera: Gadera 26,000 / Gan Yavne 22,000 / Bnei Ayish 7,000 (Likud)

SOUTHERN DISTRICT (17)

1   Eilat-Negev: Eilat 49,000 / Yeruham 9,000 / Revivim 6,000 / Mitzpe Ramon 5,000 (Likud)
2   Arad – Dimona: Dimona 33,000 / Arad 25,000 (Likud)
3   Negev North: Tel as-Sabi 19,000 / Kuseifa 19,000 / Ar'arat an-Naqab 16,000 (Joint List)
4   Ofakim: Ofakim 25,000 / Eshkol 13,000 / S'dot Negev 9,000 (Likud)
5   Be'er Sheva North (Likud)
6   Be'er Sheva Central (Likud)
7   Be'er Sheva South (Likud)
8   ak Kasom: ak Kasom 20,000 / Flura 19,000 /

Lakiya 11,000 / Omer 7,000 / Meitar 7,000 (Joint List)

9   Rahat: Rahat 62,000 (Joint List)

10   Kiryat Kat: Kiryat Kat 50,000 Lakish 10,000 / Lehavim 6,000 (Likud)

11   Nevivot-Sderot: Sderot 23,000 / Neviot 31,000 (Likud)

12   Kiryat Malakhi: Kiryat Malakhi 21,000 / Be'er Tuvia 18,000 (Likud)

13   Ashdod North (Likud)

14   Ashdod Central (Likud)

15   Ashdod South (Likud)

16   Ashkelon North (Likud)

17   Ashkelon South (Likud)

_____

NORTHERN DISTRICT (20)

1   Beit She'an-Gilboa-Jezreel Valley: Beit She'an 17,000 (Likud)

2   Afula: Afula 45,000 / Megido 12,000 (Likud)

3   Tiberias: Tiberias 42,000 / Yavine'el 4,000 (Likud)

4   Migdal HaEmek: Migdal HaEmek 25,000 / Ein Mahil 12,500 / Daburiyya 10,000 / Ilut 7,500 (Joint List)

5   Nazareth: Nazareth 60,000 (Joint List)

6   Nazareth North – Nazareth Illit: Nazareth Illit 40,000 / Nazareth North 15,000 (Joint List)

7   Kfar Kanna: Kfar Kanna 21,000 / Reineh 18,000 / Tur'an 13,000 / Mash'had 8,000 (Joint List)

8   Yokneam: Yokneam Ilit 21,000 / Bir al-Maksur 8,500 / Zazir 7,500 / Basmat 7,000 / Ka'abbiye 5,000 (Joint List)

9   Shefar'am: Shefar'am 40,000 / Kafar Manda 19,000 / Ibillin 13,000 (Joint List)

10   Sakhnin-Arraba: Sakhnin 29,000 / Arraba 24,000 / Bu'eine Nujeidat 9,000 / Deir Hanna 9,000 (Joint List)

11   Tamra: Tamra 32,000 / Kabul 13,000 / Shaab 7,000 (Joint List)

12   Acre: Acre 47,000 (Likud)

13   Nahariya: Nahariya 54,000 (Likud)

14   Jadeidi-Makr: Jadeidi-Makr 20,000 / Abu Sinan 13,000 / KfarYasif 9,000 / Julis 6,000 (Joint List)

15   Ma'alot-Tarshiha: Ma'alot-Tarshiha 21,000 / Kisra-Sumei 8,000 / Shlomi 6,000 / Fassuta 3,000 (Joint List)

16   Yarka: Yarka 16,000 Majd al-Krum 15,000 / Bi'ne 8,000 / Kfar Vradim 5,500 (Joint List)

17   Karmiel: Karmiel 45,000 / Nahf 12,000 (Joint List)

18   Mount Meron: Maghar 22,000 / Bayt Jan 11,000 / Rame 7,000 / Hurfesh 6,000 (Joint List)

19   Safed: Safed 33,000 / Hatzor Hagilit 9,000 / Tuba-Zangariyye 6,000 (Likud)

20   Golan – Kiryat Shmona: Kiryat Shmona 23,000 / Majdal Shams 10,500 (Likud)

_____

JERUSALEM DISTRICT (7)
Excludes annexed occupied east Jerusalem

1   Beit Shemesh: Beit Shemesh West and Central 75,000 (Likud)

2   East-Jerusalem Corridor: East Beit Shemesh 25,000 / Mevasseret Zion 24,000 / Abu Gosh 12,000 / Tzur Hadassah 7,500 (Likud)

3   Jerusalem North Central [predominately census area 8]: Me'a Sherim (United Torah Judaism)

4   Jerusalem North-West [predominately census area 9] (United Torah Judaism)

5   Jerusalem West [predominately census area 10] (Likud)

6   Jerusalem South-West [predominately census area 11, part 12] (Likud)

7   Jerusalem South-East [predominately census area 13, part 12] (Likud)

_____

JUDEA AND SAMARIA MAP (14)

Includes settler populations of annexed occupied east Jerusalem including Palestinian non-citizens of municipal residents of east Jerusalem

1   Alfe Menashe – Ariel: Ariel 18,700 / Alfe Menashe 8,000 / Oranit 8,000 / Karnei Shomron 7,000 / Elkana 4,000 (Likud)

2   Modin Ilit: Modin Ilit 60,000 (United Torah Judaism)

3   Samaria-Northern West Bank: Givat Ze'ev 16,000 / Beit El 6,000 / Geva Binyamin 5,000 / Eli 4,000 / Kedumin 4,000 / Har Adar 4,000 / Talmon 4,000 (Habayit Hayehudi)

4   Ramot: Ramot 50,000 (United Torah Judaism)

5   Ramat Schlomo: Ramat Schlomo 20,000 / South Pisgat Ze'ev 15,000 / Ramat Eshkol 6,800 / French Hill 6,600 (United Torah Judaism)

6   Pisgat Ze'ev: Pisgat Ze'ev 35,000 / Neve Yakov 24,000 (Likud)

7   Ma'ale Adumim: Ma'ale Adumim 40,000 / Kfar Adumim 4,000 (Likud)

8   Gilo-Har Homa: Gilo 40,000 / Har Homa 25,000 / Givat Hamatos 25,000 (Likud)

9   Beitar Ilit: Beitar Ilit 49,000 / part Gush Etzion 20,000 (United Torah Judaism)

10   Judea South West Bank: part Gush Etzion (south Jerusalem) 45,000 / East Talpiot 15,000 / Kiryat Arba 7,000 (Likud)

11   east Jerusalem – Beit Hanina: Beit Hanina 29,000
      (Joint List)
12   east Jerusalem – Shuafat: Shuafat 39,000 (Joint
      List)
13   east Jerusalem – Silwan: Silwan 40,000 / At Tur-As
      Sawana 24,000 (Joint List)
14   east Jerusalem: Jabel Mukaber 14,000 / Abu Tor
      14,000 / Sur Baher 15,000 / Um Tuba 4,000 (Joint
      List)

———

HAIFA (14)

1   Haifa West [predominately census areas 4, 5]
      (Likud)
2   Haifa North [predominately census areas 3, 6]
      (Labor)
3   Haifa South [predominately census areas 8, 9]
      (Labor)
4   Haifa East [predominately census areas 1, 2, 7]
      (Labor)
5   Mount Carmel: Tirat Carmel 19,000 / Kiryat Tivon
      18,000 / Daliyat el-Carmel 17,000 (Labor)
6   Kiryat Ata: Kiryat Ata 55,000 / Ibitin 3,000 (Likud)
7   Kiryat Bialik: Kiryat Bialik 39,000 / Nesher 23,000
      (Likud)
8   Kiryat Motskin-Yam: Kiryat Motskin 40,000 /
      Kiryat Yam 39,000 (Likud)
9   Zihron Ya'akov: Zihron Ya'akov 22,000 / Fureidis
      12,000 (Labor)
10   Hadera North: Hadera 25,000 / Ork Akiva 17,000 /
      Jisr az-Zarqa 14,000 / Caesarea 5,000 (Likud)
11   Hadera South: Hadera 65,000 (Likud)
12   Pardes Hana-Kakur: Pardes Hana-Kakur 38,000 /
      Kafir Qar'ia 18,000 / Binyamina Giv'at Ada 15,000
      (Labor)
13   Umm al-Fahm: Umm al-Fahm 52,000 / Ma'ale
      Iron 14,000 / Basma 9,000 (Joint List)
14   Baka el-Garbiya: Baka el-Garbiya 28,000 / Ar'ara
      24,000 / Jatt 11,000 (Joint List)

———

OVERALL ELECTION RESULT, 2015

Likud: 60
Labor (Zionist Union):   25
Joint List: 25
United Torah Judaism: 8
Shas: 1
Habayit Hayehudi: 1
Yesh Atid: 0
Yisrael Beiteinu: 0
Kulanu: 0
Meretz: 0

References

abbreviations

CBS   Israel Central Bureau of Statistics
PCBS   Palestinian Central Bureau of Statistics
FPRI   Foreign Policy Research Institute
Census 2008   Population Census 2008, Israel Central
               Bureau of Statistics, http://www.cbs.gov.
               il/census/census/
Q1 / Q3   first quarter / third quarter of year

INTRODUCTION

[1]   Greater Tel Aviv is understood as comprising at least the
      Tel Aviv District (1.3 million), Census 2008, Table 2a:
      Localities with 10,000 residents and more. Metropolitan
      Tel Aviv (depending on geographical definition) has over
      3.6 million residents.
[2]   Eran Razin and Igal Charney, 'Metropolitan dynamics in
      Israel: an emerging "metropolitan island state"?', *Urban
      Geography*, 36:8, 2015, 1131-48 (published online 17 Nov
      2015, http://dx.doi.org/10.1080/02723638.2015.1096117).
[3]   *ibid*. 6% of all settlers live with a 25km radius of down-
      town Tel Aviv. The figure rises to 10% if Ariel is included.
      Some 20% of Ariel residents commute to Tel Aviv to work.

———

1 – DOES SIZE MATTER?

1.1 – WHERE IS TEL AVIV?

[1]   Technically the municipality Jerusalem is Israel's largest
      city, with a population of 759,000, compared to the mu-
      nicipality Tel Aviv-Yafo, with 402,000. Greater Tel Aviv is
      understood as comprising at least the Tel Aviv District (1.3
      million), Census 2008.
[2]   Metropolitan Tel Aviv (depending on geographical defi-
      nition) has over 3.6 million residents, yet some 56% of
      municipal Jerusalem is outside of Israel proper (annexed
      east Jerusalem is 70km² out of 125km²) See Chapter 4.6 –
      Up the Road: the Semi-Detached City.
[3]   wikitravel.org (see note 1 above).
[4]   'The Bubble' is a long-established local moniker for Tel
      Aviv (a movie of the same name was released in 2006).
      Example of a typical media reference to the Tel Aviv
      Bubble is Michal Yudelman O'Dwyer, 'Secular, Israeli and
      Proud to Live in a Bubble', *Haaretz*, 26 March 2015.
      Our 'Contiguous Tel Aviv' map (page 46) extends into the
      West Bank to include commuter settlements. Israel

proper is understood as existing within the Green Line.

5. 'Bauhaus Tel Aviv' or the 'White City of Tel Aviv' is generally understood as a broad geographic area of central or downtown Tel Aviv. Technically the UNESCO 2003 designation (The White City of Tel Aviv – The Modern Movement) refers to three distinct geographic areas covering 140 hectares, generally bounded by Ben Gurion Boulevard to the north, Ibn Girol Street to the east, Allenby Street to the west, Begin Road to the south, whc.unesco.org/en/list/1096.

6. Ibid.

7. A total of 30.7% of residents of Tel Aviv-Yafo are aged between 20 and 34. In the most central part of the city, Census Area 3 (the heart of the 'White City'), it is 45.4%, Census 2008, Table 2a: Tel Aviv-Yafo – Percentage of those aged 20-24, 25-29, 30-34. A total of 24.3% of Tel Aviv-Yafo Jewish residents claim African and Asian descent. In Census Area 3 it is 19.3%; Area 4, 16.7%; and Area 5, 22.1%. Census 2008, Table 3a: Tel Aviv-Yafo – Percentage of Jews whose continent of origin is Africa and Asia.

8. Our 'Real Tel Aviv' population is calculated as follows (in thousands) : areas 32 (15.6), 33 (10.7), 34 (18.1), 51 (18.7), 52 (4.9), 54 (5.2), 55 (2.0), Census 2008, Table 3a: Statistical Areas (population in thousands). Note: only Israeli citizens are counted in the Israeli census; see Chapter 2.3 – Mapping the 'missing' persons of 'Postcards from Tel Aviv'.

9. Meretz is a member of the Socialist International and an observer member of the Party of European Socialists. Meretz has been defined as 'Israel's traditional secular-leftist party', Washington Post, March 2015, www.washingtonpost.com/news/worldviews/wp/2015/03/13/these-are-the-political-parties-battling-for-israels-future/?utm_ term=.da2db92d754c.

10. In the five immediate and contiguous Census Statistical Areas 51, 54, 55, 61 and 81, the Meretz vote exceeds 25% – the highest concentration in the country outside a handful of isolated kibbutzim in the north of the country. Tel Aviv-Yafo as a city voted for the centre-left (47.4%) in the 2015 elections – Zionist Union (Labor Party and Hatnua, 34.3%) and Meretz (13.1%) – over the parties of the non-Harridim political right – the Likud Party, Habayit Hayehudi and Yisrael Beiteinu (23.7%). Nationally the vote was reversed with the non-Haredi right receiving 35.2% versus the centre-left at 22.6%.

11. Tel Aviv is generally accepted to have been founded in 1909 as an extension to the port city of Jaffa or Yafo. www.tel-aviv.gov.il/en/aboutthecity/pages/history. aspx.

12. A total of 24.3% of Tel Aviv-Yafo Jewish residents claim African and Asian descent, Census 2008, Table 3a: Tel Aviv-Yafo – Percentage of Jews whose continent of origin is Africa and Asia.

13. ibid.

14. See note 2 above.

15. Israeli Census House Price Index: Year 2016, Q3 index for Tel Aviv (2,631), Gush Dan or Greater Tel Aviv Region (1,733), and Israel as a whole (1,429). This compares to Year 2001, Q1 index Tel Aviv (1,042), Gush Dan or Greater Tel Aviv Region (1,733), and Israel as a whole (644). That represents a 152.5% increase in Tel Aviv and a 12.9% increase in Israel, www.cbs.gov.il/ts/databank/search_databank_e.html?input_databank?input_ databank=housing.

16. The largest cities in Tel Aviv District include Tel Aviv-Yafo (pop. 402,000), Holon (185,000), Bnei Brak (172,000) and Ramat Gan (153,000), www.cbs.gov.il/ census/census.

17. See map 'Density Tel Aviv' (page 44). This maps a contiguous area of Greater Tel Aviv with a minimum density of 5,000 people per km².

18. Natalia Presman and Arie Arnon, 'Commuting patterns in Israel 1991-2004', Research Department, Bank of Israel, Discussion Paper no. 2006.04, August 2006.

19. Eran Razin and Igal Charney, 'Metropolitan dynamics in Israel: an emerging "metropolitan island state"?', Urban Geography, 36:8, 2015, 1131-48 (published online 17 Nov 2015, http://dx.doi.org/10.1080/02723638.2015.1096117).

20. Ibid.

21. It is estimated that 5% of the Qalqilya workforce work in Israel proper, Qalqilya City Profile, Applied Research Institute – Jerusalem, 2013.

22. 90% derived from following: Israelis are free to travel in all Israel proper and 40% of the West Bank (Area C, Oslo Accords). Gaza is 365km², the West Bank 5,655km². Gaza and the West Bank make up 22% of historic Palestine.

23. Metropolitan Los Angeles, 'Annual Estimates of the Resident Population: April 1, 2010 to July 1, 2013 – United States, Metropolitan Statistical Area; and for Puerto Rico', US Census Bureau, archived from the original on 15 August 2014; retrieved 29 August 2014.

24. UrbanRail.Net>Europe>Russia>Moskva Metro.

25. For comparison: London has an area of 1,569 km², pop. 8.5m, density 5,400 persons per km². Berlin has an area of 892 km², pop. 3.6m, density 4,000 persons per km².

_____

1.2 – THE LIE OF THE LAND

1. UrbanRail.Net>Europe>Russia>Moskva Metro

_____

2 – PICTURE TEL AVIV

2.2 – POSTCARDS FROM TEL AVIV

1. For visual simplicity we have used bands of percentages, e.g. 20-24, 25-29 rather than over use of "Less than, Greater than signs etc. For example, where the data is 24.6 or 24.8 etc we have included the cell/area in the 20-24 band.

2. Census 2008, Table 2a: Percentage of Jews born abroad who immigrated from 2002 and after.

3. Census 2008, Table 2a: Percentage of Jews whose continent of origin is Africa and the Percentage of Jews whose continent of origin is Asia. Note: the term Mizrahi (Eastern) technically refers to Jews descended from the Middle East and Asia; Sephardi refers to Jews of north African origin. In Israel today it is common for the term Mizrahi to apply to both.

4. Census 2008, Table 3b: Percentage of Jews born abroad who immigrated in 1990-2001.

5. Census 2008, Table 2a: Percentage of main religion.

6 Census 2008, Table 3b: Percentage of homes with just 1 room, Table 3b: Percentage of households with 1-room and 2-room dwellings.
7 Census 2008, Table 3b: Percentage of those aged 15 and over who walked as their main means of getting to work in the determinant week.
8 Census 2008, Table 3b: Percentage of those over 15 who are unskilled workers, Shapira and Neve Sha'anan, small statistics areas 814, 815, 816.
9 Census 2008, Table 3b: Percentage of households with one person in the household.
10 Census 2008, Table 2a: Males total thousands, Females total thousands.
11 Census 2008, Table 2b: Percentage of households with children up to age of 17.
12 Census 2008, Table 2b: Percentage of households residing in self-owned dwellings, and Percentage of households residing in rented dwellings, Statistical Area 943 (Kfar Shalem).
13 Census 2008, Table 3b: Percentage of households using two cars or more.

2.3 – MAPPING THE 'MISSING' PERSONS OF 'POSTCARDS FROM TEL AVIV'

1 www.tel-aviv.gov.il/en/Live/NewResidents/Pages/Olim ResidentDepartment.aspx.
2 www.cbs.gov.il/shnaton61/st_eng02.pdf, p.27 'Definitions: Persons not listed in the Population Register were not included in the population estimates, even if they had been staying in the country for more than one year. The population estimates also do not include foreign workers with work permits.'
3 Centre for International Migration and Integration, www.cimi.org.il.
4 www.ardc-israel.org/refugees-or-infiltrators.
5 How many foreigners work in Israel? www.ynetnews.com/articles/0,7340,L-4412537,00.html.
6 www.africanglobe.net/headlines/anti-african-sentiment-boils-israel/ and http://poliscihuji.wiki.huji.ac.il/ images/Immigration_Policy_Toward _Non_Jewish.pdf.
7 91.7% of the (2008 Census) population of Tel Aviv-Yafo is Jewish, with 27.2% of them foreign-born. The remaining 8.3% are split between Palestinians, almost all of whom are locally born, and ex-Soviet immigrants and their children who are not considered Jewish, the overwhelming proportion of whom were born abroad. Most of the additional 10% of 'missing persons' not counted by the Census are foreign-born (their children who were born in Israel make up a small proportion of that 10%). Taken together this generates an overall foreign-born population of approximately 33%.
8 Census 2008, Table 3a: Percentage of Jews born abroad (27.2%), and 'The Newest New Yorkers', NYC Planning 2013, https://www1.nyc.gov/site/planning/ data -maps/nyc-population/newest-new-yorkers-2013.page.
9 'Tel Aviv Global City – Work Process' 2011-2012, Tel Aviv-Yafo Municipality Global City Unit.

2.4 – 508 IMMUTABLE ZONINGS?

1 These 508 Zonings or land-use classifications are shared by all municipalities and are taken from the 'National Planning Administration Land Use Purpose Plan'. The computerized system is called MAVAAT http://iplan.gov.il/Pages/Professional%20Tools/Regulation2006/working_aids/Designated_land_nispachim.aspx.
2 A detailed review of role of the 'TABA process' is outlined in *Is Public Participation making Urban Planning more Democratic? The Israeli Experience*, 185-202; published on-line 9 Dec 2010. www.tandfonline.com/doi/citedby/10.1080/14649350307979?scroll=top &need Access=true.

2.5 – THE GREEN CITY?

1 Tel Aviv City Council and World Cities Culture Forum, www.worldcitiescultureforum.com/data/of-public-green-space-parks-and-gardens.
2 Tel Aviv Yafo City Development Plan, Table 3.2: TA/5000 Local Development (descriptive)
3 Tel Aviv Yafo City Development Plan maps and Israeli Population Census, 2008.
4 *Ibid.* Also see Chapter 2.3 – Mapping the 'missing' persons of 'Postcards from Tel Aviv'.
5 *Ibid.*
6 Hyde Park, London, is 147ha. Our city centre has an area of 3.6km² and a population of 72,000, and corresponds to the following census Small Areas: 431-433, 325-326, 334-337, 341-349, 512-513, Census 2008, pop. 72,100; overall city pop. 402,600. The population in 2015 is estimated to be 433,000.
7 Working on assumptions of a 5kmph average walking speeds, the distance is 1.2km-1.4km.
8 Ditto.
9 187,000 existing households, assuming additional 2.5% housing units (unoccupied), 3.5 residential floors per block, 2.5 homes per floor, that's 21,906 blocks, 68m² floor area per unit, and ground-floor entrance area occupying 20% of each plot.
10 Massachusetts Institute of Technology and Treepedia, http://senseable.mit.edu/treepedia.
11 The census tells us the number rooms in all the homes in Tel Aviv-Yafo: 1-room, 12.1%; 2-room, 28.4%; 3-room, 33.7%; 4-room, 17.4%; 5-room, 6.5%; 6 or more, 1.9%; Census 2008, Table 3b: Localities with 2,000 residents and more, Population Household – total (thousands). Assuming the following differential balcony spaces per unit size – 1-room, 0.25; 2-room, 0.5; 3-room, 0.75; 4-room, 1.0; 5-room, 1.25; 6-room or more, 1.5 – we then make assumptions for whether these balcony spaces are open or have been enclosed. Newer, more spacious and suburban typologies are more likely to leave balconies 'open'. The assumptions for the proportion of open balconies is as follows: 1-room, 0.5; 2-room, 0.6; 3-room, 0.7; 4-room, 0.8; 5-room, 0.85; 6-room or more, 0.9. The Census tells us there are 187,000 household in Tel Aviv-Yaffo. We assume 191,675 homes (an additional 2.5%, to account for unoccupied/newly built homes).

12 *Ibid.*
13 For our city centre areas, see note 6 above.
14 Census 2008, Table 2b: Percentage of households with one person in the household.
15 *Ibid.*

———

3 – EXTENSIONS

3.2 – THE SOIL OF ISRAEL AND THE RISE OF THE TEL AVIVIAN PENTHOUSE

1 www.emporis.com/city/100280/tel-aviv-yafo-israel.
2 *Ibid.*
3 www.timesofisrael.com/tel-aviv-to-get-israels-first-100-floor-skyscraper.
4 Ehud Barak sold his previous home in the 31-storey Akirov Towers on Pinkas Street, Tel Aviv. He apparently bought five apartments in this 34-apartment scheme, *Globes*, 10 February 2014.
5 Census of population maps http://gis.cbs.gov.il/mifkad_en/ and Election results, http://z.ynet.co.il/short/content/2015/elections_map2015.
6 www.haaretz.com/snobbism-with-a-loss-for-all-1.97414.
7 With the exception of Qiryat Malakhi, the seven most socio-economically deprived Jewish communities in Israel proper (excluding Haredi communities and Jerusalem) are all located on the periphery, either the far north or in Negev in the south. A plurality of all seven voted Likud in the 2015 Knesset elections – Zevat, Ofakim, Qiryat Malki, Mitzpe Ramon, Yeroham and Hatzor HaGlilit. The average proportion of Jews residing in these communities who claim African or Asian ancestry is 40.1%. This peaks at 48 % in Qiryat Malki, Mizpe Ramon, Yeroham. The proportion of Jews in Israel who claim African or Asian ancestry is 29.8%. Put another way, the poorest seven non-Haredi Jewish communities in Israel proper have a 40% higher proportion of residents who claim largely north African or Middle Eastern ancestry, Census 2008, Table 2a: Percentage of Jews whose continent of origin is Asia and Percentage of Jews whose continent of origin is Africa. The Israeli CBS in 2013 ranked 255 Israeli local authorities in order of their 'socio-economic' development, www.cbs.gov.il/hodaot2016n/24_16_33 0t1.pdf.
8 Can you guess which Israeli party's voters support settlements the most? 83% of voters of United Torah Judaism (almost exclusively Haredi Akenazi Party) favoured settlement expansion – more than in any other party, www.haaretz.com/israel-news/.premium-1.771242.
9 Census 2008, Table 2a: Percentage of Jews whose continent of origin is Asia and Percentage of Jews whose continent of origin is Africa.
10 Census 2008, Table 2a: Percentage of Jews whose continents of origin are America and Oceania. Mizrahi Jews outnumber Ashkenazi North American Jews by a ratio of 6:1 in Israel. In the six settlements of Beit El, Ofra, Shilo, Eli, Talmon and Tekoa, Ashkenazi North American Jews marginally outnumber Jews of African and Asian (Middle Eastern) descent.

3.3 – CHASING SPACE IN THE WHITE CITY OF TEL AVIV

1 'Israeli protests: 430,000 take to streets to demand social justice', www.theguardian.com/world/2011/sep/04/israel-protests-social-justice.
2 OECD, analytical house prices indicators, https://stats.oecd.org/Index.aspx?DataSetCode=House_Prices#.
3 *Ibid.*
4 *Ibid.*
5 *Ibid.* Israeli Housing Index was as follows: 82.7 (2003), 78.6 (2008), 116.7 (2013).
6 World Bank, data.worldbank.org/country/Israel.
7 CBS Database for Construction: Construction Homes Finished, 2017.
8 www.globes.co.il/serveen/fcurrency/historyrates.asp?Currency=USD&Month=8&Year=2012/.
9 www.forbes.com/sites/jessecolombo/2014/04/29/why-israels-boom-is-actually-a-bubble-destined-to-pop/#2dbc38bc1e63/. In early 2009 the US Dollar was worth 4.2 NIS; by mid-2011 it was worth 3.4 NIS.
10 *Ibid.*
11 www.timesofisrael.com/did-a-little-noticed-tax-exemption-law-turn-israel-into-a-criminals-paradise/
12 See note 7 above.
13 Jphn Benzaquen, 'The state of Israeli real estate: problems and solutions, *Jerusalem Post*, 2 Julu 2017.
14 *Ibid.*
15 See note 7 above.
16 2015 Israeli population estimate, Israeli CBS, List of localities, in alphabetical order (pdf), www.cbs.gov.il/ishuvim/reshimalefishem.pdf, retrieved 16 October 2016.
17 Israeli Census House Price Index: Year 2016, Q3 index for Tel Aviv (2,631), Gush Dan or Greater Tel Aviv Region (1,733), Israel as a whole (1,429). This compares to Year 2001, Q1 index Tel Aviv (1,042), Gush Dan or Greater Tel Aviv Region (1,733), Israel as a whole (644). That represents a 152.5% increase in Tel Aviv and a 12.9% increase in Israel, www.cbs.gov.il/ts/databank/search_databank_e.html?input_databank?input _databank=housing.
18 See note 7 above.
19 Jewish Virtual Library, Settlements Population (Judea Samaria, excl. annexed east Jerusalem, was 303,900), www.jewishvirtuallibrary.org/jewish-settlements-population-1970-present.
20 Census 2008, Table 2b – Percentage of households with one person in the household.
21 Census 2008, Table 2b – Percentage of households with 6 persons in the household.
22 OECD, fertility rates, Israel, https://data.oecd.org/pop/fertility-rates.htm.
23 Tel Aviv District largest cities: Tel Aviv-Yafo, Holon, Bnei Brak, Ramat Gan and Bat Yam.
24 Population density of Israel is 377 person per km². Of those nation states with a population greater than 5 million people, Israel is the 12th most densely populated nation on earth. Combined, Israel and Palestine has a density of population that would place it 7th.
25 For detailed explanation and critique of TAMA 38 see Bimkom – Israeli Planning Association, http://bimkom.

org/eng/wp-content/uploads/Tama-38-English.pdf.

26 *Strategic Policy for Underground Uses*, Amos Brandeis, Planning & Architecture for Tel Aviv-Yafo Municipality (2017)

27 www.emporis.com/city/100280/tel-aviv-yafo-israel

28 See note 18 above.

29 World Cities Culture Forum, Percentage of public green space and gardens www.worldcitiescultureforum.com/data/of-public-green-space-parks-and-gardens.

30 *Ibid.*

31 Census 2008 tells us there are 187,000 households in Tel Aviv-Yafo. With average building heights 4 storeys, and 4 units per floor, that's an estimated 11,688 residential blocks. A fifth of these is 2,338 blocks; 4 extra residential units (1 additional floor) amounts to 9,350 new homes.

32 House construction in Tel Aviv District: 2016: 6,776 residential units; 2015: 6,941; and 2014: 6,007. See note 5 above.

33 Census 2008, Table 3b (col. FZ): Percentage of homes with two rooms or less.

34 Census 2008, Table 3b (col. FZ): Statistical Area 3 (Tel Aviv-Yaffo) has 39,900 households and 61,000 people. Homes with two rooms or less is 61.4%. Statistical Area 5 (Tel Aviv-Yafo) has 21,600 households with 36,600 people. Homes with 2 rooms or less is 54.4%.

35 Census 2008, Statistical areas 3 and 5 (Tel Aviv-Yafo). More than 50% of all households are single occupancy. Table 2b – Percentage of households with one person in the household.

36 www.numbeo.com/property-investment/ rankings.jsp.

_____

3.4 – SUICIDAL GEOGRAPHY

1 B'Tselem, Israeli Information Center for Human Rights in the Occupied Territories, www.btselem.org/ statistics.

2 This figure includes suicide bomb-attacks only, and excludes non-suicide bomb-attacks, such as the June 2016 Tel Aviv shooting at Sarona Market when four people were murdered by gunfire by Palestinians assailants.

3 See note 1 above.

_____

3.6 – ELEVEN AND A HALF ROTHSCHILDS

1 In the five immediate and contiguous Statistical Areas (51, 54, 55, 61, 81), the Meretz exceeds 25% of the vote, Census 2008, http://gis.cbs.gov.il/ mifkad_en, and election results, http://z.ynet.co.il/short/content/2015/ elections_map2015/. This is the highest in the country outside a handful of isolated *kibbutzim* in the north of the country.

2 Deir Ballut Town Profile, Applied Research Institute – Jerusalem, 2013, http://vprofile.arij.org/ salfit/pdfs/vprofile/Deir%20Ballut_ tp_en.pdf.

_____

3.7 – BNEI BRAK AND THE ARCHITECTURE OF EXPANSION

1 Bniei Brak, pop. 183,000 in 2015, second to Tel Aviv-Yafo

and Holon in the Tel Aviv District, Israeli CBS, List of localities, in alphabetical order, www.cbs.gov.il/ishuvim/reshimalefishem.pdf, retrieved 16 October 2016.

2 Census of population maps http://gis.cbs.gov.il/mifkad _en/, and election results, http://z.ynet.co.il/ short/content/2015/elections_map2015/.

3 https://en.wikipedia.org/wiki/List_of_cities_ by_population_density.

4 The density of population in Kolkata is 24,000 persons per km², Census of India, 'Kolkata Municipal Corporation Demographics', retrieved 3 June 2016.

5 Israeli CBS, List of localities, in Alphabetical order (pdf), www. cbs.gov.il/ reshimalefishem.pdf, retrieved 16 October 2016. Tel Aviv-Yafo had a population of 433,892.

6 Census 2008, Table 2a: Statistical Area 2 (43,100), Area 3 (37,700), and Area 4 (44,800) only (82.7% of pop.).

7 Kowloon, Hong Kong, density of 43,000 persons per km² (pop. 2 million, area 47km²).

8 Census 2008, Table 3b: Percentage of households with 4 children up to age 17 in the household.

9 Census 2008, Table 2a: Percentage of those aged 0 to 19.

10 Census 2008, Table 2b: Percentage of households residing in a housing density of 2 persons or more per room.

11 CBS, Reference Table 1, Socio-economic index 2013 of local authorities in ascending order of index values, index value, rank and cluster. Of 255 ranked Israeli local authorities, Bnei Brak is ranked 17th poorest.

12 Israeli Census House Price Index – Year 2016, Q3 index for Tel Aviv (2,631), Gush Dan or Greater Tel Aviv Region (1,733), and Israel as a whole (1,429). This compares to Year 2001, Q1 index Tel Aviv (1,042), Gush Dan or Greater Tel Aviv Region (1,733), and Israel as a whole (644). That represents a 152.5% increase in Tel Aviv and a 12.9% increase in Israel, Israeli Census house prices www.cbs. gov.il/ts/databank/search_databank_e.html?input_databank?input_databank=housing.

13 Census 2008, Table 3b: Percentage of households with five-rooms dwellings or more.

_____

4 – GREEN LINE EXURBIA

4.1 – THE EXURBAN GEOGRAPHY OF TEL AVIV – ALFE MENASHE

1 Defined as 'quality-of-life settlers who came to the settlements for their low housing prices and relatively high quality of life, rather than for ideological reasons', http:// peacenow.org.il/en/west-bank-settlements-facts-and-figures.

2 Census 2008, Table 3b: Percentage of Households with 5 or more rooms (Israel 19.8%). Of the hundreds of communities, *moshavim*, settlements, towns and cities listed in the Israeli census, only Kfar HaOranim, pop. 2,700 (87.8%), and Tel Mond, pop. 11,900 (87.8%) have larger homes. (Note: 2 rooms in Israel is usually a 1-bedroom apartment with separate kitchen.)

3 Peace Now put the figures as follows: Ideological 39%, Extreme Ideological 1%, Not Ideological 31%, Ultra-Orthodox 29%. Are quality-of-life settlements, by defini-

tion, non Ultra Orthodox? Is largely secular Ma'ale Adumin, east of Jerusalem, pop. 38,000, where 47% voted Likud and a further 12% voted left and centre-left (Meretz, Labor-Zionist Union and Yesh Atid) a quality-of-life settlement? Is Ariel, a settlement 16km inside the West Bank, which also has similar voting pattern? http://peacenow.org.il/ en/west-bank-settlements-facts -and-figures.

4   Election results 2015 mapped, http://z.ynet.co.il/ short /content/2015/ elections_map2015/.

5   See Google map of Qalqilya, page 160.

6   Census 2008, Table 2a: Percentage of main religion.

7   *Ibid.*

8   *Ibid.*

9   *Ibid.*

───────

4.2 – AN ISRAELI CITY OVER THE GREEN LINE

1   Benjamin 'Bibi' Netanyahu speech to the US Congress, Washington DC, 24 May 2011, www.theglobeandmail. com/news/world/transcript-of-prime-minister-netanyahus -address-to-us-congress/article635191/? page=all.

2   *Ibid.*

3   Ravi Regal and Eyal Weizman (eds), *A Civilian Occupation – the politics of Israeli architecture* (Verso, 2003).

4   Census 2008, Table 3b (col. CK): Percentage of those aged 15 and over who worked in 2008 outside of their residential locality.

───────

4.3 – BACK DOOR TO THE SEAMLESS ZONE

1   BADIL, Resource Center for Palestinian Residency & Refugee Rights 2012 http://reliefweb.int/sites/reliefweb. int/files/resources/Bulletin-25.pdf.

───────

4.4 – SEAMLESS SEGREGATION
AND GREATER TEL AVIV

1   Census 2008, Table 5a: Localities with up to 500 residents.

2   *Ibid.* Type of Locality.

3   A note on 'Non-Jews and Ex-Soviet Union Immigrants': A significant portion of the immigrants from the former Soviet Union either lack official religious-ethnic classification or are considered 'Non-Jews' as they are from mixed-marriage families of some Jewish origin. The city of Ashkelon is 'just' 89.3% Jewish, with 44.2% of its Jewish population born abroad. Of those born abroad, 55.6% arrived between 1990 and 2001, a period that coincides with the break up of the Soviet Union and mass immigration to Israel. Over one million arrived to Israel during this period. By comparison, in Tel Aviv-Yafo 27.2% of its Jewish population was born abroad, and of those born abroad just 28.4% arrived between 1990 and 2001. Ariel, a settlement of 18,000 in the West Bank, is 81.6% Jewish, but revealingly some 77.3% of its Jewish immigrant population arrived between 1990 and 2001. There are unlikely to be many Palestinians living in Ariel. Conversely the wealthy city of Ra'anana is 98.1% Jewish. Just 30.9% of those were born abroad and just 27.5% of those born abroad arrived between 1990 and 2001. It is clear that predominantly Jewish Israeli cities with very high levels of Jewish immigration in 1990s (ex-citizens of the USSR) have relatively lower levels of Jews as a proportion of their overall population.

4   See note 3.

5   The High Court of Justice in Israel in September 2014 upheld a law (by 5 to 4) allowing small communities to screen potential new members via admissions committees. www.haaretz.com/israel-news/.premium-1.616391.

6   Census 2008, Table 3a: Localities with 2,000 residents and more.

7   *Ibid.*

8   *Ibid.*

9   *Ibid.*

10   Census 2008, Table 5a: Localities with up to 500 residents.

11   *Ibid.* Main Religion – Moslem or Christian or Jewish or Druze

12   *Ibid.* Percentage of Main Religion.

13   Census 2008, Table 4a: Localities with 501-1,999 residents.

14   Malkit Shoshan, *Atlas of the Conflict, Israel-Palestine* (010 Publishers, Rotterdam, 2010) p.340.

15   In January 2015 the Israeli Interior Ministry gave figures of 389,250 Israeli citizens living in the West Bank and a further 375,000 Israeli citizens living in east Jerusalem. www.breakingisraelnews.com/26966/jewish-population-in-judea-and-samaria-growing-significantly/#1XZZdXz ITyBjVZd3.97. Arutz Sheva (Israeli National News), www. israelnationalnews.com/Articles/Article.aspx/18210#. VpK885scTIU.

16   Btselem, www.btselem.org/settlements/statistics, updated May 2015. There are an estimated 547,000 settlers in the West Bank. This figure is derived from two sources. According to data provided by Israel's CBS, at the end of 2013, 350,010 people were living in the settlements of the West Bank, excluding east Jerusalem. According to data provided by the Jerusalem Institute for Israel Studies, the population of the Israeli neighborhoods in east Jerusalem was 196,890 at the end of 2012.

17   As reported in *Haaretz* newspaper, October 2016, www. haaretz.com/israel-news/premium-1.746087.

18   The number of settlers living in 128 illegal settlements in the occupied West Bank, excluding Jerusalem, has reached 406,302, an Israeli report revealed. The report was issued by former Member of the Knesset, Yaakov Katz, www.middleeastmonitor.com/20160219-israeli-report-more-than-400000-settlers-in-west-bank/.

19   The report was from 2012 – www.theatlantic.com/international/archive/2012/08/dani-dayans-war-can-israeli-settlers-control-both-the-west-bank-and-themselves/ 260672/.

20   www.jpost.com/National-News/Housing-minister-sees-50-percent-more-settlers-in-West-Bank-by-2019-352501. Construction & Housing Minister, Uri Ariel, is a member of the hardline Habayit Hayehudi (Jewish Home) party in Israeli Prime Minister Benjamin Netanyahu's conservative coalition government.

[21] Jerusalem Institute of Israel Studies, http://en. jerusalem institute.org.il/.upload/Jerusalem%20%20 English.pdf.

[22] The CBS estimated there were 8.6 million Israelis by September 2016. Somewhat confusingly this figure includes some 300,000 Palestinians of east Jerusalem, who are residents but not citizens of Israel.

_____

4.6 – UP THE ROAD: THE SEMI-DETACHED CITY

[1] The Book of Revelation (or the Revelation to John or the Apocalypse of John), 21:2.

[2] At time of writing, the United States of America announced a plan to open an embassy in Jerusalem in May 2018.

[3] In the years following the passing of the 'Basic Law: Jerusalem, the Capital of Israel' (known as the 'Jerusalem Law') by the Knesset on 30 July 1980, and the passing of the UN Security Council Resolution 478, adopted on 20 August 1980 (one of seven UNSC resolutions condemning Israel's attempted annexation of east Jerusalem), all foreign embassies in Israel relocated to the Greater Tel Aviv region. The last to relocate from Jerusalem were Costa Rica and El Salvador in 2006.

[4] CBS, List of localities in alphabetical order, www.cbs.gov.il/ishuvim/reshimalefishem.pdf.

[5] *Ibid.*

[6] Census 2008, Table 3a: Localities with 2,000 residents and more. Also Maya Choshen and Michal Korach, *Jerusalem: Facts and Trends 2009/2010* (Jerusalem Institute for Israel Studies), http://en.jerusaleminstitute.org.il/upload/ facts-2010-eng%20(1).pdf.

[7] 'After the annexation of east Jerusalem, Israel granted permanent residency status to residents in the annexed areas present at the time. Permanent residents are permitted, if they wish and meet certain conditions, to receive Israeli citizenship. These conditions include swearing allegiance to the State, proving that they are not citizens of any other country, and showing some knowledge of Hebrew. For political reasons, most of the residents do not request Israeli citizenship.' www.btselem.org/jerusalem/legal_status.

[8] See Chapter 4.4 for 'What is the true settler population?', page 184.

[9] The area of annexed east Jerusalem is 70km². The total area of Municipal Jerusalem is 125km² (55km² inside the Green Line or Israel proper). Hence, 56% of total municipal area is annexed. Between 1948 and June 1967, Jerusalem was divided in two: west Jerusalem (38km²) under Israeli control, and east Jerusalem (6km²) ruled by Jordan. In June 1967, Israel annexed some 70km², to the municipal boundaries of west Jerusalem. These annexed territories included not only the part of Jerusalem that had been under Jordanian rule, but also an additional 64km² in the West Bank.

[10] In 2008 the Tel Aviv-Yafo population was 402,000. West Jerusalem, or 'Israeli Jerusalem', part of Israel proper as recognised by international law, was 304,000 in 2008.

[11] 'The low voter turn-out in Jerusalem is in part the result of the decision of most of the Arab population to refrain from voting entirely; they view such participation as recognising Israeli control over east Jerusalem, and as co-operating with Israeli governmental and municipal authorities by taking part in their selection'. http://en.jerusaleminstitute.org.il/?cmd=datast.146&act=read &id =218#.WX2U_oiGN.

[12] Census 2008, Table 3b: Percentage of Jewish men aged 15 and over who studied in a *yeshiva.*

[13] Census 2008, Table 2a: Percentage of Main Religion by sub-quarter (sub-quarter 54 is 76.2% Jewish). The Israeli census officially counts Palestinians in annexed east Jerusalem but evidently doesn't give detailed breakdowns on any socio-economic or demographic data in Census. (Quarters 2, 3, 6, 14 and 15 are missing.)

[14] The Israeli CBS in 2013 ranked 255 Israeli local authorities in order of 'socio-economic' development. The ranking criteria included, amongst other things, the proportion of those with third-level education, employment levels, standard of living and age structure. Each settlement, city or village was given an overall score ranging from 1 (lowest) to 10 (highest).

[15] In 2016 the Municipality doubled its municipal vacancy tax. Ref: a 100m² vacant resident will now have to pay $5,800 annually to City Hall. www.jpost.com/Israel-News/Bill-to-double-property-tax-on-Jerusalems-ghost-apartments-approved-439361.

[16] Census 2008, Table 2a: Percentage of those aged 0-4, aged 5-9, aged 10-14.

[17] Official Knesset site, Current Members. Note only 86 out of 120 list their home residence. https://knesset.gov.il/mk/eng/MKIndex_Current_eng. asp? view=1.

[18] See note 2 above.

_____

4.7 – TRAM SPACE

[1] Jewish Virtual Library, www.jewishvirtuallibrary.org/comprehensive-listing-of-terrorism-victims-in-israel.

_____

5 – INVISIBLE GEOGRAPHIES

5.1 – THE ROAD TO ARIEL

[1] Census 2008, Table 2a: Localities with 2,000 residents and more.

[2] According to the PCBS, in 2007 Tulkarm had a population of 51,300 while its adjacent refugee camp had a population of 10,641.

[3] *Ibid.*

[4] In March 2017, in a 54 to 48 vote, the Knesset passed preliminary legislation on the so-called controversial 'Muzein bill'.

[5] The Ministerial Committee for Legislation voted in favour of the bill, and it will now proceed to the Knesset floor for further readings before becoming law. The bill states that 'the national language is Hebrew' and downgrades Arabic's status to 'a special status in the State,' adding that 'its speakers have the right to language-accessible state services'.

_____

5.2 – THE SHIFTING IDEOLOGY OF A SIMPLE MAP

1   Malkit Shoshan, *Atlas of the Conflict, Israel-Palestine* (010 Publishers, Rotterdam, 2010) p.35.
2   *Ibid*. West Bank and Gaza strip 6,220km²; Israel (inside the Green Line) 20,770km²; Sinai Peninsula 60,000km²; Golan Heights 1,800km².
3   See top illustration, page 227.
4   The Yesha Council (Mo'etzet Yesha), which is the Hebrew acronym for **Ye**huda **Sh**omron, **A**za (lit. 'Judea Samaria and Gaza Council'), is an umbrella organisation of municipal councils of Jewish settlements in the West Bank (and formerly in the Gaza Strip), known by the Hebrew acronym Yesha.
5   http://fathomjournal.org/1967-why-more-and-more-israeli-jews-think-the-settlements-are-in-israel/.

5.3 – MINI ISRAEL

1   Mini Israel, along with a section of Route 1 between Tel Aviv and Jerusalem, is located between two Green Lines in the Latrun region. From Ma'ale HaHamisha, west of Jerusalem, the 1949 Armistice Agreement line splits in two, running somewhat parallel, in places up to 3.5km apart, before they meet again, 40km later, near the town of Budrus.

5.4 – INVISIBLE GEOGRAPHY AND THE CENSUS

1   Census 2008, Summary file of broad geographical units, Sheet 1(a) of the Israeli census has a singular and arguably exceptional oddity. Sheet 1 (a) divides the country into 7 'Districts' and 51 'Natural Regions'. For each of these 'Districts', 'Sub Districts' and 'Natural Regions', the population, the total geographical area and density of population is calculated. Although Judea and Samaria is not an official district in Israel, it's given the code number District 7. The other six districts have areas – Jerusalem 653, Northern 4473, Haifa 866, Central 1294, Tel Aviv 172, Southern 14 185.
2   *Ibid*.
3   Palestinian residents of east Jerusalem (only) are counted in the census.
4   The settler population (outside annexed east Jerusalem) has since increased to over 400,000. See Chapter 4.4 for 'What is the true settler population?', page 184.

5.5 – CONSTITUENCY GEOGRAPHY

1   Israeli Democracy Institute, https://en.idi.org.il/articles/6916.
2   The Municipality currently has 31 councillors from 14 different groupings including members from 'City for All Faction' (1), 'Green Faction' (1), 'Social Justice Faction' (1) 'Young Faction' (3), www.tel-aviv.gov.il/en/aboutthe Municipality/Pages/City Council.aspx
3   Israel operates a single national constituency of 120

members under a party list system (closed list system where factions/parties decide). The Netherlands also operates as a single national constituency, but has 20 electoral districts that play a role in who gets elected from party lists.
4   'The general framework for the elections was laid down in article 4 of the Basic Law: The Knesset is to be elected in general, country-wide, direct, equal, secret and proportional elections. The qualifying threshold is currently 3.25%. Until the elections to the 13th Knesset, the qualifying threshold was only 1%. During the 16th Knesset, the law changed the threshold from 1.5% to 2%, and the 19th Knesset raised the threshold to 3.25%.' www.knesset.gov.il/description/eng/eng_mimshal_beh.htm.
5   Tamar Friedman, 'Reforming the Israeli Electoral System: What's needed? What's possible?', FPRI, 13 May 2015, www.fpri.org/article/2015/ 05. 'Single constituency ... makes sense in the context of the emerging Israeli state because Israel is a very small country geographically and did not have strong regional distinctions at its birth.'
6   www.jewishvirtuallibrary.org/population-of-israel-1948-present.
7   Amotz Asa-El, 'Israel's Electoral Complex', *Azure*, 31, 2008, pp.25-48, http://azure.org.il/include/print.hp? id= 419.
8   Malkit Shoshan, *Atlas of the Conflict, Israel-Palestine* (010 Publishers, Rotterdam, 2010).
9   Hasan Afif El-Hasan, *'Israel or Palestine? Is the Two-State Solution already Dead?'* (Algora Publishing, New York, 2010), p.113; Begin Menachem, *In the Underground: Writing and Documents*, 4 vols (Hadar, Tel Aviv, 1975-77) vol. 4, p.70.
10 In 1981 Israel passed the 'Golan Heights Law' which is widely accepted as an unofficial but de facto annexation by Israel.
11 The 'Jerusalem Law' is the common name for the Basic Law: Jerusalem, Capital of Israel, passed by the Knesset on 30 July 1980. Its text includes the statement that 'Jerusalem, complete and united, is the capital of Israel.' The United Nations Security Council Resolution 478, adopted on 20 August 1980, is one of seven UNSC resolutions condemning Israel's attempted annexation of east Jerusalem. Following the passing of the Jerusalem Law and the UNSC Resolution, all foreign embassies in Israel relocated (over time) from Jerusalem to the Greater Tel Aviv region.
12 See note 5 above.
13 www.jewishvirtuallibrary.org/jewish-and-non-jewish-population-of-israel-palestine-1517-present.
14 *Ibid*.
15 705,200 Israeli Palestinians live in the Northern District, which has a total population of 1,320,800. In 2008, they made up 53% of the Northern District's population, making it Israel's only district with an Arab majority. 44% of the Arab population lives in this district. CBS, 'The Arab population in Israel – 2008', https://web. archive.org/web/20100401030834/www1.cbs.gov.il/www/statistical/ arab_popo8e.pdf.
16 See 'The geography of Squeezed Zionism', page 307.
17 In 1984 a bill based on David Ben-Gurion's original model of 120 Knesset members (MKs) elected in 120 regions

passed a first reading in the Knesset. In 1958 Yosef Serlin of the General Zionists proposed an electoral reform that would divide the country into 30 regions, each of which would elect three lawmakers, while the remaining 30 MKs would be elected nationally. In 1972 a bill based on this system passed a first reading. In 1987 a bill sponsored by the Labor Party, calling for the election of 80 MKs in 20 districts, and 40 MKs nationwide, passed a first reading. In 1988 a bill sponsored by MK Mordechai Virshubski (Ratz) and 43 other MKs offered two alternatives: one proposed the creation of 20 districts that would elect four lawmakers each, while the remaining 40 would be elected nationally; the other proposed that 60 MKs would be elected in 60 districts, with the remaining 60 MKs elected nationally. This too passed a first reading.

[18] See Chapter 5.7 – Settling for Less (page 265).

[19] See election results by city, http://z.ynet.co.il/short/content/2015/elections_map2015/.

[20] Israel Democracy Institute, 'Reforming Israel's Political System: Recommendations and Action Plan', 2011, p.40, http://185.6.64.65:5300/media/2077306/PoliticalReform Booklet.pdf.

[21] See Chapter 4.4 for 'What is the true settler population?', page 184.

[22] Asa-El, 'Israel's Electoral Complex, op. cit.

[23] Israel Democracy Institute, 'Reforming Israel's Political System: Recommendations and Action Plan, op. cit.

[24] See Appendix for 120 single-seat member constituencies (page 320).

[25] www.electoralcommission.org.uk/find-information-by-subject/elections-and-referendums/past-elections-and-referendums/uk-general-elections/2005-uk-general-elect ion-results.

[26] http://esm.ubc.ca/CA93/results.html.

[27] See Chapter 4.4 for 'What is the true settler population?', page 184.

[28] 'DEFINITIONS: Persons not listed in the Population Register were not included in the population estimates, even if they had been in the country for more than one year. The population estimates also do not include foreign workers with work permits.' www.cbs.gov.il/shnaton61/ st_eng02.pdf.

[29] The Golani Druze, with just 18,000 residents, may sway our single-seat constituency of Golan-Kiryat Shmona. In and of themselves, as a single voting block, they are unlikely to deliver enough votes to elect.

[30] Jerusalem Institue for Policy Research 2008, http://en. jerusaleminstitute.org. il/?cmd =datast.146&act=read& id=218#.WX2U_oiGN. This paper discusses Palestinian voter turnout.

[31] See Chapter 4.4 for 'What is the true settler population?' page 184.

[32] Judea and Samaria map: If Israel and the occupied West Bank had electoral constituencies, the settler population would justify 10 seats in the Israeli Knesset:

1 Alfe Menashe-Ariel: Ariel 18,700 / Alfe Menashe 8,000 / Oranit 8,000 / Karnei Shomron 7,000 / Elkana 4,000 (Likud)

2 Modi'in Ilit 60,000 (United Torah Judaism)

3 Samaria-Northern West Bank: Givat Ze'ev 16,000 / Beit El 6,000 / Geva Binyamin 5,000 / Eli 4,000 / Kedumin 4,000 / Har Adar 4,000 / Talmon 4,000 (Habayit Hayehudi)

4 Ramot 50,000 (United Torah Judaism)

5 Ramat Schlomo: Ramat Schlomo 20,000 / South Pisgat Ze'ev 15,000 / Ramat Eshkol 6,800 / French Hill 6,600 (United Torah Judaism)

6 Pisgat Ze'ev: Pisgat Ze'ev 35,000 / Neve Yakov 24,000 (Likud)

7 Ma'ale Adumin: Ma'ale Adumin 40,000 / Kfar Adumin 4,000 (Likud)

8 Gilo-Har Homa: Gilo 40,000 / Har Homa 40,000 / Givat Hamatos 25,000 (Likud)

9 Beitar Illit: Beitar Illit 49,000 / Part Gush Etzion 15,000 (United Torah Judaism)

10 Judea South West Bank: part Gush Etzion (south Jerusalem) 40,000 / East Talpiot 15,000 / Kiryat Arba 7,000 (Likud).

[33] Election results 2015, http://z.ynet.co.il/short/content/2015/elections_map2015/.

[34] Official Knesset site, Current Members. Note only 86 out of 120 list their home residence. https://knesset. gov.il/mk/eng/MKIndex_ Current_eng.asp? view=1.

[35] Ibid. The settler population (including annexed east Jerusalem) is estimated to be 700,000. See Chapter 4.4 for 'What is the true settler population?', page 184.

[36] Ibid. Also CBS, List of localities in alphabetical order, population taken from 2015 census estimates, www.cbs.gov.il/ishuvim/reshimalefishem.pdf 2015.

[37] Ibid.

[38] Ibid.

[39] Ibid.

5.6 – BUTTERFLY STATE

1 http://fathomjournal.org/1967-why-more-and-more-israeli-jews-think-the-settlements-are-in-israel/.

5.7 – SETTLING FOR LESS?

[1] See Chapter 4.4 for 'What is the true settler population?', page 184.

[2] Ibid.

[3] CBS, List of localities in alphabetical order, population taken from 2015 census estimates, www.cbs.gov.il/ishuvim/reshimalefishem.pdf 2015.

[4] Ibid.

[5] Ibid.

[6] Ibid.

[7] Ibid.

[8] Ibid.

[9] The Israeli 'Disengagement Plan Implementation Law' was adopted by the Knesset in 2005 which paved the way for the evacuation of a total of 8,000 Jewish settlers from the Gaza Strip.

[10] CBS, List of localities in alphabetical order, population taken from 2015 census estimates, www.cbs.gov.il/ishuvim/reshimalefishem.pdf 2015.

11 *Ibid.*

12 *Ibid.*

13 *Ibid.*

14 The mathematical author of the formula is Derek Stynes.

15 There is, in fact, a double Green Line located west of Modi'in Ilit – the first 1.5km from the settlement, the second 2.5km.

16 Habayit Hayehudi, the radical right-wing party, received 50% of the vote in Eli, 59% in Shilo, 59% in Beit El, 72% in Ofra and 35% in Kiryat Arba. The party received just 6.7% nationwide.

17 Peter Beinart, *The Crisis of Zionism* (Melbourne University Press, 2012)

18 *Ibid.*

19 *Ibid.*

20 The Geneva Initiative (also known as the Geneva Accord), is a draft Permanent Status Agreement to end the Israeli-Palestinian conflict based on previous official negotiations, international resolutions, the Quartet Roadmap, the Clinton Parameters, and the Arab Peace Initiative. The document was finished on 12 October 2003. It was drafted by former Israeli minister Yossi Beilin and former Palestinian minister Yasser Abed Rabbo.

21 The settlement population is a 2015 estimate. CBS, www.cbs.gov.il/ishuvim/ishuvim_main.htm.

22 So-called 'quality-of-life settlers' is a Shalom Achshav (Peace Now) definition. They are 'settlers who came to the settlements for their low housing prices and relatively high quality of life, rather than for ideological reasons', http://peacenow.org.il/ en/west-bank-settlements -facts-and-figures.

23 Election results 2015, http://z.ynet.co.il/short/content/2015/elections_map2015/.

24 *Ibid.* Also CBS, Socioeconomic Index 2013 of Local Authorities, www.cbs.gov.il/hodaot2016n/24_16_330t1. pdf.

_____

6 – THE STATE OF TEL AVIV

6.1 – BURSTING THE TEL AVIV 'BUBBLE'

1 The 'Bubble' is a long-established local nickname or moniker for Tel Aviv (a movie of the same name was released in 2006). Example of a typical media reference to the Tel Aviv Bubble is Michal Yudelman O'Dwyer, 'Secular, Israeli and Proud to Live in a Bubble', *Haaretz*, 26 March 2015.

2 Meretz is a member of the Socialist International and an observer member of the Party of European Socialists.

3 Raphael Ahren, *Times of Israel*, March 2015. Meretz has been described as a 'traditional secular-leftist party' ('A guide to the political parties battling for Israel's future', *Washington Post*, 14 March 2015), and 'left-wing' ('Guide to Israel's political parties', BBC News website, 21 Jan 2013), and 'one of the last Israeli factions to consider itself leftist, campaigning on Issues of social justice, equality and peace with the Palestinians.' (J Street's one-stop resource on the 2015 Israeli Election).

4 In the five immediate and contiguous Small Area statistics units of 51, 54, 55, 61, 81, the Meretz vote exceeds 25%, the highest in the country outside of a handful of isolated *kibbutzim* in the north of the country), http://z.ynet.co.il/short/=content/2015/elections_map2015.

5 Official Results, Israeli Ministry of Foreign affairs, http://mfa.gov.il/MFA/ PressRoom/2015/Pages/Israel-votes-17-March-2015.aspx. For mapped regional results (in Hebrew only), see http://z.ynet.co.il/short/content/2015/elections_ map2015/.

6 Census 2008, Table 3a: Percentage of Jews whose continent of origin is Africa and Asia is 24.3% (for Tel Aviv-Yafo as a whole). For North Tel Aviv statistical area 11 it is 20.8%; statistical area 12, it is 18.1%; and statistical area 13, it is 15.4% (area 11, 12, 13 pop. 51,000).

7 http://z.ynet.co.il/short/content/2015/elections_map2015/.

8 *Ibid.* Labour got more than 40% of the vote in 29 out of the 31 small census district areas north of Bograshov Street, exceeding 50% in five of these areas. In the southwest and south-east of the city, in 26 contiguous Small Area statistics areas or neighbourhoods stretching from Yafo (Jaffa) in the south-west to Yad Eliyahu in the southeast, the party didn't get above 25% in any area.

9 Palestinian, Druze, Bedouin and Religious Orthodox (Haredi) communities make up 48 of the poorest 50 communities in Israel (the other two being Zefat and the settlement of Kiryat Arba). CBS, Socioeconomic Index 2013 of Local Authorities, http://www.cbs.gov.il/hodaot2016n/24_16_330t1.pdf.

10 Shas 'wants to see progress for poorer citizens, particularly those not of Ashkenazi descent' in 'A guide to the political parties battling for Israel's future', *Washington Post*, 14 March 2015. 'Works to end prejudice against the Sephardic community and highlights economic issues and social justice' in 'Guide to Israel's political parties', BBC News website, 21st January 2013.

11 Israeli 2015 Knesset election results (cities):

	Zionist Union	Likud, Shas
	Meretz	UTJ Habait YaYudi
	Yesh Atid	Yisrael Beiteinu
Haifa	41.5%	39.4%
Netanya	25%	59%
Ashdod	17.7%	69.4%
Be'er Sheva	20.8%	63.3%
Petah Tikva	31.4%	55%
Rishon LeZion	39.3%	46.5%
Rehovot	36.7%	48.6%
Ashkelon	17.8%	68.3%
Beit Shemesh	6%	82%

Official Results, Israeli Ministry of Foreign afairs, op. cit.

12 *Ibid.*

13 *Ibid.*

14 *Ibid.*

15 Lahav Harkov and Ariel Ben Solomon, 'Tel Aviv Mayor Ron Huldai: Palestinian celebrations of terror result of Occupation, *Jerusalem Post*, 9 June 2016, http://www.jpost.com/Arab-Israeli-Conflict/Tel-Aviv-Mayor-Ron-Huldai- blames- occupation-for- attack-456351.

16 Euromonitor International Tel Aviv City report, 2018

17 'Israeli High Tech is Maturing' – *Haaretz*, January 2017. Number of High Tech by Head office and Haaretz January

2016 (Hagai Amir)

[18] "The Marker" and Start up nation Central January 2018) City Seed Capital Funding for start-ups 2014-2016

[19] The nine cities are Holon, Ramat Gan, Bnei Brak, Rehovot, Bat Yam, Givatayim, Herzliya, Kiryat Ono, Ramat HaSharon.

[20] Natalia Presman, Arie Arnon, 'Commuting patterns in Israel 1991-2004', Research Department, Bank of Israel, Discussion Paper no.2006.04, August 2006. www.boi.org.il/deptdata/mehkar/papers/dp0604e.pdf.

6.2 – WORLD'S FIRST JEWISH GLOBAL CITY

[1] The population of Tel Aviv-Yafo in 1983 had declined to a low of 325,000. The proportion of those aged over 65 peaked at 19.2%. In 2008 the population rose to 402,000 with just 14.2% aged over 65. Census 2008, Table: Comparison Between Censuses – comparison between 1972, 1983, 1995 and 2008 Censuses), Percentage of those aged 65+.

[2] For a critical review on the myths surrounding the origins of Tel Aviv, see Sharon Rotbard, *White City, Black City: Architecture and War in Tel Aviv and Jaffa* (MIT Press, 2015).

[3] In 2003 'The White of Tel Aviv – The Modern Movement' was designated a UNESCO world heritage site (http://whc.unesco.org/en/list/1096). 'The authenticity of architectural design has been fairly well preserved, proven by homogeneous visual perception of urban fabric, the integrity of style, typology, character of streets, relationship of green areas and urban elements, including, fountains, pergolas and gardens.'

[4] *Ibid.*

[5] Baruch A Kipnis, 'Tel Aviv, Israel – A World City in Evolution: Urban development at a dead end of the global ecomomy', GaWC (Globalization and World Cities Research Network) Research Bulletin 57, 2004.

[6] Israeli Census House Price Index: Year 2016, Q3 index for Tel Aviv (2,631), Gush Dan or Greater Tel Aviv Region (1,733), and Israel as a whole (1,429). This compares to Year 2001, Q1 index Tel Aviv (1,042), Gush Dan or Greater Tel Aviv Region (1,733), and Israel as a whole (644). That represents a 152.5% increase in Tel Aviv and a 12.9% increase in Israel, www.cbs.gov.il/ts/databank/search_databank_e.html?input_databank?input_databank=housing.

[7] See Karima Kourtit, Peter Nijkamp and Roger R. Stough (eds), *The Rise of the City: spatial dynamics in the urban century*, New Horizons in Regional Science series (Edward Elgar Publishing, Cheltenham, UK, 2015). See also Saskia Sassen, *The Global City: New York, London, Tokyo* (Princeton University Press, 1991, later eds 2001, 2013); Richard Florida, *The Rise of the Creative Class ...and how it's transforming work, leisure, community and everyday life* (Basic Books, New York, 2002).

[8] Pricewaterhouse Coopers valued Tel Aviv's economy at $122 billion at PPP, 'Global City GDP rankings 2008-2025', 'Global City GDP Rankings 2008-2025', May 2011. Tel Aviv is ranked 53 (Jerusalem doesn't make the top 128 list) in 'Global Cities 2017: Leaders in a World of Disruptive Innovation', AT Kearney Global Cities Reports, www.atkearney.com/research-studies/global-cities-index/full-report/.

[9] The use of 'Global City', as opposed to 'megacity', was popularised by sociologist Saskia Sassen, *The Global City*, op. cit.

[10] See AT Kearney Global Cities Reports, op. cit.

[11] 'The World According to GaWC 2012', www.lboro.ac.uk/gawc/world2012t.html.

[12] See AT Kearney Global Cities Reports, op. cit.

[13] S Sade, 'Europe's Silicon Valley', *Haaretz*, 6 June 2001.

[14] *Ibid.*

[15] 'The Global Financial Centres Index 18', Qatar Financial Centre, www.longfinance.net/images/GFCI18_23Sep2015.pdf.

[16] World Bank http://data.worldbank.org/country/israel.

[17] Emporis www.emporis.com/city/100280/tel-aviv-yafo-israel.

[18] Kipnis, 'Tel Aviv, Israel – A World City in Evolution', op. cit.

[19] Designated in 2013 'The White of Tel Aviv – The Modern Movement', UNESCO world heritage site, http://whc.unesco.org/en/list/1096.

[20] In 1984 Tel Aviv's premier art museum hosted a seminal exhibition titled *White City, International Style Architecture in Israel – Portrait of an Era* and 'Tel Aviv – The White City' concept was born. The city's architectural heritage was championed over the next decade and beyond by Nitza Szmuk (city conservation architect) with vocal support from by Esther Zanberg (journalist with *Haaretz*). In 1994 the Tel Aviv Municipality organised a DOCOMOMO and UNESCO-sponsored international conference on the 'the values of the Modern Movement in architecture and the International Style in Tel Aviv'. Five years later the 12th International ICOMOS-UNESCO Congress recommended that the Tel Aviv Municipality propose 'The White City' as a World Heritage Site. Formal UNESCO adoption eventually took place in 2003.

[21] Rotbard, *White City, Black City*, op. cit.

[22] That rediscovery has been attributed by some as part-reaction to the electoral success of the Likud Party in 1977 and the rise of the voting power of a long politically dispossessed Mizrahi and Sephardic Jewish majority.

[23] See note 6 above.

[24] 'Frishman Tower – Frishman Dizengoff Street' (Moore Yaski Sivan Architects), www.haaretz.com/israel-news/tel-aviv-high-rise-is-a-black-spot-in-the-white-city.premium-1.431611.

[25] 'Tel Aviv – A Global City', www.tel-aviv.gov.il/en/aboutthe City/Pages/TelAvivGlobal.aspx.

[26] Simon Anholt (The Place Brand Observer), http://place-brandobserver.com/ 2015-city-brands-index-reputation-ranking-anholt-gfk- roper/.

[27] Bruce E Stanley, ' "Going Global": Wannabe World Cities in the Middle East', in Wilma A Dunaway (ed.), *Emerging Issues in the 21st Century World-System*: Volume 1, crises and resistance in the 21st century world-system (Praeger, Westport, CT, 2003), 151-70.

[28] 'The World According to GaWC 2012', www.lboro.ac.uk/gawc/world2012t.html.

[29] 'Tel Aviv, the Brand Story', www.tel-aviv.gov.il/en/ about theCity/Pages/ TelAvivBrand.aspx

30 'Tel Aviv Is in Top Three Cities in the World, Says Lonely Planet', https://www.haaretz.com/1.5133373.

31 GayCities.com and American Airlines, www.haaretz.com/israel-news/travel/tel-aviv-declared-world-s-best-gay-travel-destination-1.406699.

32 Richard Florida, 'The World's Leading Startup Cities', Citylab.com, www.citylab.com/life/2015/07/the-worlds-leading-startup-cities/399623/.

33 Nasdaq.com, www.nasdaq.com/screening/regions. aspxlsrael.

34 Kipnis, 'Tel Aviv, Israel – A World City in Evolution', op. cit.

35 Pricewaterhouse Coopers valued Tel Aviv's economy at $122 billion and Cairo at $145 billion at PPP, 'Global City GDP rankings 2008-2025', May 2011. Brookings valued the following cities' economics (billion US dollars at PPP): Tel Aviv 153, Dubai 83, Cairo 102, Kuwait 166, Brookings Institution, 8 May2015.

36 Ben Guion Airport, www.telaviv-airport.com/departures. php.

37 Global Edge Israel Trade Statistics, https://globaledge. msu.edu/countries/israel/tradestats

38 'Global Cities 2017: Leaders in a World of Disruptive Innovation', AT Kearney Global Cities Reports, www. atkearney.com/research-studies/global-cities-index/full-report/.

39 Ibid.

40 '2015 Airport Traffic Statistics', Airport Council International

41 'Tel Aviv Global City – Work Process' 2011-2012, Tel Aviv-Yafo Municipality Global City Unit, pp.5, 25.

7 – AUTONOMY

7.1 – THE LOOMING DIVORCE

1 'Can you guess which Israeli party's voters support Settlements the most?', www.haaretz.com/israel-news /.premium-1.771242. 83% of voters of United Torah Judaism favoured settlement expansion – more than in any other party.

2 For overview of Neo-Zionism (and Post-Zionism), see Uri Ram, *Israeli Nationalism: social conflicts and the politics of knowledge* (Routledge, 2010). Neo-Zionism is generally considered a right-wing, nationalistic and religious ideology that appeared in Israel following the Six-Day War in 1967.

3 In February 2017 the Knesset passed (60 votes to 52 votes) the so-called 'Regularization Law'. The law ostensibly seeks to 'regulate settlement in Judea and Samaria and allow its continued establishment and development'. In effect, it legalises government expropriation of privately owned Palestinian land retroactively. In March 2017 the Knesset passed (46 votes to 28 votes) the so-called 'Anti-BDS Entry Law' which bars entry to Israel to those calling for 'Boycott, Divestment and Sanctions' against Israel. In April 2017 the Religious Services Ministry published a government bill to grant the Rabbinical Courts full judicial authority in arbitration cases (if both parties consent). The bill is seen as creeping Judaising of Israeli secular jurisprudence. In May 2017 the Justice minister Ayelet Shaked (Habayit Hayehudi) announced the formulation of a new 'Civil Law Bill' which seeks to extend Israeli Civil Law rights to settlements and settlers (only) in the West Bank. The bill is seen as creeping Annexation of Israeli jurisprudence in the occupied West Bank. A draft of the new controversial 'Nation State Bill' approved by the Ministerial Committee for Legislation in May 2017 revokes Arabic as an official language of the state and gives precedence for the Jewish character of the state over its democratic form of government.

4 Jonathan Lis, 'Israeli Minister Proposes Annexing Large Settlement East of Jerusalem', *Haaretz*, 2 Jan 2017.

5 Following the 2009 election, Bibi Netanyahu and the (right-wing) Likud replaced (centre-right) Kadima (under Ehud Olmert) as the primary governing party. Labor remained part of the coalition but lost a third of its seats in the 2009 election. Following the 2013 election Labor left the governing coalition. Following the 2015 election (centrist) Yesh Atid was replaced by Religious Orthodox parties (Shas and United Torah Judaism) in the governing coalition. The Likud Party List also drifted rightward during this period.

6 See 3 above.

7 Revisionist Zionism is a faction within the Zionist movement developed by Ze'ev Jabotinsky and associated with the non-religious right and the Likud Party. See Nadav G. Shelef, 'From "Both Banks of the Jordan" to the "Whole Land of Israel": Ideological Change in Revisionist Zionism', *Israel Studies*, vol. 9, no.1, Spring 2004, 125-148,

8 See Efraim Inbar, 'The decline of the Labour Party', *Israel Affairs*, vol. 16, 2010, pp.69-81.

9 Ibid.

10 See note 2 above.

11 See note 3 above.

12 The Palestinian-Israeli Pulse: A Joint Poll (June-July 2017), a joint poll conducted by the Tami Steinmetz Center for Peace Research and the Palestinian Center for Policy and Survey Research (funded by the EU). Answer to question IV23: 'support for the two-state solutions and three alternative options among Israeli Jews was Israeli Jews' was Two State 46.7%; One-State 11.6%; Apartheid 14.9%; Expulsion 14.8%; Other 12%.

13 See Habayit Hayehudi election youtube video 2013, 'Tranquilizing Plan', which calls for full annexation of Area C, West Bank (61%) and 'self-rule' for Palestinians, www.youtube.com/ watch?v=tJo2QTeRpbw.

14 'Tel Aviv Global City – Work Process' 2011-2012, Tel Aviv-Yafo Municipality Global City Unit.

15 See Chapter 7.2 – The Geography of Regional Zionism.

16 Census 2008, Table 3a and Table 4a: Percentage of Jews born abroad who immigrated from 2002 and after. North American Jewish immigrants make up just 4.4% of Israeli population – in Eli 9.1%, Ofra 10.2%, Beit El 13.1%, and Shilo 15.1%. Tables 3a and 4a: Percentage of Jews whose continents of origin are America and Oceania.

17 Forbes Magazine 2013, www.forbes.com/sites/peter cohan/2013/03/23/5-steps-that-turned-israel-from-social-ism-to-start-up-haven/ #685cacaf5fc6.

18 Paltiel Ari, Michel Sepulcre, Irene Kornilenko, Martin Maldonado, 'Long-range population projections for

Israel: 2009-2059', technical paper, CBS, March 2012, www.cbs.gov.il/ www/publications/tec27.pdf.

19 OECD fertility rates, https://data.oecd.org/pop/fertility-rates.htm#indicator-chart.

20 Census 2008, Table 5a: Localities with up to 500 residents. Qalya / Kalya: 290, Argaman: 170, Mehola: 350.

21 See Chapter 4.4 for 'What is the true settler population?' page 184.

22 See note 6 above.

23 Pricewaterhouse Coopers valued Tel Aviv's economy at $122 billion at PPP, 'Global City GDP rankings 2008-2025', 'Global City GDP Rankings 2008-2025', May 2011. That represented approximately 50% of entire Israeli economy in 2011.

24 Carlo Strenger, 'The federalization of Israel is an existential necessity', Haaretz, 16 Sept 2016, www.haaretz.com/opinion/.premium-1.742296

25 Official Results, Israeli Ministry of Foreign affairs, http://mfa.gov.il/MFA/ PressRoom/2015/Pages/Israel-votes-17-March-2015.aspx. For mapped regional results (in Hebrew only), see http://z.ynet.co.il/short/content/2015/elections_map2015/.

26 Israeli 2015 Knesset election results, see 6.1 – Bursting the Tel Aviv 'Bubble', note 10.

27 By comparison, metropolitan Madrid (6.5 million) and Barcelona (5.5m) account for 2% of the Spanish population (46m). Rome (4.3m) and Milan (5.2m) account for 16% of the Italian population (60.6m).

28 Census 2008, Table 3b: Percentage of Jewish men aged 15 and over who studied in a yeshiva.

29 Ibid. In 5 of the 11 Small Area statistical geographic areas in Jerusalem, the percentage of Jewish men who studied in a yeshiva ranges from 43% (area 5) to 76% (area 7).

30 Census 2008, Table 3b: Percentage of households with 4 children up to age 17 in the household.

31 Dan Senor and Saul Singer, Start-up Nation: the story of Israel's economic miracle (Hachette Book Group, 2009)

32 Census 2008, Table 3b: Percentage of those aged 15 and over who worked in 2008 in the 'Public administration' and 'Education' industry etc.

33 CBS, Socioeconomic Index 2013 of Local Authorities, www.cbs.gov.il/hodaot2016n/24_16_330t1.pdf. The Israeli CBS in 2013 ranked 255 Israeli local authorities in order of 'socio-economic' development. The ranking criteria included, amongst other things, the proportion of those with third level education, employment levels, standard of living and age structure. Each settlement, city or village was given an overall score ranging from 1 (lowest) to 10 (highest).

34 Ibid.

35 Richard Florida, 'The World's Leading Startup Cities', Citylab.com, www.citylab.com/life/2015/07/the-worlds-leading-startup-cities/399623/. Tel Aviv was ranked 5th in the Global High Tech start-up cities.

36 In 2016, 10,3511 moved into the city but 17,091 people left the city (net migration loss of 6,740). CBS and also Maya Choshen and Michal Korach, Jerusalem: Facts and Trends 2009/2010 (Jerusalem Institute for Israel Studies), http://en.jerusaleminstitute.org.il/.upload/facts-2010-eng%20(1).pdf.

37 U.S. chip giant Intel bought Israeli driverless technology firm Mobileye, based in a Jerusalem high-tech park, for $15.3 billion in 2017.

38 The percentage of Tel Aviv household with internet subscription (in 2008) was 95%. In Jerusalem it was just 62%, with many neighbourhoods with some of the highest yeshiva study rates (Statistical Area 9) not reaching above 40%. Census 2008, Table 3b: Localities with 2,000 residents and more, Statistical Areas.

39 'Mehadrin' bus lines was a type of bus line in Israel serving Haredi population centres and in which gender segregation and was observed. In January 2011 the Israeli High Court of Justice ruled that gender segregation was unlawful. 'A public transportation operator, like any other person, does not have the right to order, request or tell women where they may sit simply because they are women,' Supreme Court Justice Elyakim said. https://en.wikipedia.org/wiki/Mehadrin_bus_lines

40 Read more: Yair Ettinger, 'High Court: Gender segregation legal on Israeli Buses – but only with passenger consent', 6 Jan 2011, https://www.haaretz.com/1.5104449; and Nir Hasson, 'Jerusalem Bus Companies decide to ban all ads featuring People – Men or Women', 4 July 2013., https://www.haaretz. com/.premium-no-human-images-on-egged-j-lem-buses-1.5291185.

41 For background, see Mike Boehm, 'Israeli court OKs Museum of Tolerance's controversial branch', Los Angeles Times, 29 Oct 2008.

42 Report of State Comptroller, Joseph Shapira, Nov 2016.

43 Census 2008, Table 3a: Percentage of those aged 0-17.

44 The report was in response to a resolution adopted in 2016 by the UN Human Rights Council that called for the creation of a database of all companies doing business with the Israeli settlements, which the United Nations considers illegal under international law.

45 The Labor party (primary representative of the centre-left) has not win a plurality of the vote, nor office of Prime Minister in the Knesset elections of 2003, 2006, 2009, 2013 or 2015. The last Labor Prime Minister was Ehud Barak (1999-2001).

46 See note 5 above.

47 According to the CBS forecast, the Ultra-Orthodox population will number 1.1 million people by 2019, compared with 750,000 in 2009. By 2059 there will be anywhere between 2.73 million and 5.84 million Haredi – a 264% to 686% increase. Ari et al, 'Long-range population projections for Israel: 2009-2059', op. cit., www.cbs. gov.il/www/publications/tec27.pdf.

48 See note 3 above.

49 Germany severely criticized Israel's 'Regularization Law' (see note 3 above) in February 2017, www.timesofisrael.com/germany-dissapointed-lost-confidence-in-israel-after-outpost-law/.

50 See note 3 above.

51 See Gili Cohen, 'Ex-Mossad chief says occupation is Israel's only existential threat', Haaretz, 22 March 2017, www.haaretz.com/israel-news/1.778650.

52 Ari et al, 'Long-range population projections for Israel: 2009-2059', op. cit., www.cbs.gov.il/www/publications/tec27.pdf.

53 *Ibid.*

54 CBS, 'On the Eve of Israel's 69th Independence Day – 8.7 Million Residents in the state of Israel', www.cbs.gov.il/reader/newhodaot/ tables_template_eng.

55 *Ibid.*

56 OECD Working Age, Fertility Rates, Young Population, Population, https://data.oecd.org/pop/working-age-population.htm#indicator-chart

57 data.oecd.org.

58 Ibid, data.oecd.org https://data.oecd.org/socialexp/social-spending.htm#indicator-chart.

59 Ibid, data.oecd.org.https://data.oecd.org/socialexp/family-benefits-public-spending.htm

60 Ibid, data.oecd.org https://data.oecd.org/ tax/tax-on-personal-income.htm#indicator-chart

61 The Palestinian-Israeli Pulse: A Joint Poll (see note 12 above). Interestingly for all Palestinians (West Bank and Gaza), some 53% favour a two-state solution over a one-state (11%), apartheid (10%) or expulsion of Jews (15%).

7.2 – THE GEOGRAPHY OF REGIONAL ZIONISM

1 Israel Ministry of Foreign Affairs, 'Israeli Democracy: how does It work?', May 2013, www.mfa.gov.il.

2 2015 Israeli population estimate: CBS, List of localities in alphabetical order, www.cbs.gov.il/ ishuvim/reshimale-fishem.pdf.

3 PCBS, Estimated Population in the Palestinian Territory Mid-Year 1997-2016, www.pcbs.gov.ps.

4 Yesh Atid has been described as belonging to 'centrist, secularist parties' (Ishaan Tharoor, 'A guide to the political parties battling for Israel's future', *Washington Post*, 14 March 2015) and to 'represent the secular centre' ('Guide to Israel's political parties', BBC, 21 January 2013).

5 See note 2 above.

6 For election results mapped (in Hebrew only) see http://z.ynet.co.il/short/content/2015/elections_map2015/, Official Results, Israeli Ministry of Foreign Affairs, http://mfa.gov.il/MFA/ PressRoom/2015/Pages/Israel-votes-17-March-2015.aspx.

7 CBS, Socioeconomic Index 2013 of Local Authorities, www.cbs.gov.il/hodaot2016n/24_16_330t1.pdf. Ratings included 255 local authorities, 201 of which are cities and local councils, and 54 district councils. Values for the socio-economic index vary from minus 2.344 for the Neve Midbar local council to plus 3.058 for Savyon. The socio-economic level for the population in each local authority is measured by combining its educational level, standard of living, employment, and age. 132 local councils containing 46% of the population had a negative index value (below the general average), while 123 local authorities containing 54% of the population had a positive index value (above average).

8 *Ibid.*

9 See note 6 above.

10 See note 7 above.

11 See note 6 above.

12 See note 2 above.

13 See note 7 above.

14 See note 6 above.

15 See note 2 above.

16 See note 7 above.

17 The census tells us that Morocco, Ethiopia, Algeria and Tunisia make up 84.7% of 'Africa', and Iran, Iraq, Yemen, Turkey make up 60% of 'Asia'.

18 Census 2008, Table 3a: Percentage of Jews whose continent of origin is Asia and Africa, Localities with 2,000 residents and more.

19 Mark Muro and Sifan Liu, 'Another Clinton-Trump divide: high-output America vs low-output America', Brookings Institute, 29 November 2016.

20 Census 2008, Table 3b: Percentage of those aged 15 and over with up to 8 years of schooling, and Percentage of those aged 15 and over with 16 or more years of schooling, Localities with 2,000 residents and more.

21 *Ibid.*

22 *Ibid.*

23 See note 6 above.

24 See note 20 above.

25 See note 2 above.

26 See note 7 above.

27 See note 6 above.

28 Results of General Election 2015 (% right v % centre-left): Haifa 39.4 v 41.5, Rishon LeZion 46.5 v 39.3, Petah Tika 55 v 31.4, Holon 50 v 35, Rehovot 48.6 36.7, Hadera 53 v 28. Election results mapped (in Hebrew only) http://z.ynet.co.il/short/content/2015/elections_map2015/, Official Results, op. cit.

29 Of these largest 30 Palestinian 'cities', 10 are located in the Gaza Strip, including Gaza City itself (pop. 570,000), Khan Yunis (pop. 179,000) Jabalia (pop. 165,000) and Rafah (pop. 158,000). The largest Palestinian city (outside of Jerusalem) in the West Bank is Hebron (pop. 209,000). PCBS, Estimated population in the Palestinian Territory Mid-Year 1997-2016, www.pcbs. gov.ps.

30 Our 11 federal states are as follows:
    (state name / supra-national identity / geography of Zionism / largest cities):

    1 State of Tel Aviv / Israeli / Permissive Zionism / Tel Aviv, Ramat Gan

    2 State of Jerusalem / Judean / Neo-Zionism / Jerusalem, Bnei Brak

    3 State of Haifa / Israeli / Exurban Zionism / Haifa, Hadera

    4 Gush Dan / Israeli / Exurban Zionism / Rishon LeZion, Petah Tikva, Holon

    5 Negev Midbar / Israeli / Exurban Zionism / Eilat, Arad

    6 Galilee / Israeli / Squeezed Zionism / Kiryat Ata, Nahariya, Akko

    7 Southern State / Israeli / Squeezed Zionism / Ashdod, Be'er Sheva

    8 Galilee / Palestinian / Non-Zionism / Nazareth, Umm al Fahm

    9 West Bank / Palestinian / non-voting or disenfranchised cities / Jerusalem, Hebron, Nablus

    10 State of Gaza / Islam / non-voting or disenfranchised cities / Gaza City, Khan Yunis

    11 Bedouin / Bedouin/ Non- Zionism / Rahat.

The Authors

MOTTI RUIMY was born in Petah Tikva, Israel, in 1975. He is an architect, interdisciplinary artist and author. He studied architecture at Bezalel Academy of Art & Design, Jerusalem (graduating 2007), where he previously studied fine art (graduating 2000). He has exhibited in museums, galleries and public spaces. He divides his time between Dublin and Tel Aviv. He was a speaker at TEDxJaffa 2013.

PAUL KEARNS was born in Dublin in 1966. He is an urban planner, author, journalist and university lecturer with extensive experience as both a practitioner and a creative researcher in the discipline of city making. He is a graduate of University College Dublin, with a BA in economics and geography (1988) and a Masters in urban planning (1990). Between 2002 and 2004, based in Jerusalem, he was the Israeli-Palestinian correspondent for the *Sunday Tribune* newspaper. He worked as a planner with Dublin City Council until 2018. He now lives in Tel Aviv.

Paul and Motti are authors of two critically acclaimed books on Dublin – REDRAWING DUBLIN (Gandon Editions, 2010) and BEYOND PEBBLEDASH – THE PUZZLE OF DUBLIN (Gandon Editions, 2014), both of which received an 'Engaging with Architecture' award from the Department of the Environment and The Arts Council / An Chomhairle Ealaíon.

Their creative interest primarily lies in the playful merging and synthesis of urban policy and public art. Their work can be described as 'Action Urbanism'.

In 2011 Motti and Paul initiated the URBAN PARTY – TALKING CITIES platform, which has since been hosted in Dublin (Complex Theatre and National Museum of Ireland), Tel Aviv (Port) and Jerusalem (Museum on the Seam).

They are twice recipients of Department of Foreign Affairs (Ireland) Culture Ireland grants including for the exhibition in Cooper Union, POSTCARDS OF OUR CITY – New York Dublin (Cooper Union, New York, 2013).

In 2014 their six-month BEYOND PEBBLEDASH project, hosted by the National Museum of Ireland, included the largest-ever sculptural installation constructed in the NMI's major outdoor public space at Collins Barracks.

In 2015 they initiated and co-designed the MAPPING BEAUTY web app to model inner city regeneration (partners: School of Geography UCD, Workday Ireland, Dublin City Architects).

In 2016 they set up and taught an interdisciplinary research module on urban regeneration in the School of Geography, University College Dublin (Master of Urban Studies).

They have contributed to many publications and are regular contributors to *Architecture Ireland*. They have been guest lecturers at NCAD and GradCAM (Dublin), Queen's University Belfast Columbia University and Cooper Union (New York city).

Further information on their work can be found on their Redrawing Project website, http://redrawingproject.com/